Life on the Lake

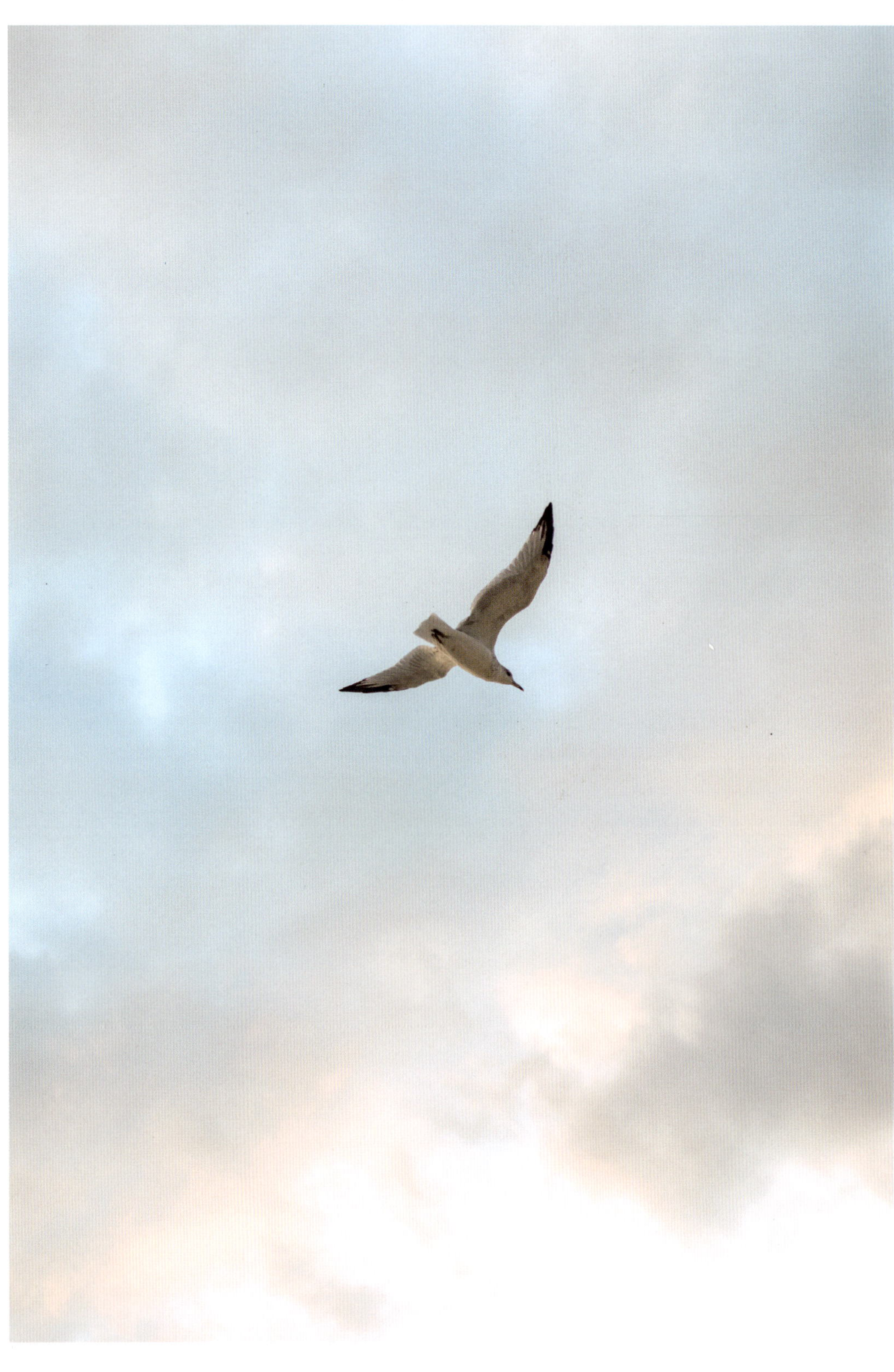

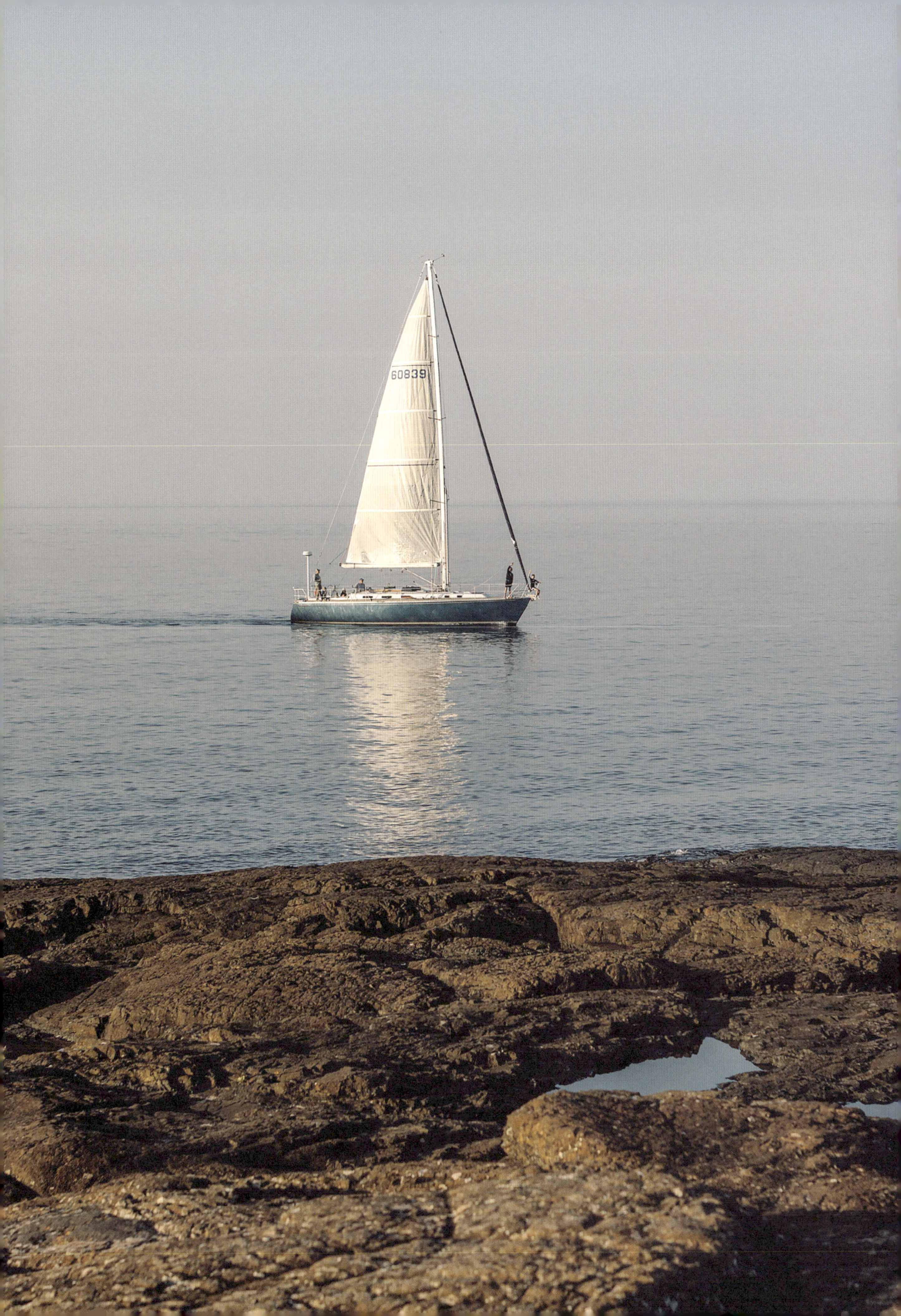
60839

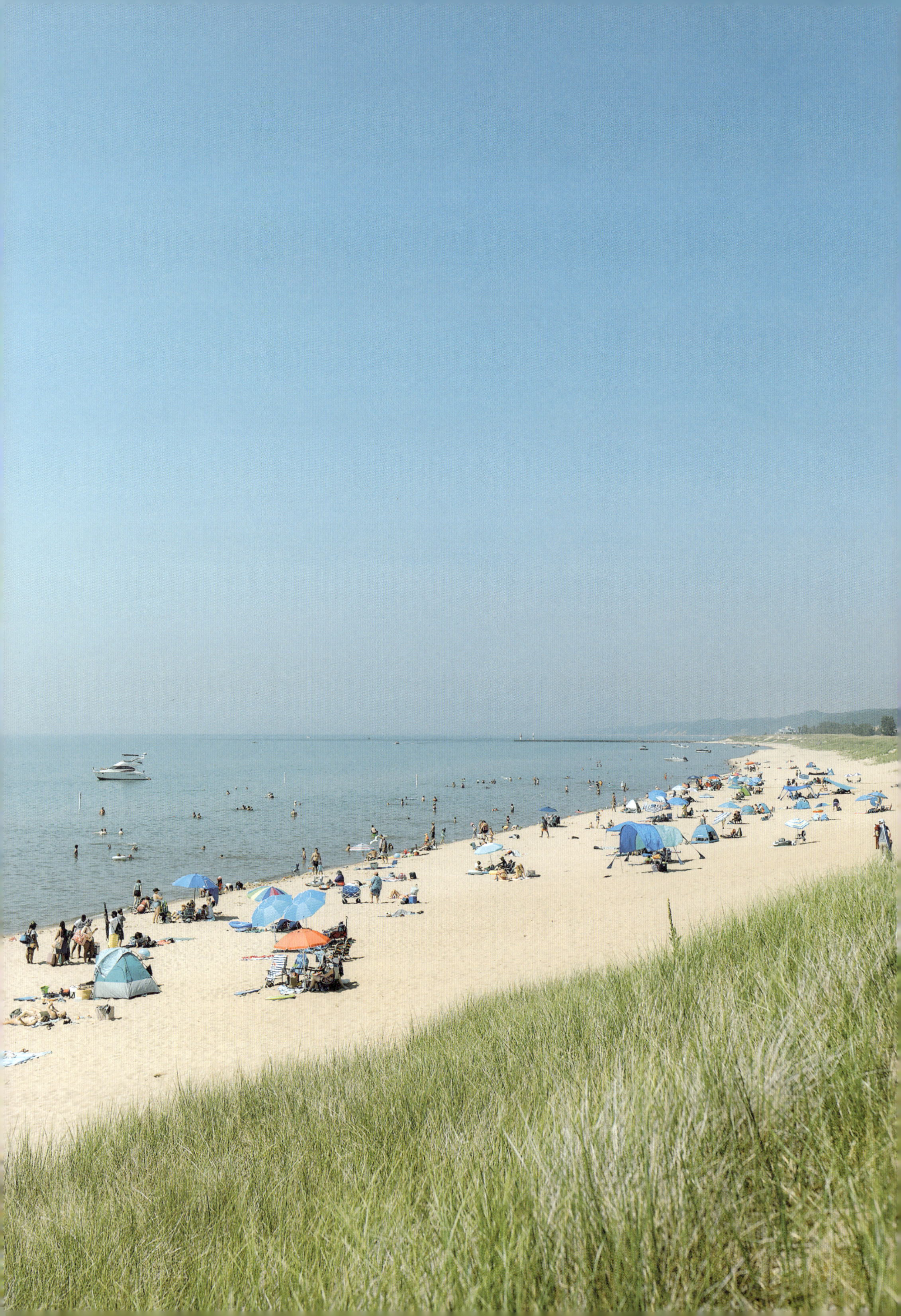

Life on the Lake

savoring days on freshwater shores

Tylee Shay

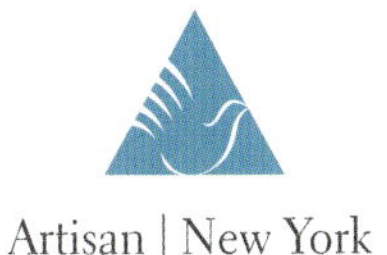

Artisan | New York

Copyright © 2026 by Tylee Shay
Photos copyright © 2026 by Tylee Shay

Hachette Book Group supports the right to free expression and the value of copyright. The purpose of copyright is to encourage writers and artists to produce the creative works that enrich our culture.

The scanning, uploading, and distribution of this book without permission is a theft of the author's intellectual property.

If you would like permission to use material from the book (other than for review purposes), please contact permissions@hbgusa.com. Thank you for your support of the author's rights.

Library of Congress Cataloging-in-Publication Data is on file.

ISBN 978-1-64829-531-7 (hardcover)
ISBN 978-1-64829-533-1 (ebook)

Design by Jane Treuhaft

Published in association with Joy Eggerichs Reed of Punchline Agency

Artisan books may be purchased in bulk for business, educational, or promotional use. For information, please contact your local bookseller or the Hachette Book Group Special Markets Department at special.markets@hbgusa.com.

The publisher is not responsible for websites (or their content) that are not owned by the publisher.

The Hachette Speakers Bureau provides a wide range of authors for speaking events. To find out more, go to hachettespeakersbureau.com or email HachetteSpeakers@hbgusa.com.

Published by Artisan,
an imprint of Workman Publishing,
a division of Hachette Book Group, Inc.
1290 Avenue of the Americas
New York, NY 10104
artisanbooks.com

The Artisan name and logo are registered trademarks of Hachette Book Group, Inc.

Printed in China (TLF) on responsibly sourced paper

First printing, April 2026

Cover © 2026 Hachette Book Group, Inc.

10 9 8 7 6 5 4 3 2 1

To Gavin—for not only encouraging me to pursue my dreams, but holding my hand and pursuing them alongside me

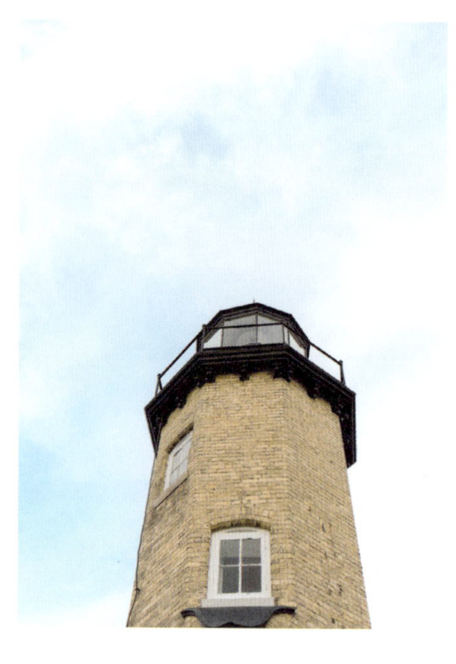
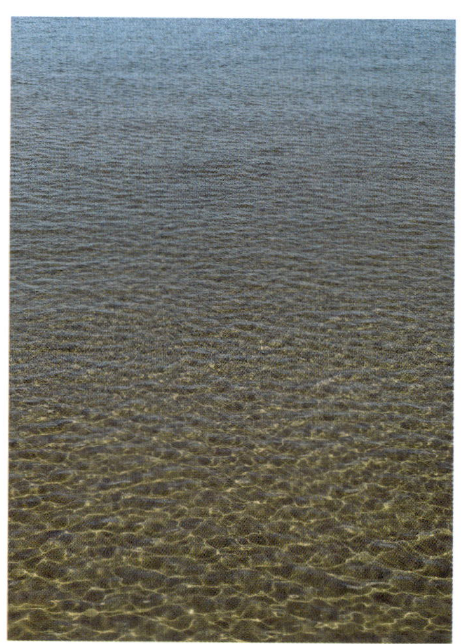

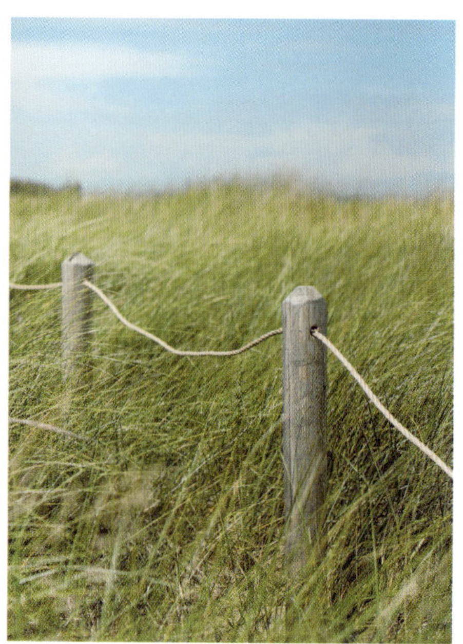

Contents

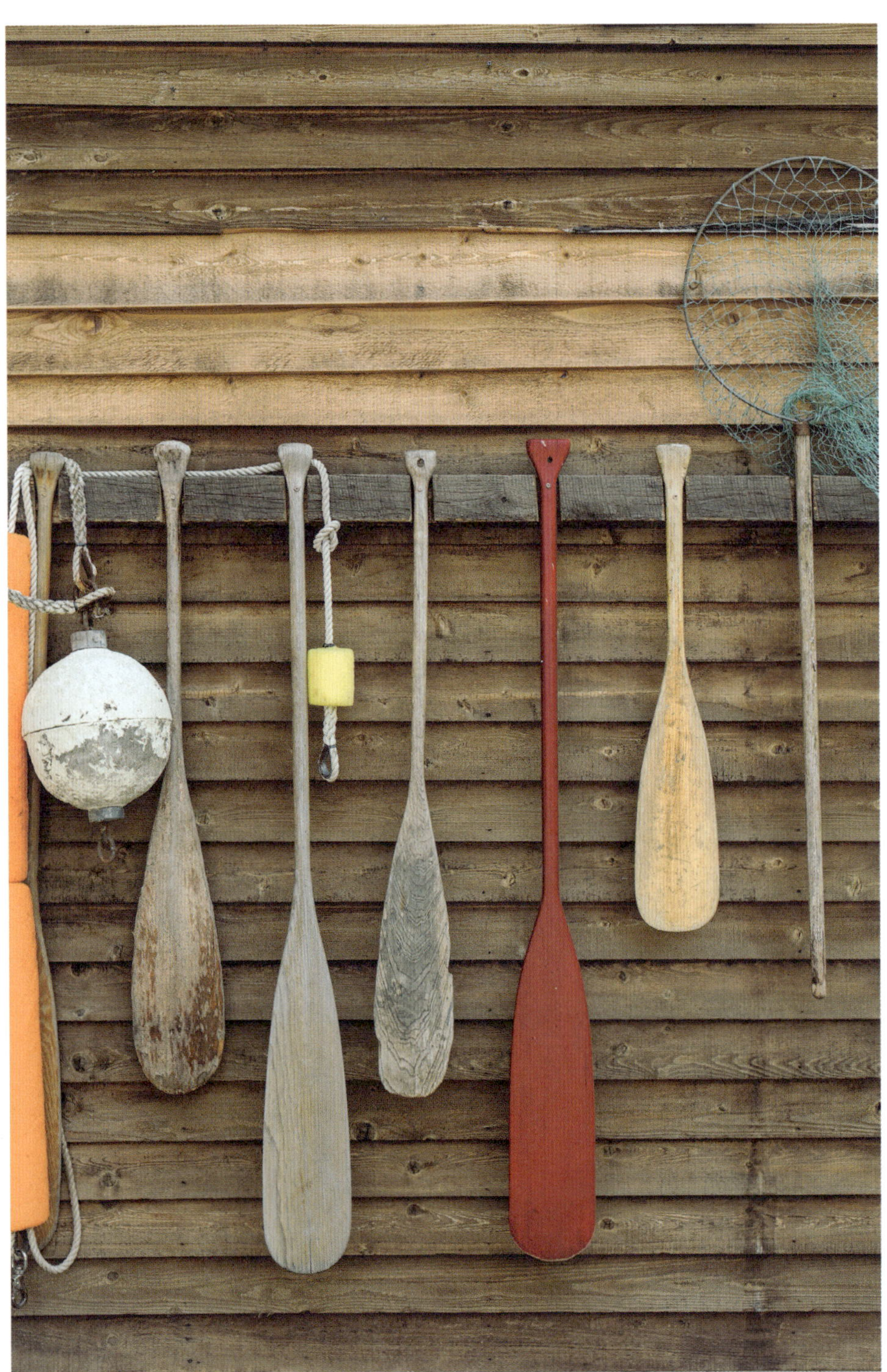

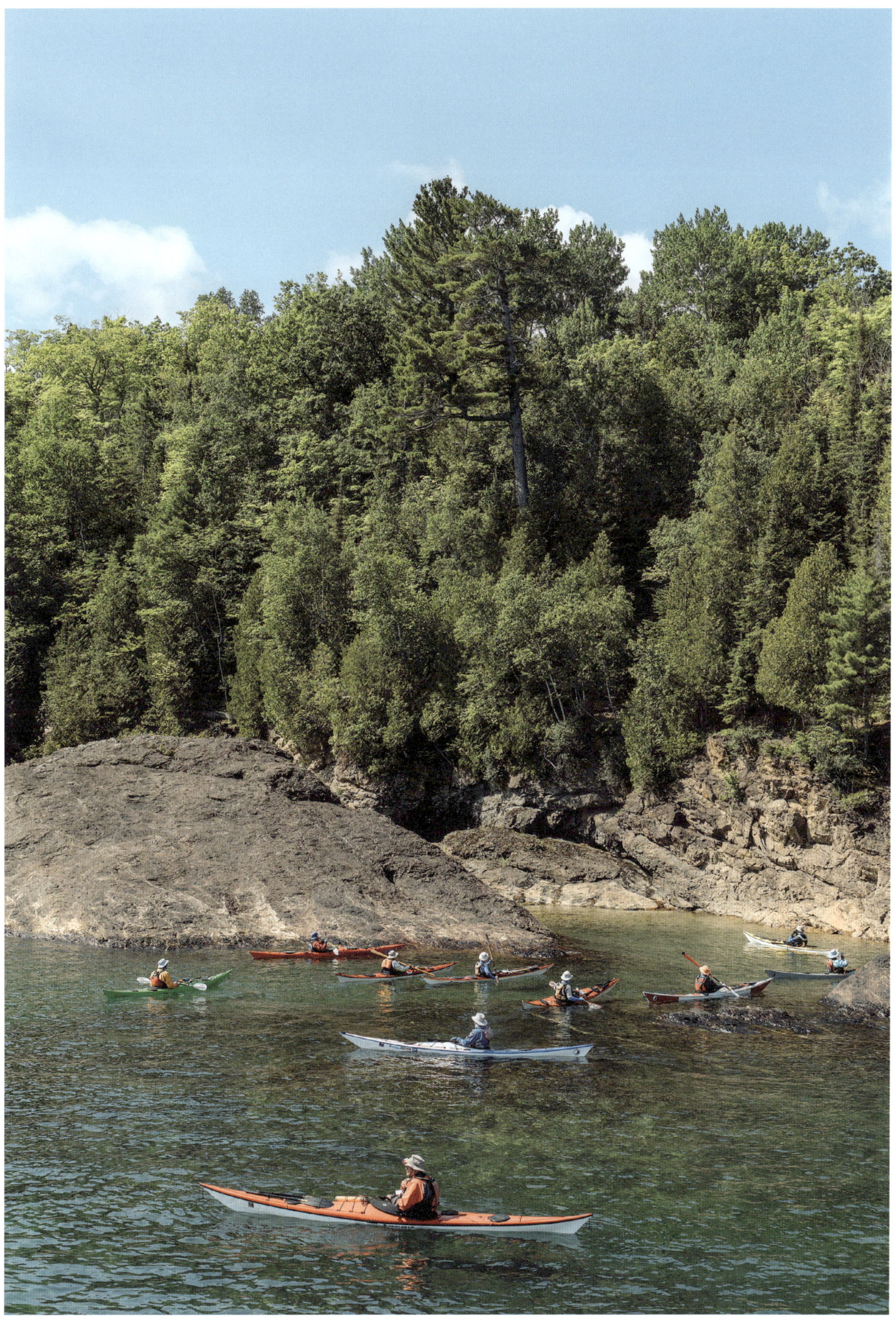

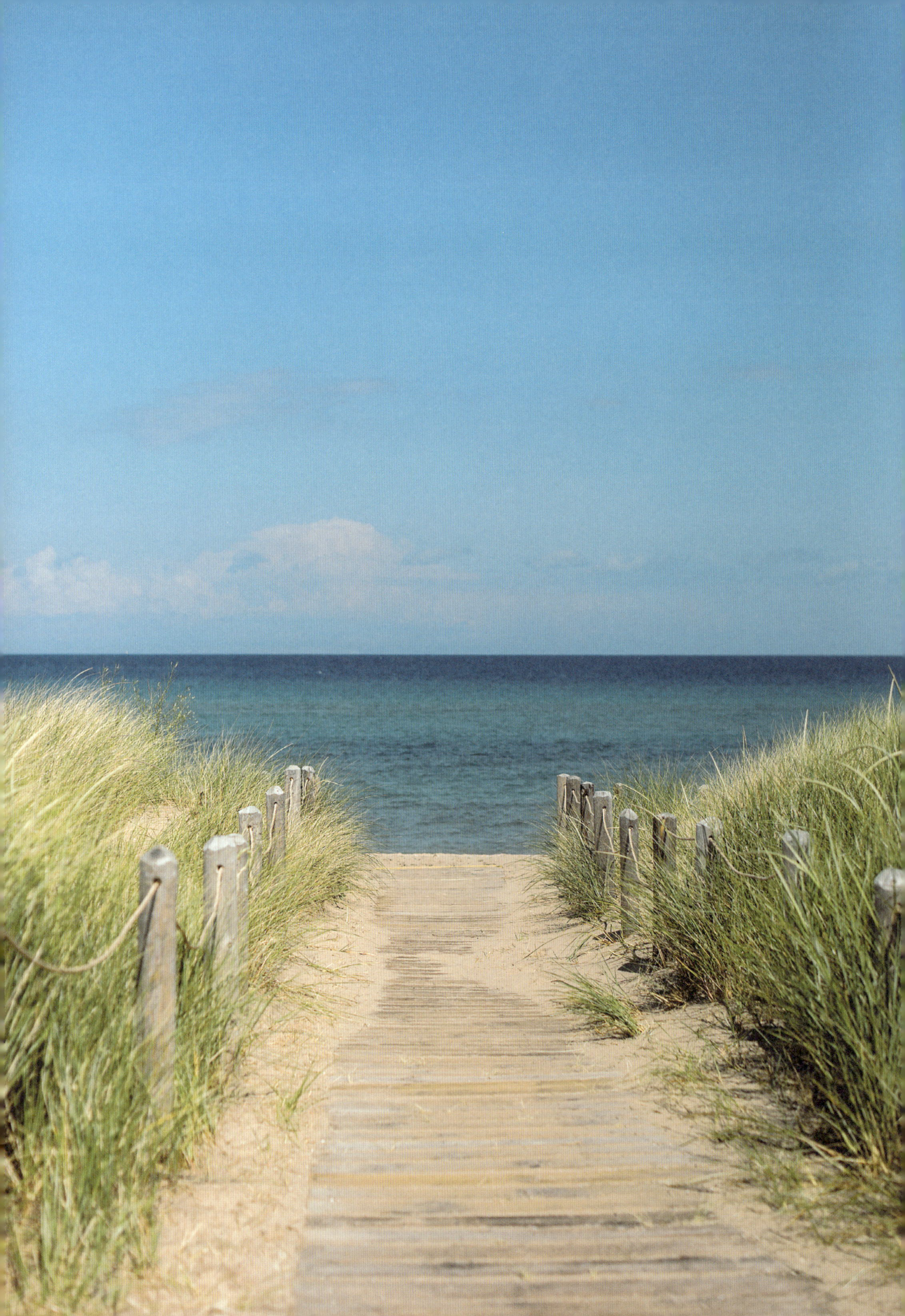

Introduction

Summer at the lake is everything summer should be.

Boat rides followed by bonfires. Sweatshirts over swimsuits. S'mores and ice cream cones. Splashing in shimmering waves by day, then watching the colors of the sunset reflect on a rippling surface by night.

Many lakes offer this idyllic summer lifestyle, but for me, it's always been Lake Michigan. I grew up on a freshwater coast with miles and miles of soft sandy shores and bright blue waves. My childhood was marked with beach days and bare feet, sandcastles and seagulls, family and friends.

I also grew up with a deep respect for summer, an awareness that it is short and sacred. For those of us who live in a northern climate, we have four distinct seasons, with harsh winters and fleeting summers. But that's why our appreciation for summer runs so deep; its brevity only makes it more magical. Locals and visitors alike share a strong conviction to cherish each warm and golden day at the lakeshore.

As I've gotten older, this conviction has grown too, in tandem with my love for the lake. The sunny days may be sparse here in Michigan, but that's why I spend every one of them lakeside, face aglow, listening to the waves, and never missing an opportunity to jump in while the water's warm.

Whether your lake has sandy beaches and dune grass dancing in the wind, or pebbles along the shore and lily pads in the shallows... whether your lakeside retreat is a sentimental family cottage or a state park campground... whether it's a vast Great Lake with faithful waves or a quaint inland lake with a serene surface... whatever your lake may look like, I hope these pages will help you to rediscover your love for summer days on freshwater shores.

This book can be read cover to cover, taking you through one summer season—June, July, August, and September—or enjoyed out of order, at random, one heartening page at a time. Each section includes inspiring essays along with prompts, guides, and recipes to help you cherish that momentary month at the lakeshore.

Whether you have five minutes or a whole afternoon, take this outside and into the sunlight. Take it to the lake and let it get a little sandy. Keep it on your coffee table to be perused on a whim.

Through my photos, I hope you'll see the beauty in both the magical and mundane aspects of lake life.

Through my words, I hope you'll take in valuable lake lessons—life lessons tenderly taught by the lake to those who pay attention.

Through it all, I hope this book will help you to make the most of your own lakeside summer, wherever that may be.

Because I believe every season of life should be savored, but especially summer.

And there's no better place to spend summer than at the lake.

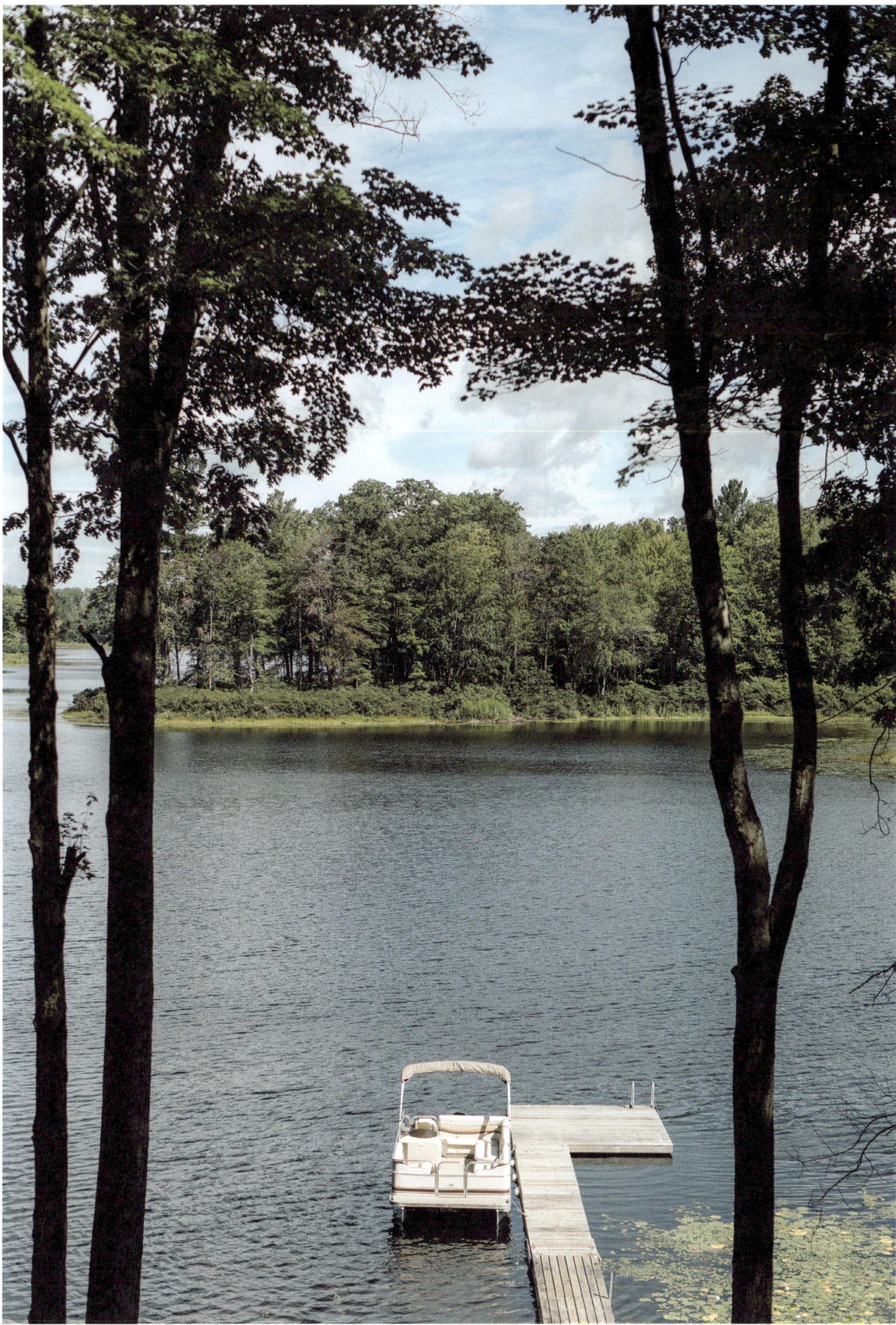

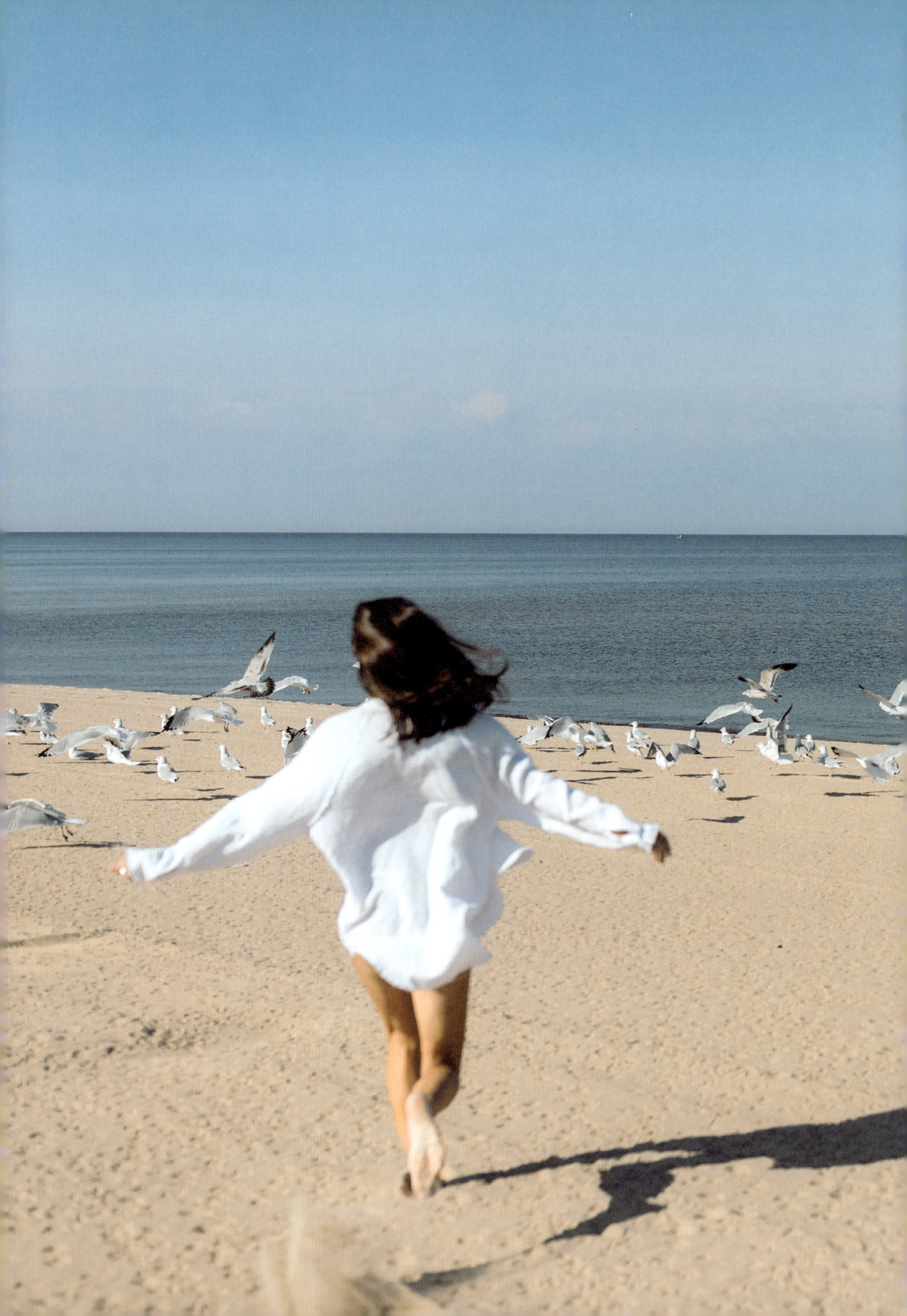

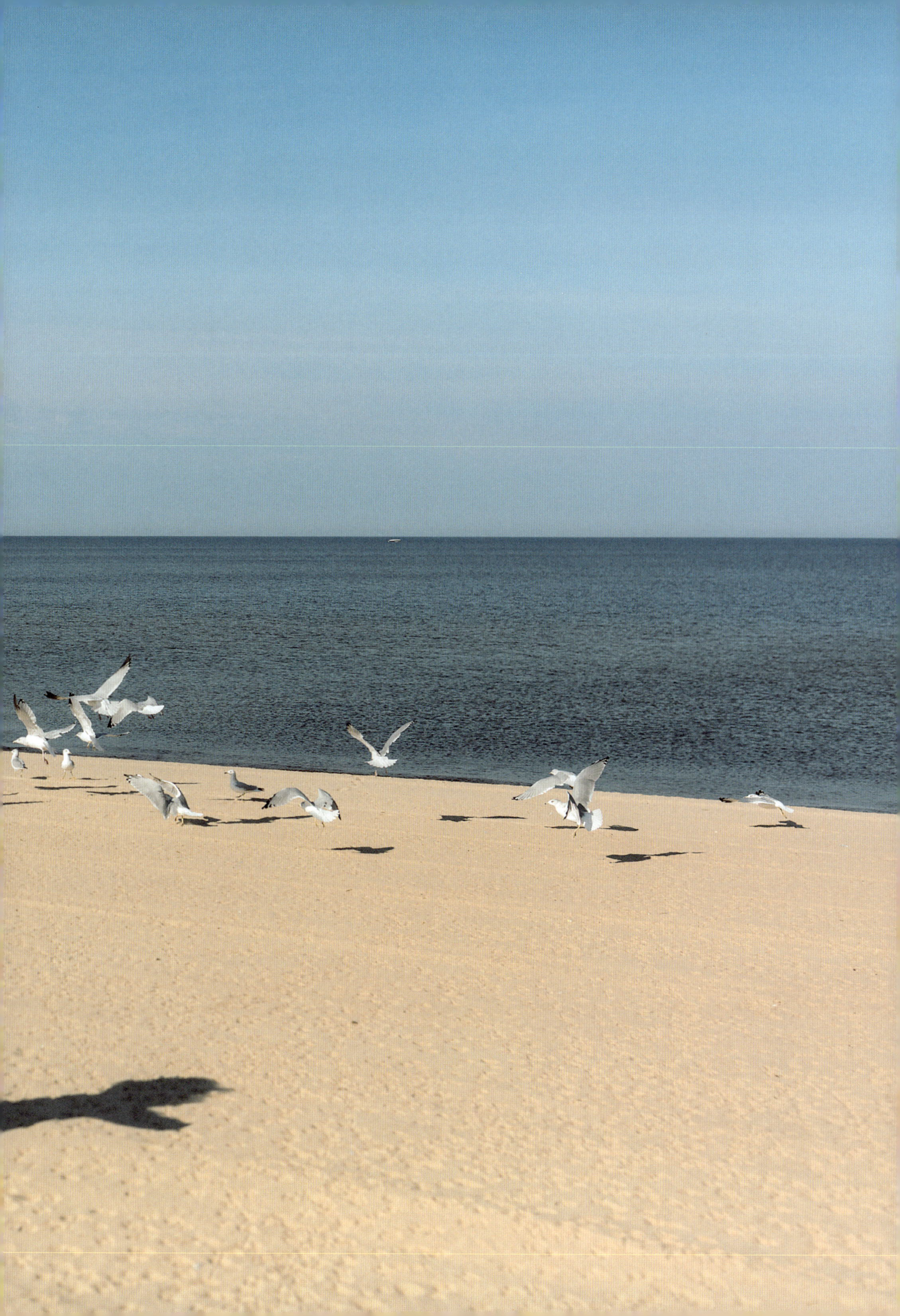

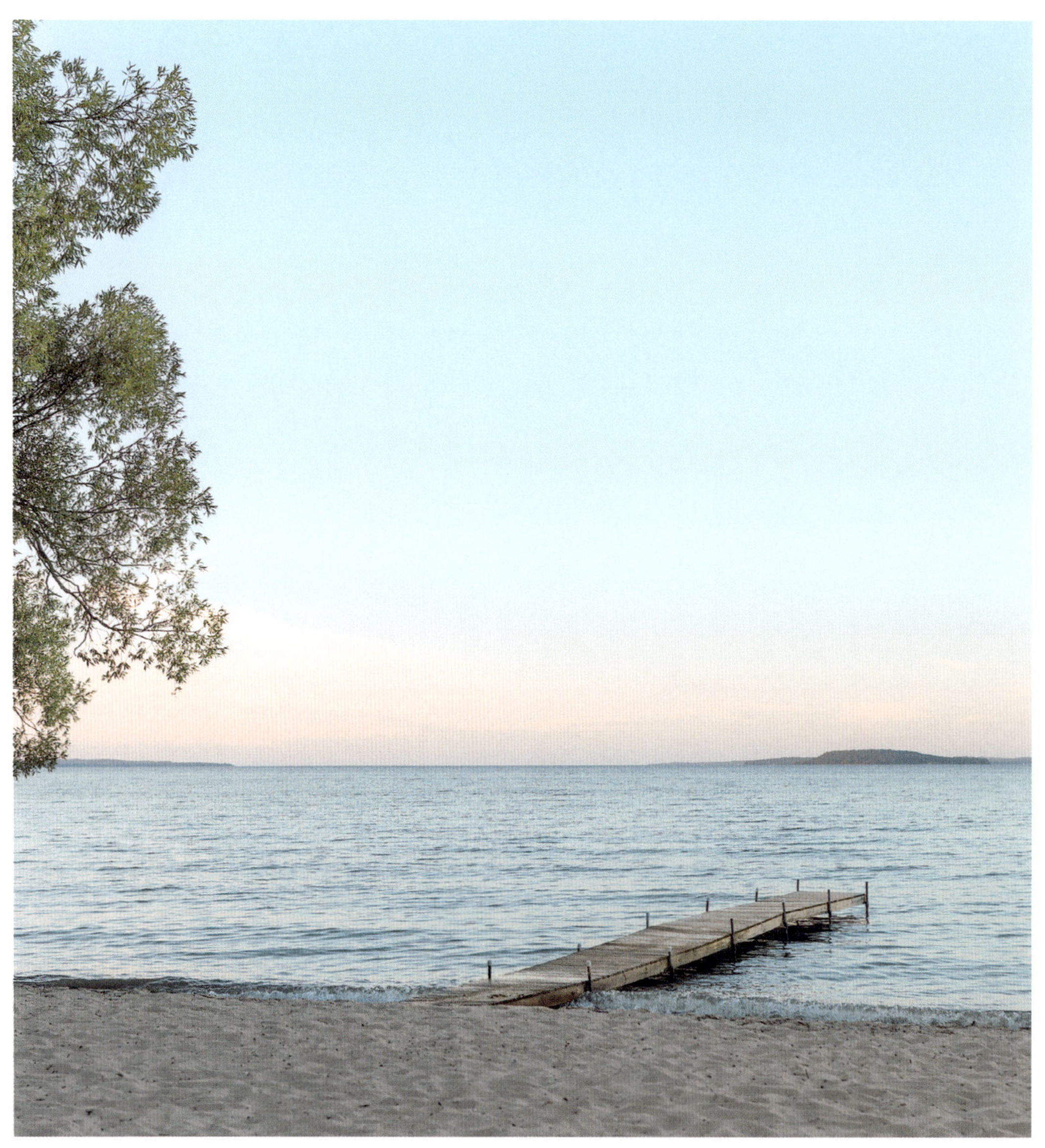

June

June at the lake feels like the first day of vacation—it's the knowing that we've finally arrived paired with a bone-deep sense that so much good has yet to come. Summer in the Midwest starts slow and steady, with longer days, later sunsets, and warm wind. It begins with the first sixty-degree day and short sleeves. The earth goes from brown to green, the lake from gray to blue, and we start getting our color back, too. There's a deep sense of comradery after surviving another long hard winter and collectively putting our faces back in the sun. Docks are reinstalled, boats are launched back in the water, and mudrooms transform into sandy entryways with boots swapped for sandals, coats for life jackets, backpacks for beach bags stocked and ready to take to the lake on a whim. June is for sweatshirts worn in the cool of the morning, forgotten in the afternoon, and rediscovered at dusk. For long lines at the ice cream shop, nostalgia twisting with anticipation, knowing the biggest decision we'll make today is choosing between a cup or a cone. June feels like that first lick of ice cream, a jolt of sugary energy and mouthwatering delight. And the sweetest part is, June is only the beginning. Summer has just begun. So much good has yet to come.

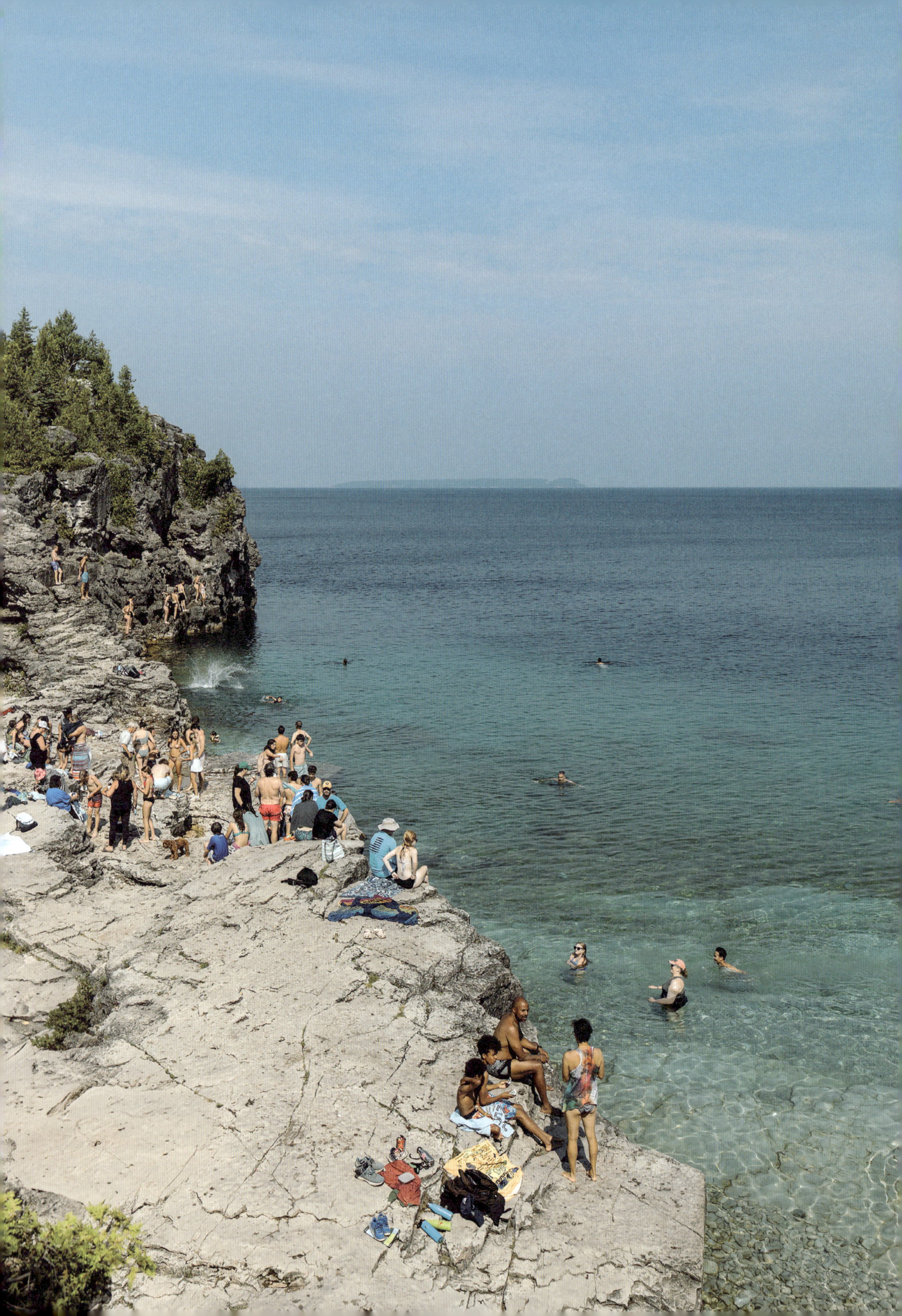

Bucket List

MAKING THE MOST OF SUMMER

It's a warm Saturday morning. I'm waking up with a cappuccino and an early June breeze drifting through my kitchen window. I smell the fresh-cut peonies by my sink, listen to the soft birdsong, admire the pastel sunrise painting the sky, and take a deep breath of gratitude, knowing that the only things on my agenda for this weekend are to pick strawberries at a little local farm, relax at the lake, and spend time around a campfire with my family.

But it wasn't always this way.

I used to have an annual midsummer moment of panic. Each year the realization that summer was halfway over would be followed by the discovery that I hadn't done most of my favorite quintessential summer activities yet. I'd be overcome with dread that sweet summertime was ticking away with so much I still wanted—needed—to do.

Without even realizing it, my schedule would always seem to fill up with busy summer plans, all fun and wonderful things, but suddenly I wouldn't have a single free weekend until October.

I'd have no margin left in my calendar for unhurried beach days or impromptu drives to the lake, for that leisurely road trip or relaxing staycation I desired, for lingering at lakeside grottoes or the freedom to simply spend an evening watching the sunset. The slow-paced weekends, lazy afternoons in the sun, spontaneous ice cream runs—these are the things that make summer, summer! And I was always too busy for them.

So I started making a bucket list. I now begin each summer by creating a list of things I want to do, places I want to visit, memories I want to make, flavors I want to enjoy while they're in season, traditions I want to uphold, and simple summer experiences that just make my heart happy. Then I schedule these things in my calendar before it's too late. I've learned that if

I don't put things in my calendar, they'll never happen. And if I don't fill my schedule, then others will fill it for me, especially in these sacred summer months.

It may seem odd to block off a calendar day for something as casual as a swim or a drive to your favorite lakeside town or an afternoon picking berries, but a little planning goes a long way in maximizing these precious few months. Sometimes, savoring your summer means going against the grain. It can feel like a true act of resistance to say no to the busyness and obligations in order to say yes to the slow, the simple pleasures, the things that will actually make your summer feel significant.

Throughout the course of summer, I try to be as devoted to my bucket list endeavors as I am to my formal RSVPs. It's like keeping a promise to myself, a pinkie promise, and it enables me to enjoy my summer to the fullest—slow, intentional, and savored.

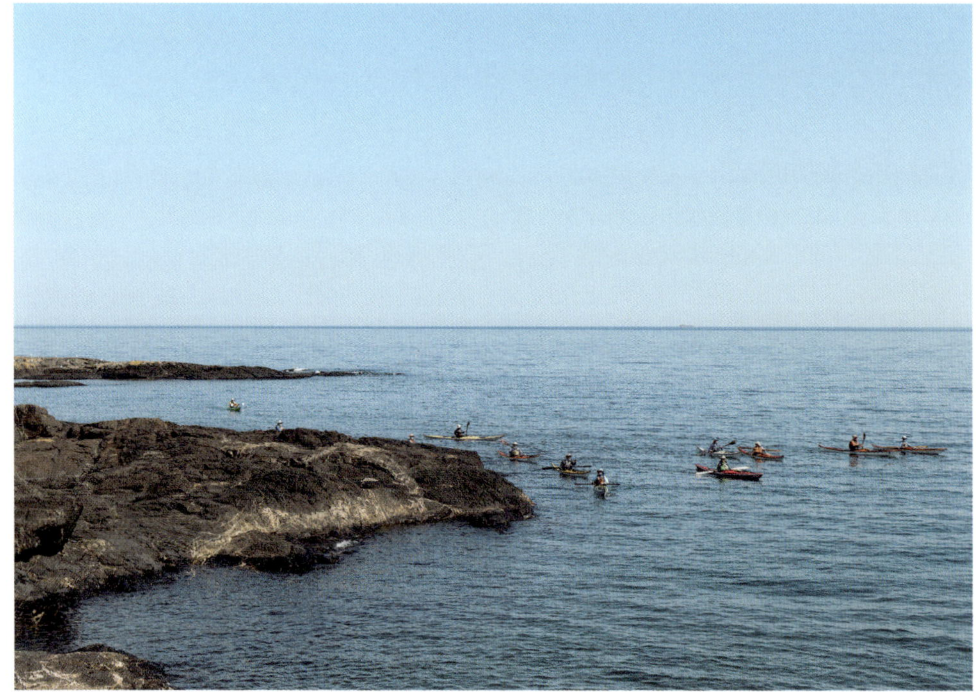

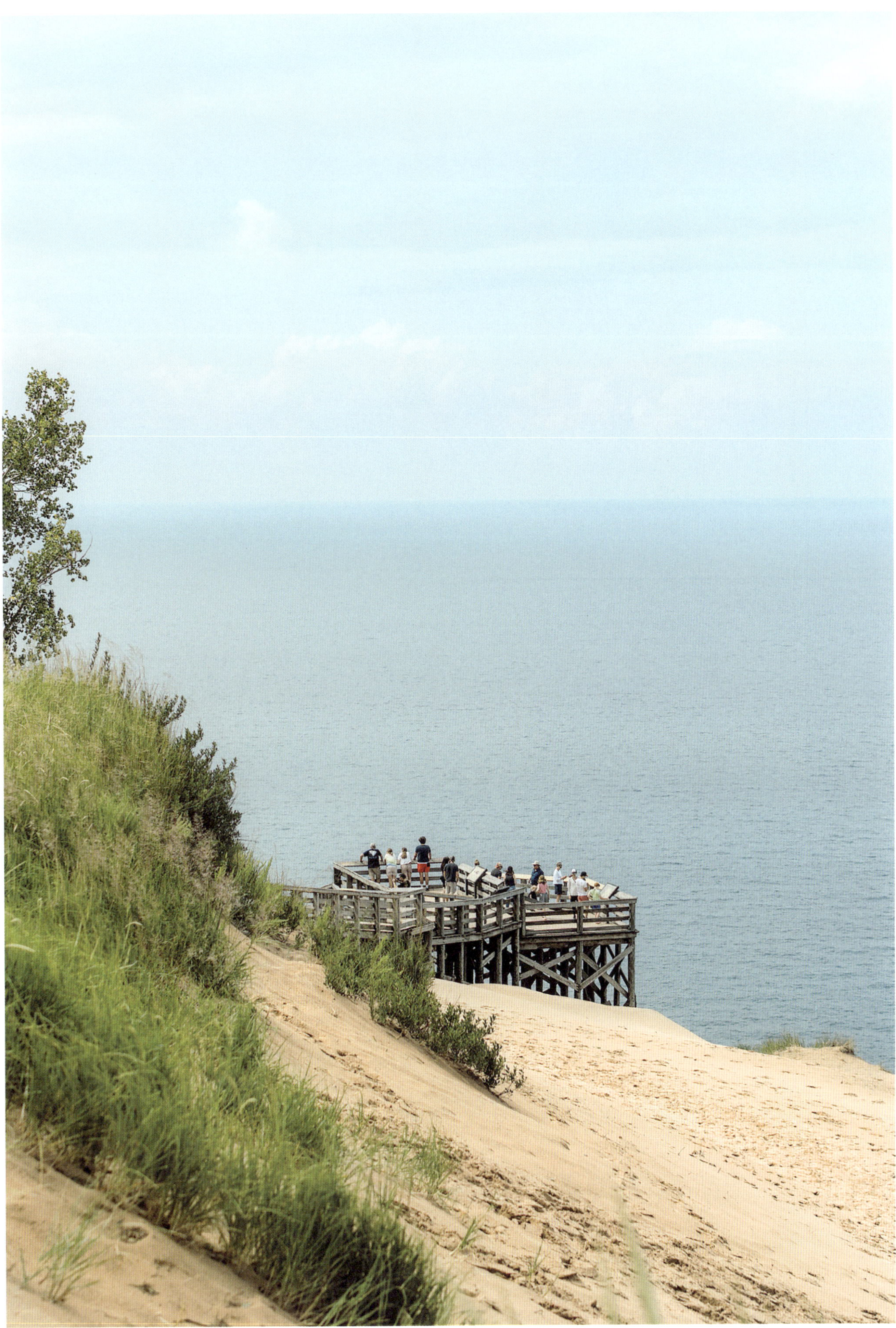

my summer bucket list:

Maybe you also live in a place where summer is fleeting. Maybe, like me, summer is your favorite season and you're wanting to be more intentional with where that time goes. Here are some of the things I add to my bucket list; I hope it gives you some ideas and motivates you to make your own.

- Sunset swim in Lake Michigan
- Kayak on Reeds Lake
- Attend a lakeside outdoor summer concert
- Boat ride with Dad
- Staycation Up North (see pages 47 and 77)
- Visit a new lakeside lighthouse
- Picnic on the beach with friends
- Go to a baseball game (eat Dippin' Dots)
- Volunteer at a nonprofit farm
- Attend a lakeside sunset yoga class
- Golf at our favorite course
- Watch a sailboat regatta at the local yacht club
- Have a dinner date at our favorite lakeside restaurant (and be willing to wait extra long for a waterfront table!)
- Visit my favorite lake towns (see page 144)
- U-pick local summer fruits while they're in season (see page 41)

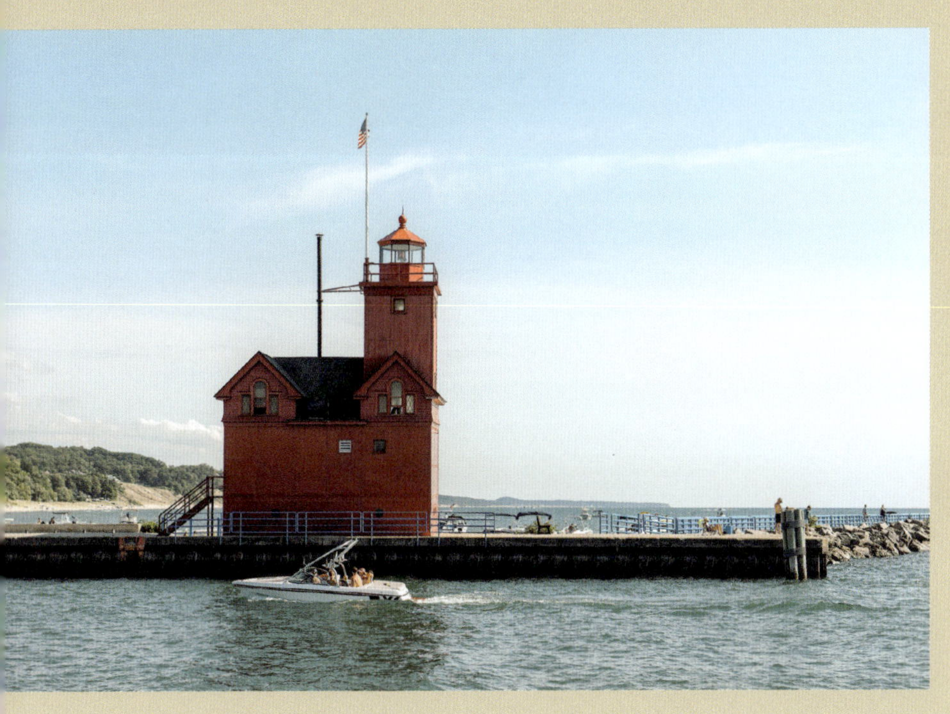

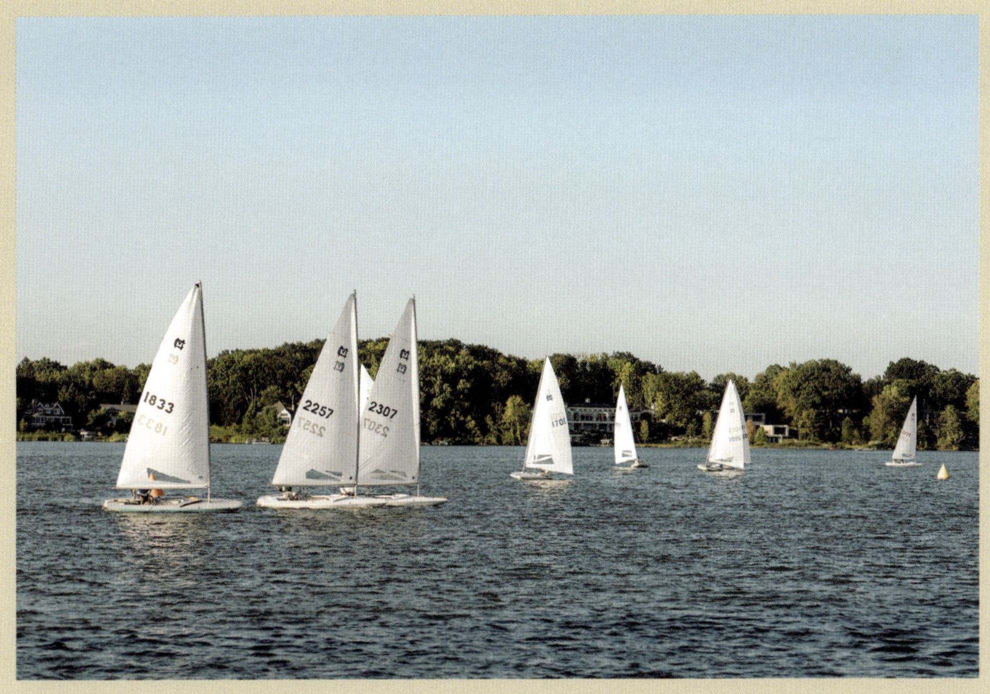
1833
2257
2307

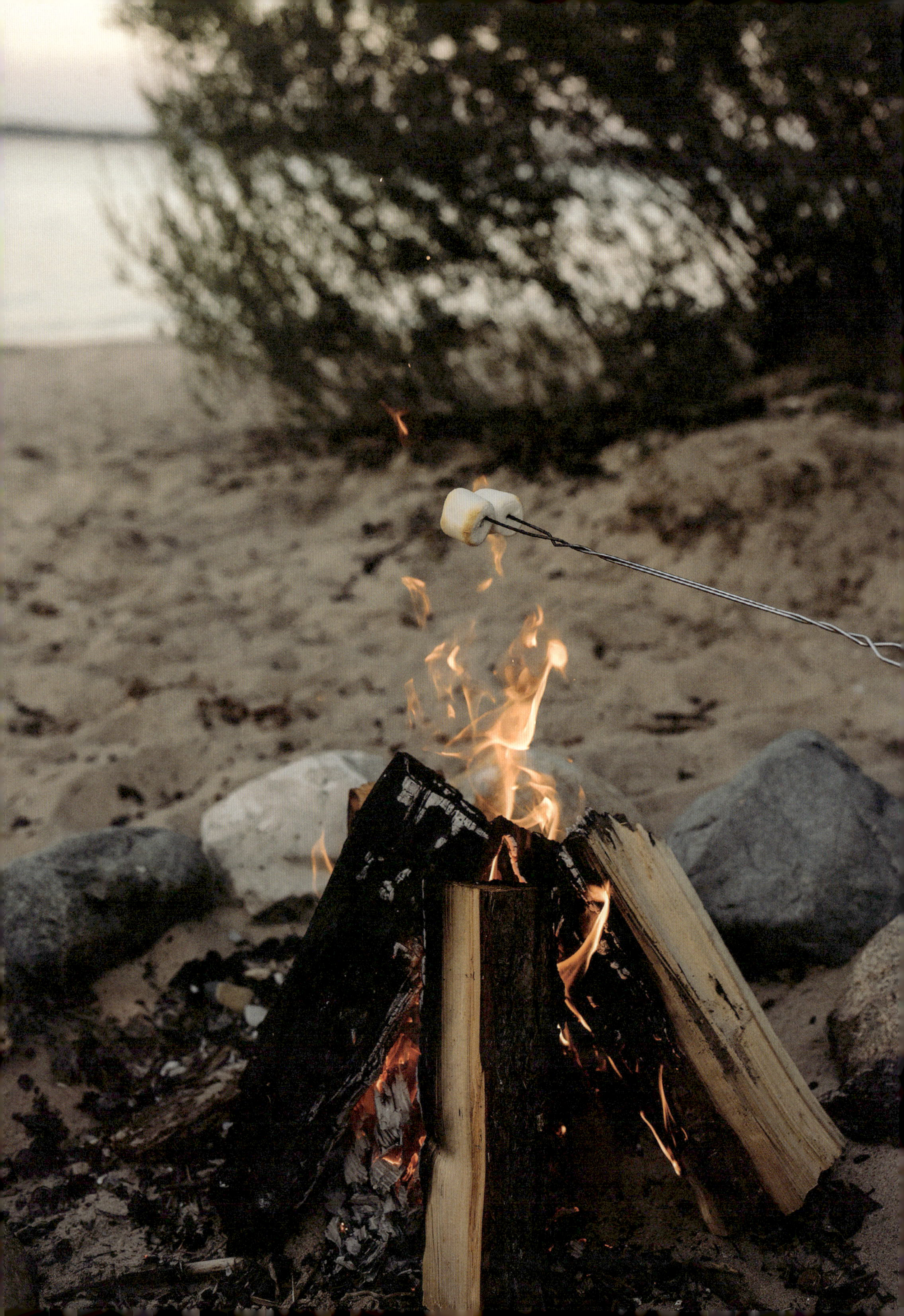

S'mores

SPREADING SUMMER DELIGHT

Summertime is bountiful and generous with us—in sunsets that are masterful works of art, in wildflowers that are sheer delight, in warm sunshine and natural shade from a thousand leaves, in extra daylight and bonus hours to play. All this abundance in the summer season inspires me to pay it forward, to share the magic, to throw it around like candy at a parade.

I decided that s'mores would be my thing. So one day I got a cute basket from the thrift store, and I filled it with supplies. Graham crackers, both classic and gluten free. Marshmallows, the jumbo-sized square ones that perfectly ooze into every corner of the cracker. Hershey's chocolate bars and Reese's peanut butter cups. All organized and arranged into a little woven basket and lovingly stored in the center of my pantry, ready to grab as I dash out the door to cookouts and campfires.

My family and friends have learned that if there's any event planned with an open fire, I will be bringing the s'mores. It fills me with joy every time I see my basket passed around the circle; roles are assigned as roasters or chocolate-cracker assemblers, and sticky smiles sing a chorus of approval. It's my small, simple, sugary way of spreading the summer delight.

I'd encourage you to decide what your "thing" will be this summer—what you'll be known for—and share it every chance you get, because there's more than enough joy and sweetness to go around.

Maybe it's flowers from your yard, like my aunt's dahlias and zinnias and sunflowers, lovingly grown in her garden, tended to for months, just to be snipped and shared. No one leaves her house in the summertime without a mason jar of fresh-cut blooms.

Maybe it's lakeside concerts, like the local bands in my town who offer free shows in the park on Monday nights. The whole community will bring a chair or anchor their boats and listen from the water.

Maybe it's a lemonade stand, like the house down my street that always has a beverage station out on their sidewalk for walkers, bikers, and joggers to find refreshment on warm days, as well as a water dish and treat jar for the neighborhood pups.

Maybe it's every little thing all year long, like my sweet grandmother, the most generous person I know. I've witnessed her give away the jacket off her back and the earrings out of her ears when strangers complimented them, and I think the world might be a better place if we all lived this openhanded and openhearted, leaving a trail of goodness wherever we go.

Decide one way that you'll magnify the summer delight, then spread it far and wide, like ripples on the lake after a cannonball.

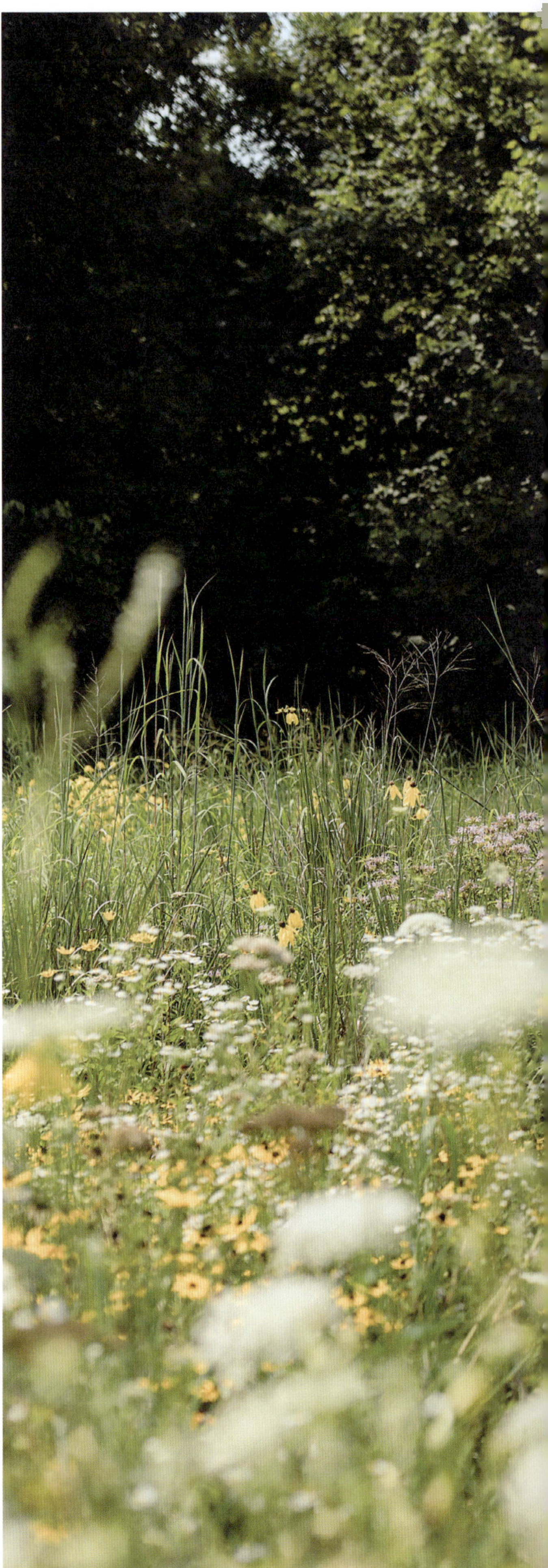

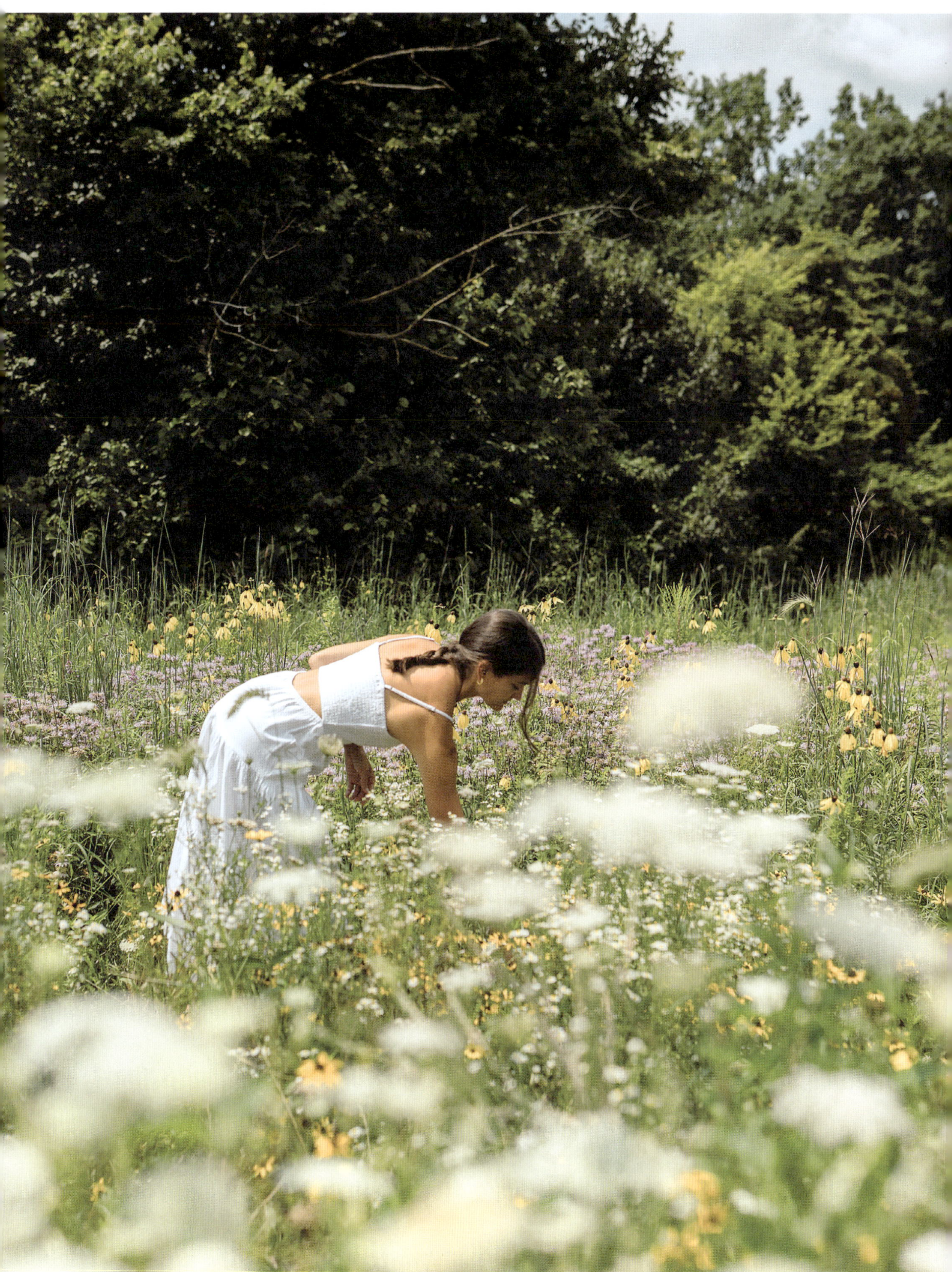

ideas for sharing summer cheer:

— Paddle around the lake with a cooler full of Popsicles to pass out to boaters and dockside neighbors.

— Plant more than you need in your vegetable garden and pass along produce to others when you have a surplus of green beans, tomatoes, or cucumbers.

— Become the designated fireworks expert on your lake (after reviewing local firework ordinances) and light off a spectacular show on holidays for everyone across the water to sit back and enjoy.

— Fire up the grill and text the neighborhood group chat "free hot dogs while supplies last."

— Go to a U-pick farm and gather an extra bucket of berries to drop off at a friend's house.

— Cut some fresh flowers from your yard and deliver a bouquet.

— Make a double batch of summer treats and share with loved ones.

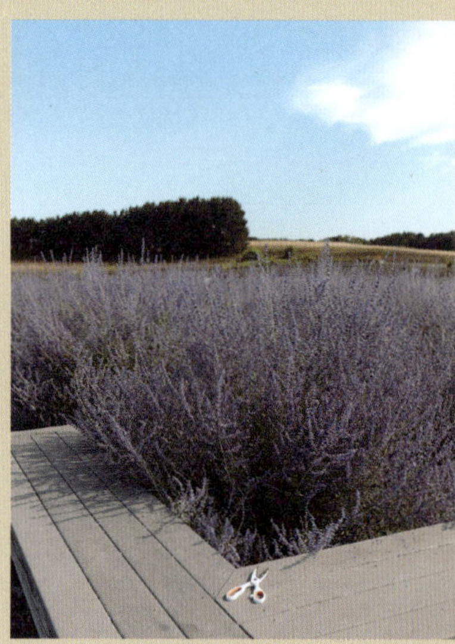

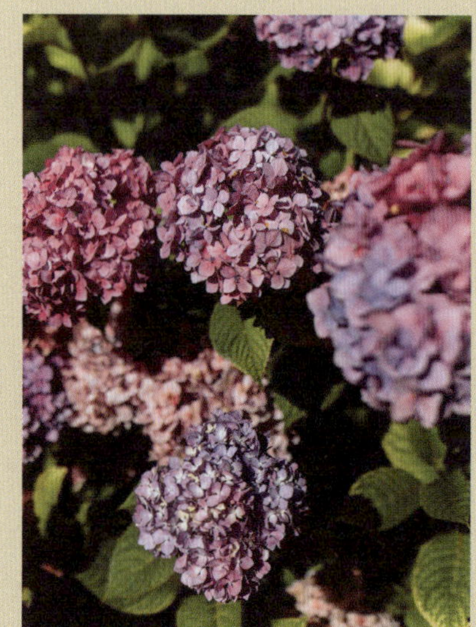

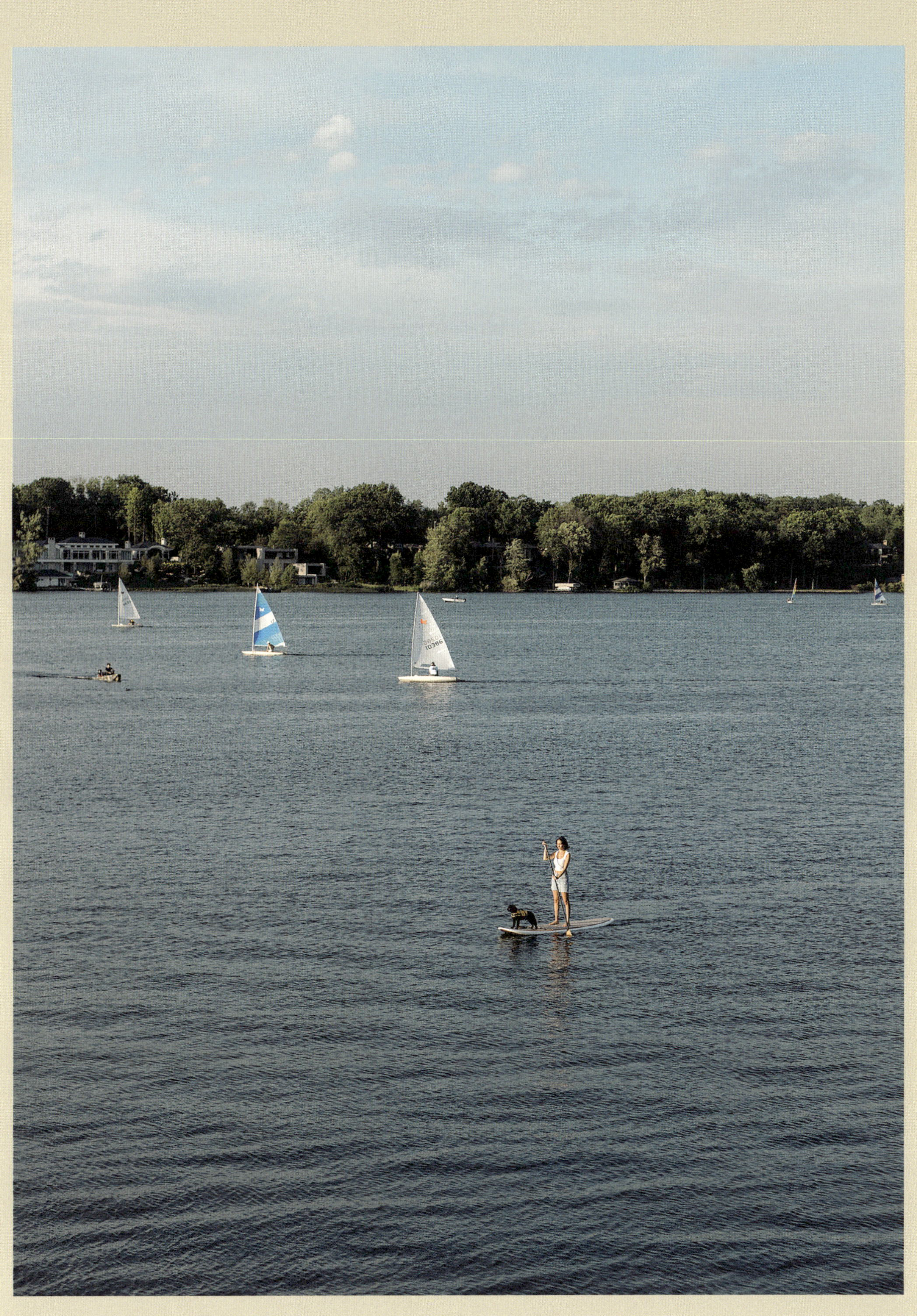

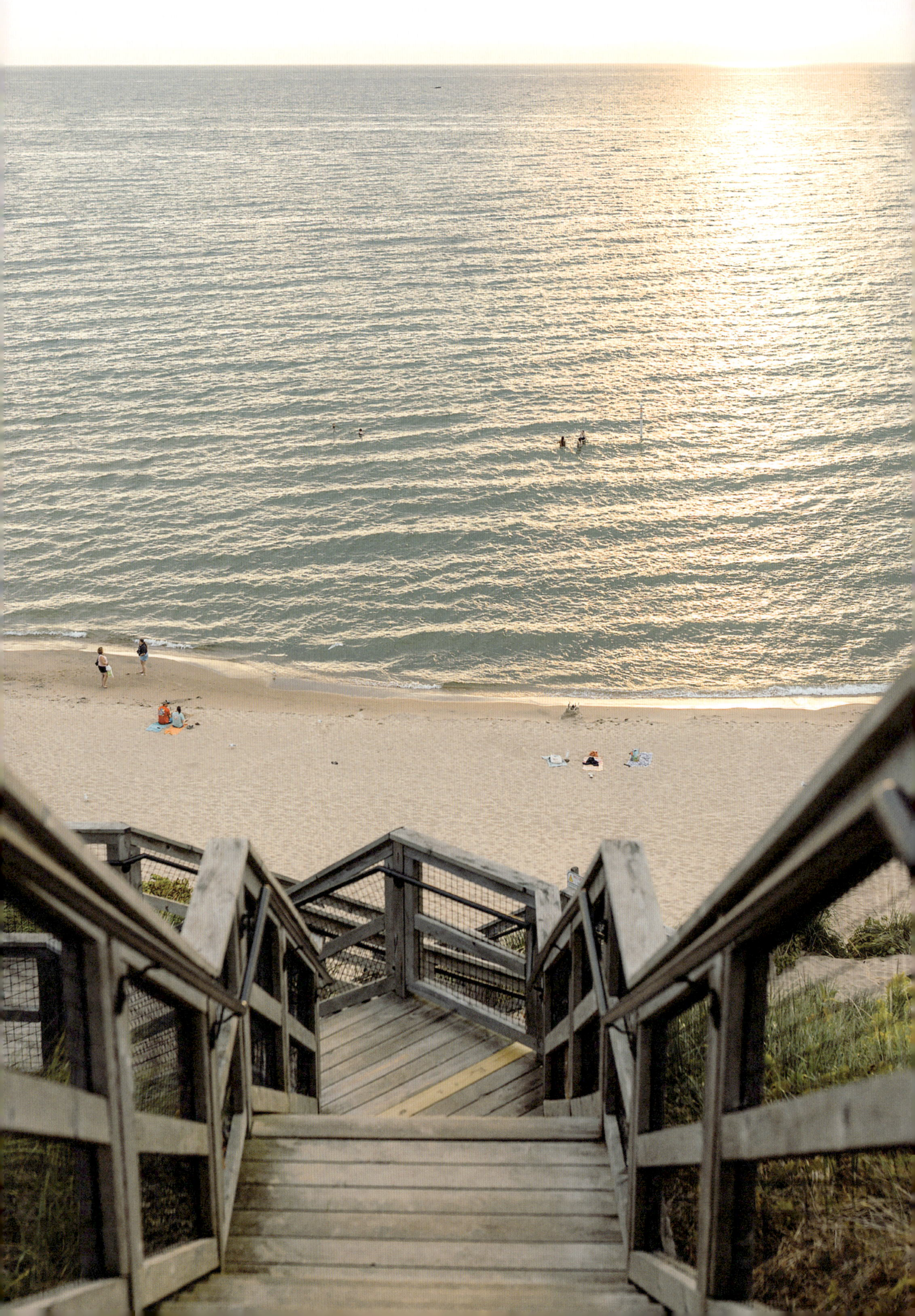

Solstice

THE FORMAL INVITATION

My first lake day of the year always feels both foreign and familiar. The sand is strange between my toes, a sensation I'd forgotten about after a winter spent in socks. The lake breeze is surprisingly gentle on my face after months of frigid air. Towels and bedsheets and beach chairs are scattered across the shoreline, in a mutual agreement that we're all content to just be here for a while, and I'm reminded of the ways that water gathers us.

The lake may still feel wintery cold in June, but that doesn't stop each of us from enjoying it in our own way—in boating or floating, in brave squeals or silent reverence. I make my way to the water's edge, starting ankle-deep and slowly working myself in, giving my body a moment to adjust before each step further and deeper.

While we've been gradually easing ourselves into summer with ever-rising temperatures and ever-increasing daylight, wading into chilly lakes one slow stride at a time, there's something about the solstice that makes things feel official.

When the calendar marks the summer solstice in the northern hemisphere, the earth bends toward the sun at its greatest angle and we get to experience the longest day of the year. The brightest light and the shortest night. The earth at its maximum tilt, the sun at its maximum intensity, the days at their maximum potential.

The solstice means that summer is no longer soon, almost, around the corner. It's here and now, and you're invited.

Consider the solstice a formal invitation to throw away comfort zones and routines, to splash and be silly, to take the scenic route and go on the spontaneous adventure, to do something a little bold, a little brave, a little wild.

The solstice is my permission slip to take a swim even if I didn't bring my swimsuit. To stray from my usual pastel palette and paint my nails something bright and

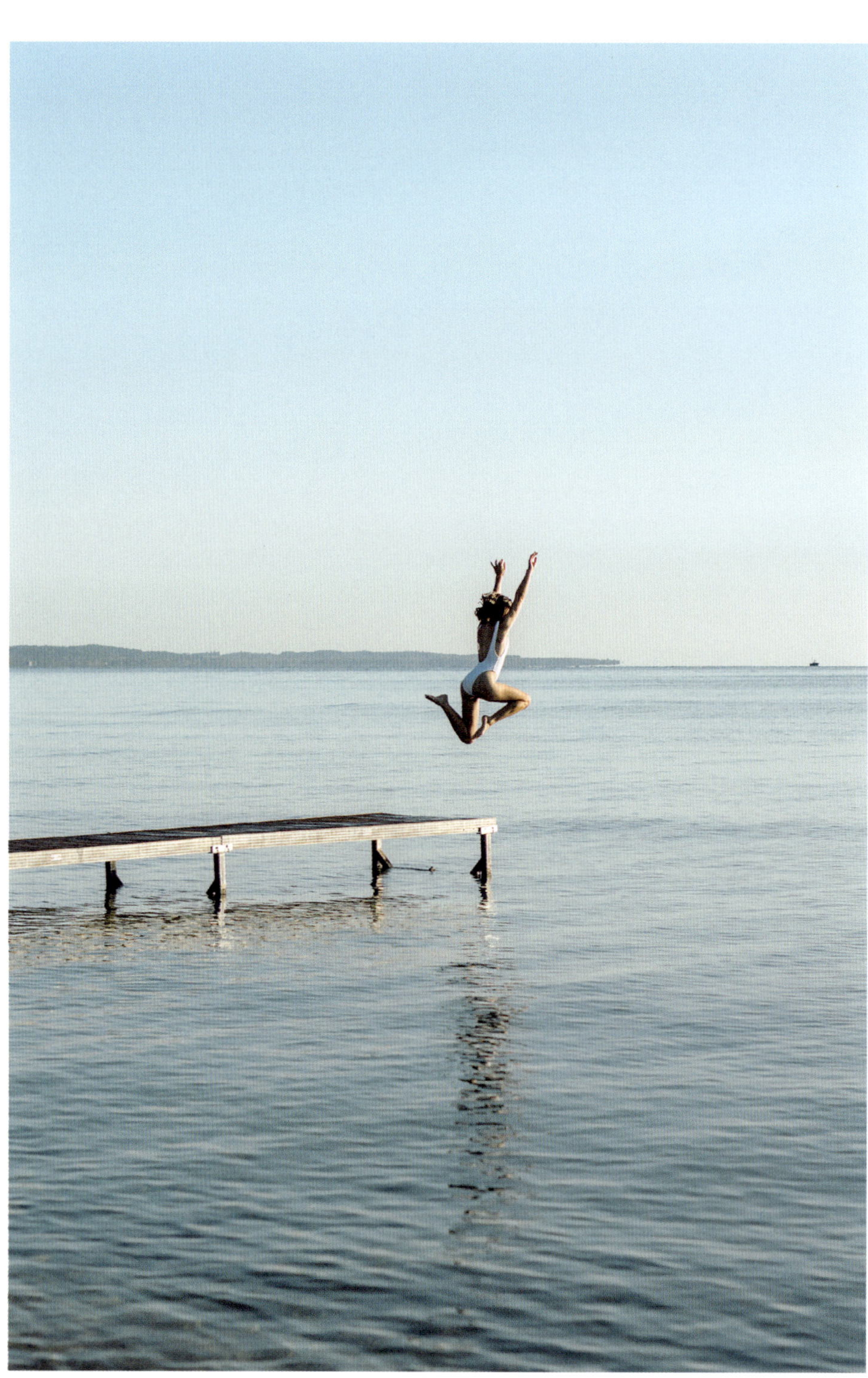

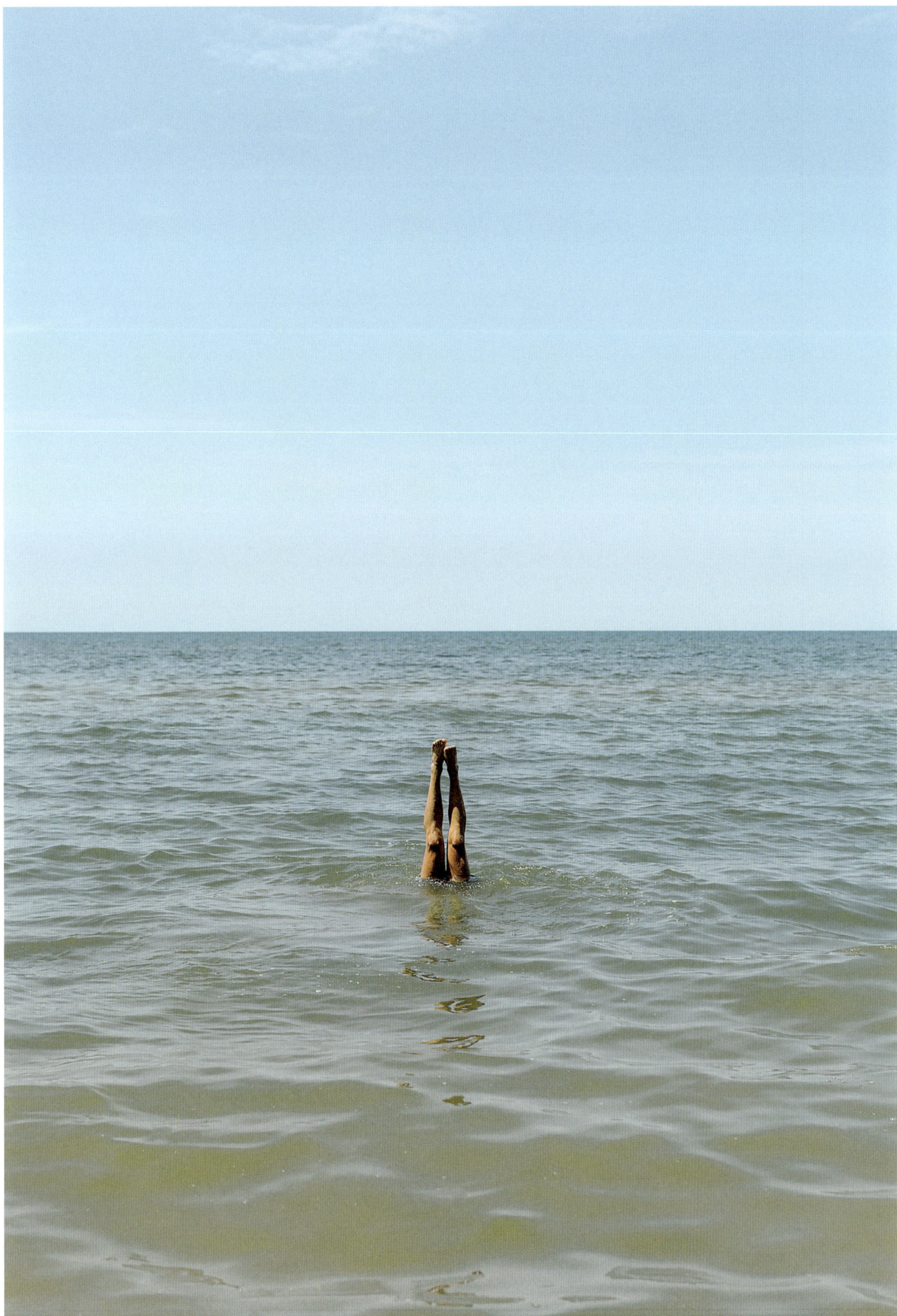

The solstice means that summer is no longer soon, almost, around the corner. It's here and now, and you're invited.

unapologetic, like the exact red-pink shade of an overripe watermelon. To drop whatever I'm doing when I get a last-minute invitation. To run full speed down a sand dune until my legs are moving so fast I don't have control of them anymore.

Each year I want summer to be seared in my memory. I want these long radiant days and intense sunrays to fill my phone storage and scrapbook and heart with memories. And the only way to do that is by being carefree, maybe even a little reckless.

By letting go and jumping in.

Making a mess and eating every last crumb.

Running out of breath and laughing until it hurts.

Doing cartwheels and underwater handstands.

Roasting another marshmallow and staying up late.

Painting nails hot pink and swimming with your clothes on.

Bending toward the sun, just because it's summer.

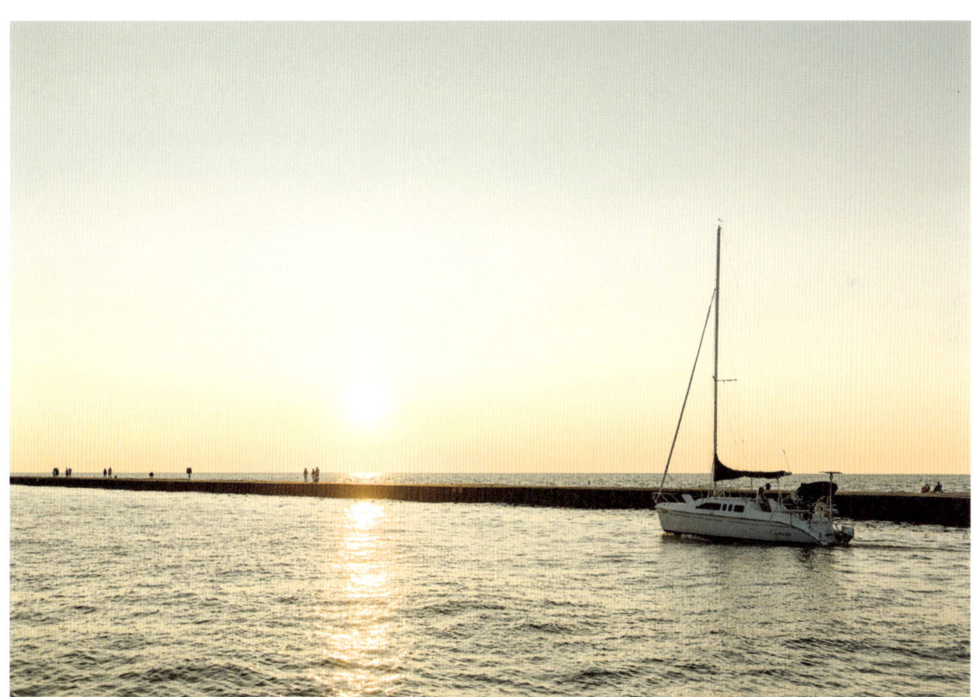

summer spontaneity checklists:

THE BEACH BAG

Keep a beach bag stocked and ready with these items for any race-you-to-the-lake moments:

- Sunscreen
- Book
- Sunglasses
- Snacks
- Towels and a flat bedsheet
- Sand toys
- Sun hat or baseball cap
- Bag or jar for rock treasure collecting
- Deck of cards
- Checkerboard or tic-tac-toe game mats—mine are DIYed with fabric paint and old linen napkins, and I forage the shore for game pieces

THE CAR TRUNK

Maximize your summertime spontaneity by keeping some of these items in your car:

- Camp chairs
- Picnic blanket
- Bug spray
- Sun umbrella
- Rain umbrella
- Pickleball paddles or tennis racquets
- Spare swimsuit, so you never miss an opportunity to jump in

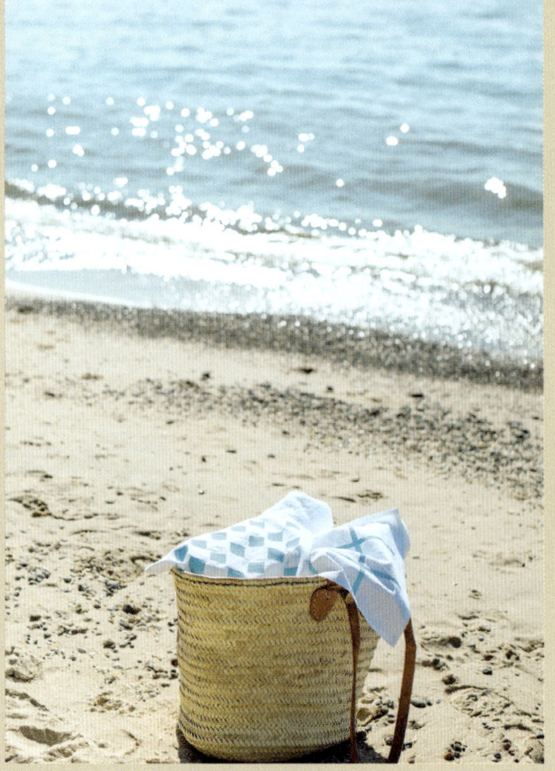

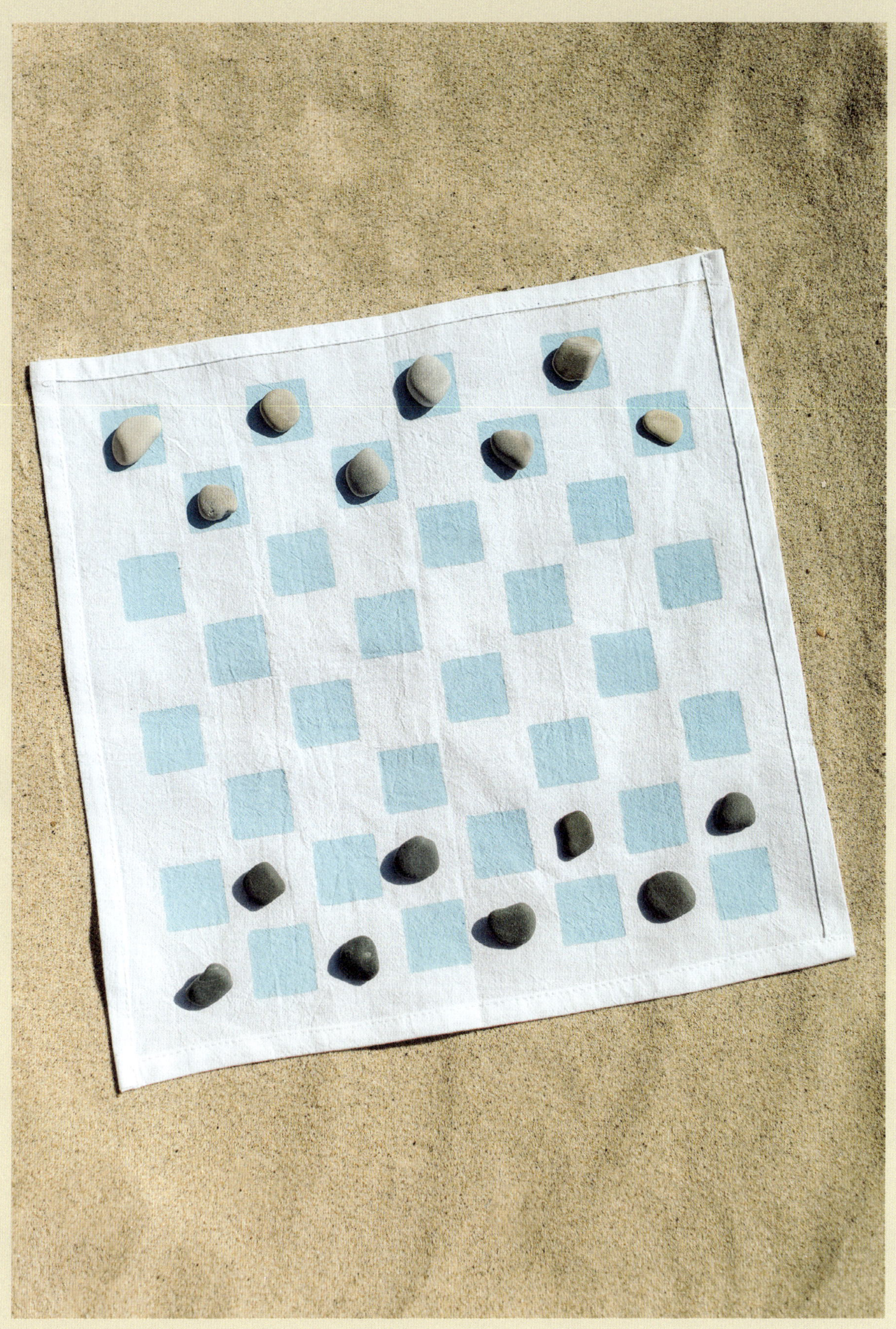

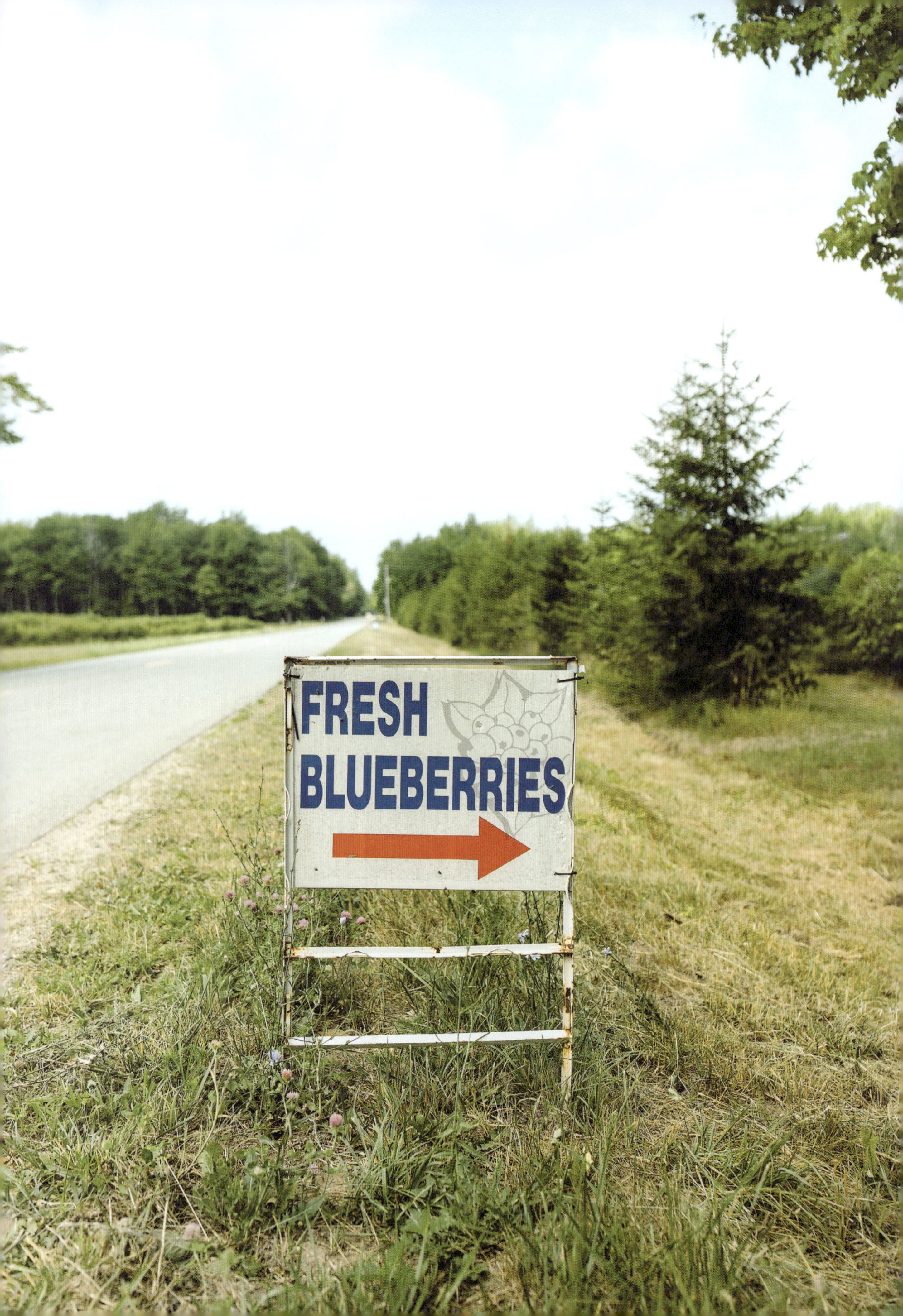
FRESH
BLUEBERRIES

U-Pick

FRESH AIR AND FRESH BERRIES

I grew up picking blueberries at my grandparents' house every summer. A few blueberry bushes grew in the back corner of their yard, and they would give each of us kids repurposed plastic Cool Whip containers to fill with berries—although more berries would end up in our bellies than our bins.

I remember those blueberry-picking afternoons with my brothers and cousins like they were yesterday. I can still feel the grass beneath my feet, the sun on my shoulders, and the warm burst of juice from a fresh-picked blueberry, sampling bites straight from the branch while they still tasted like sunshine.

These days, I drive around my little corner of Michigan in pursuit of those same feelings: fresh air and fresh berries, blue skies and berry-stained fingertips. I'm a regular at my local U-pick farms in the summer season. Whether it's blueberries or dark sweet cherries, strawberries or peaches, I love searching for the ripest, juiciest ones and feeling the satisfaction of a full bucket.

I also joined a CSA for the summer: a community-supported agriculture program through a local farm. I visit every week to pick up a variety of vegetables, and I love rummaging through the leaves to find the perfect tomatoes, snap peas, green beans, peppers. Often, by the time I get back in my car, I notice that my thumb has turned green from popping the veggies off their stems. It feels so great to leave with a literal green thumb and a basket of fresh organic produce in my passenger seat.

Living in a region where the earth is barren for half of the year, I've learned to never take for granted the summer harvest. The colors and flavors of the season deserve to be relished, and these afternoons on the farm leave me feeling fulfilled like nothing else can.

A whole new level of slow-paced is unlocked when you spend a few sun-soaked hours picking your own produce, one single bite at a time. And a deeper gratitude is discovered for the things that nourish us when we get some dirt under our nails.

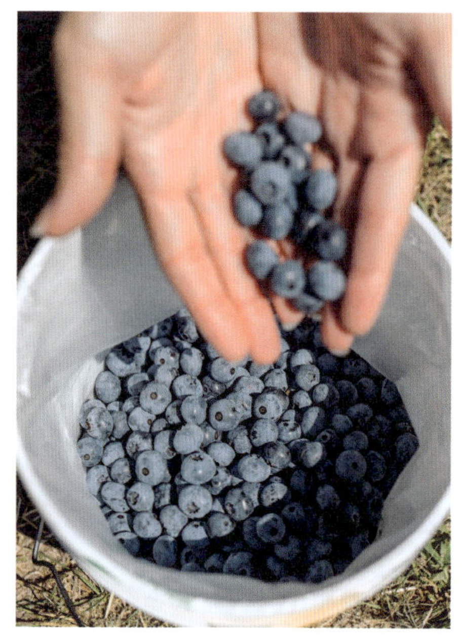

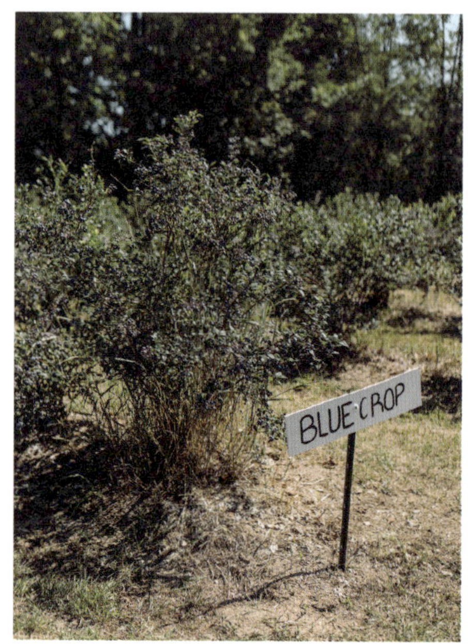
BLUE CROP

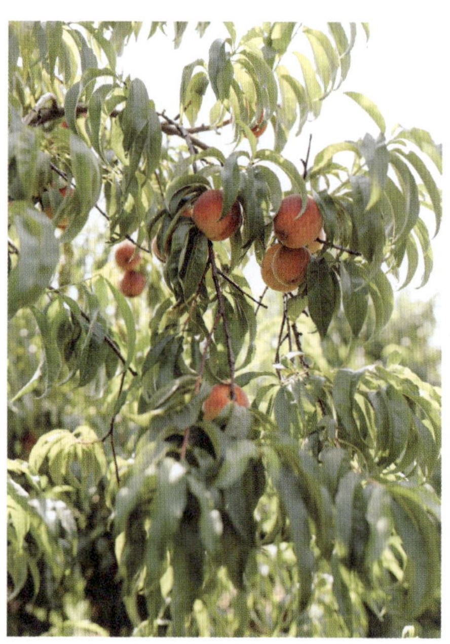

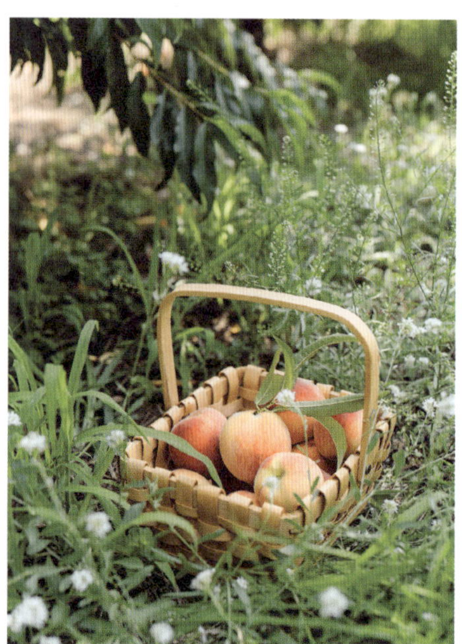

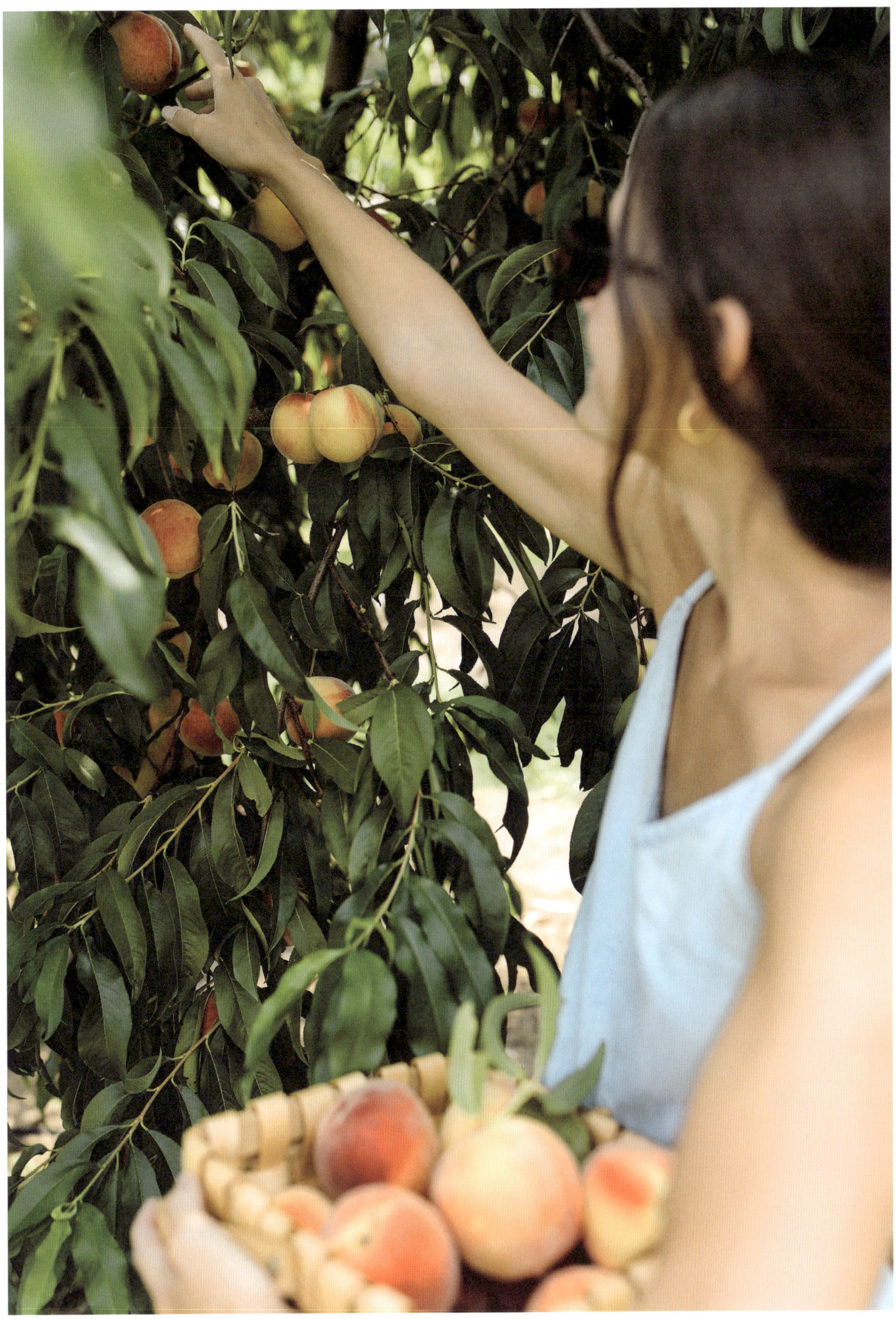

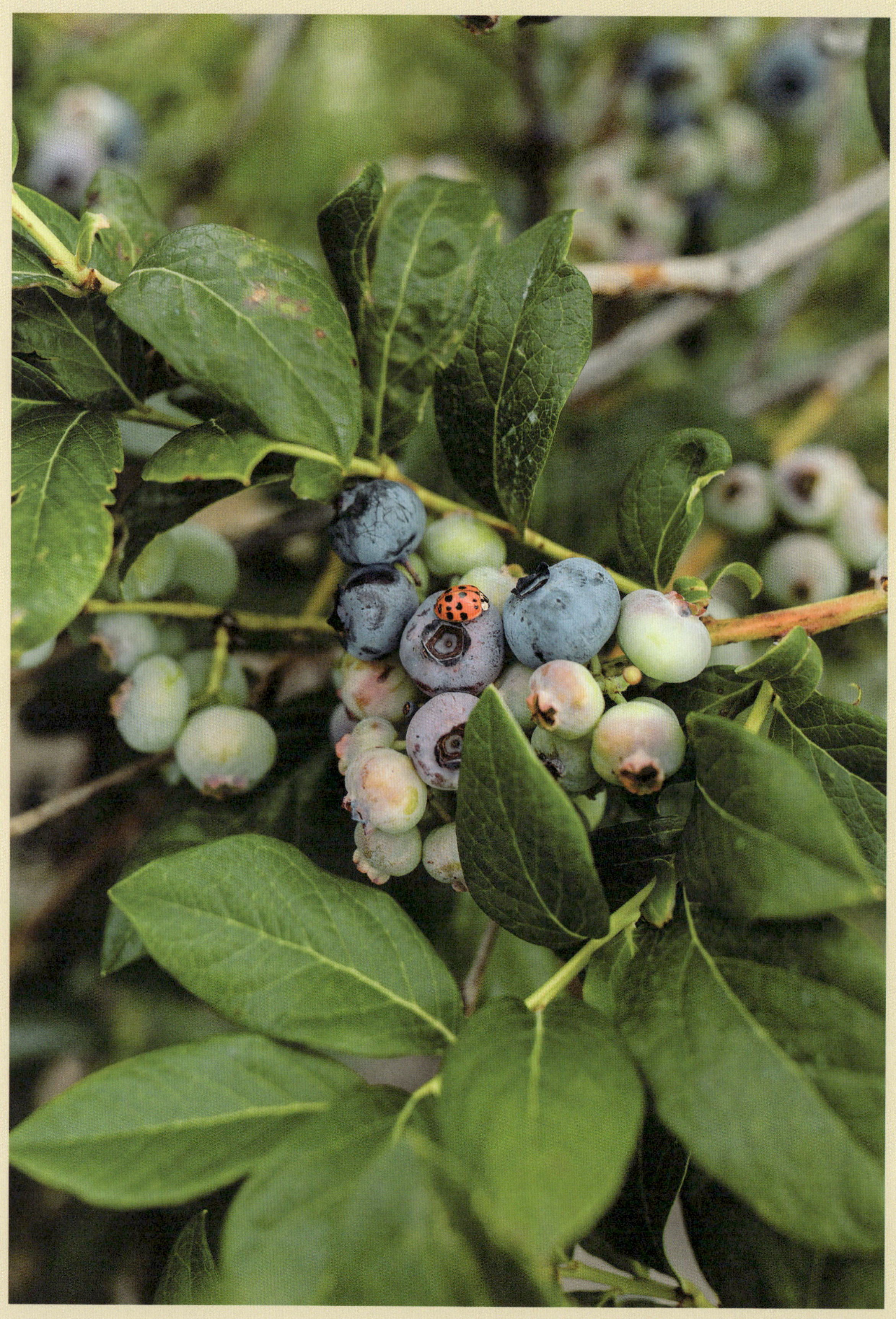

u-pick produce calendar:

These are some of my favorite fruits to pick. Ripening times fluctuate from year to year and location to location throughout the Midwest, so be sure to reach out to your local farms for more accurate harvesting schedules. You'll discover more ways to cook, bake, and enjoy these fresh flavors in the pages to come.

- June: strawberries
- July: blackberries, blueberries, cherries, raspberries
- August: blueberries, peaches
- September: apples, pears

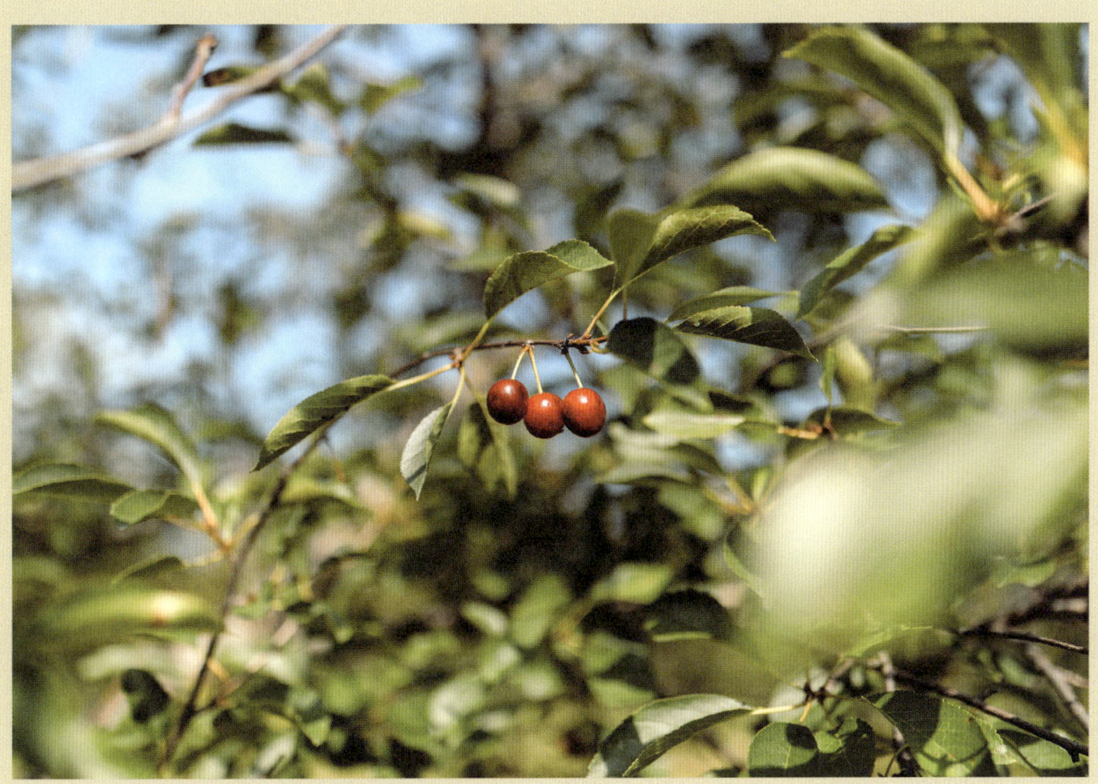

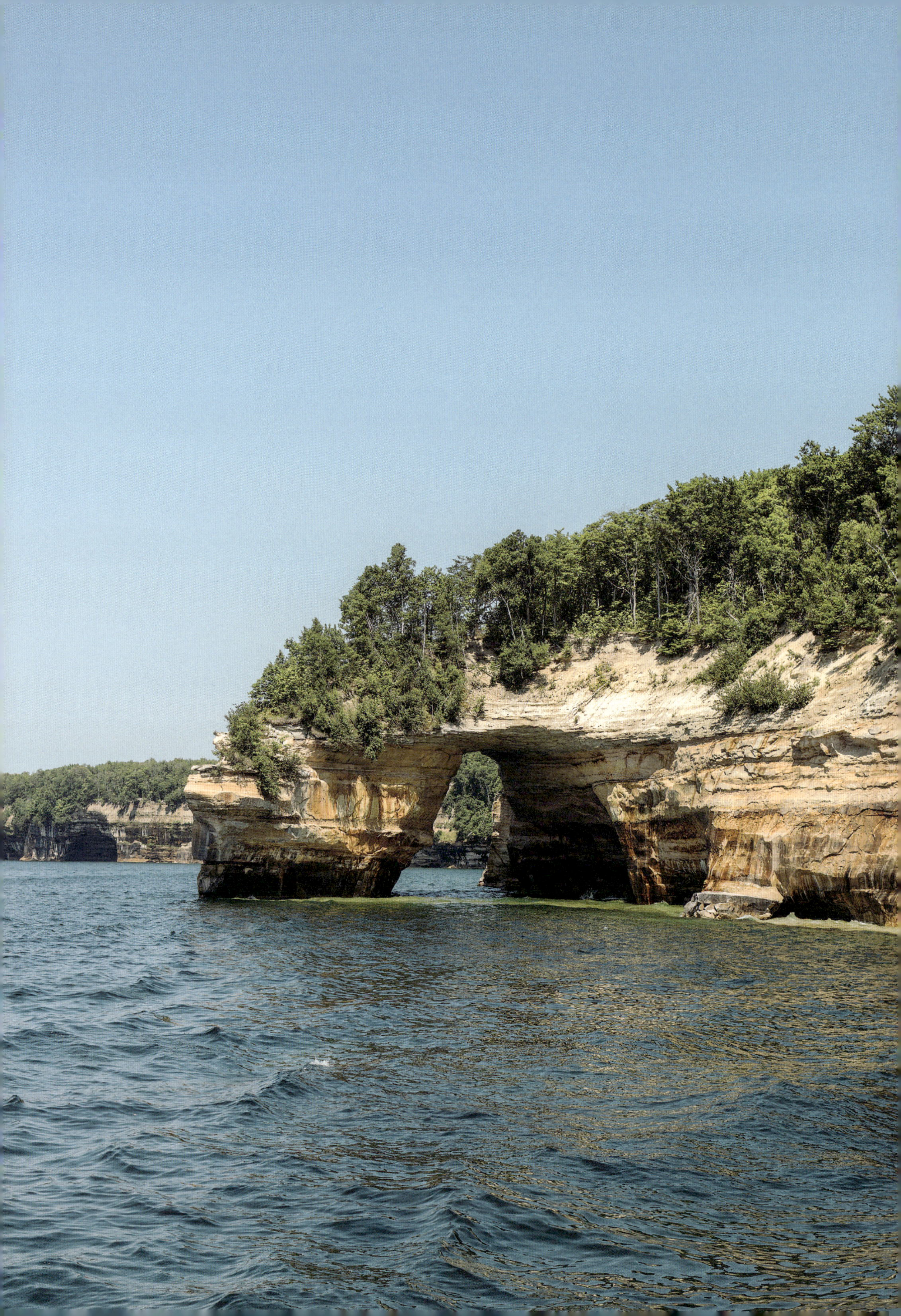

Staycation

TRAVELING THE LAKESHORE

The Great Lakes region remains understated and often underrated, a true hidden gem. Endless fresh water and crisp northern air. Pristine beaches with rolling dunes, as well as rocky cliffs and rustic shores. Wide-open skies and waterfront sunsets, starry constellations and northern lights. It's the perfect summertime destination.

Plus, each of the Great Lakes has its own unique offerings. Lake Michigan is visited for its warm swimming water, sandy coast, and beloved summer towns. Meanwhile, Lake Superior is known for its rugged shoreline, waterfalls, and cliff jumping into its cold waters. Lake Huron offers coastal hiking trails and grottoes, plus several historic shipwreck sites and scuba diving. Lake Erie holds half of all the Great Lakes' fish, making it a fisherman's paradise. And Lake Ontario, although the smallest, boasts many picturesque islands and scenic boating.

In addition to the five Greats, the region also contains thousands of inland lakes too, many of which are just as beautiful and worth visiting. These smaller inland lakes often have calm waters and laid-back coastal communities. They're the perfect place for recreational activities like tubing and waterskiing, kayaking and paddleboarding, sailing and wake surfing. Midwestern friendliness can be found on the land and on the water, with strangers striking up conversations and waving from boat to boat.

I feel so grateful to have been born and raised in such a place as this. And yet, I'm a victim of wanderlust. I love to travel, and all too often I have the misconception that the farther I go, the more fun I will have. Sometimes I falsely believe happiness is out there, far far away, on a flight to a foreign destination.

My husband, Gavin, and I take a trip every year on our wedding anniversary, and this past year we were really torn on where to go. With his job benefits as a pilot and the world at our fingertips, we truly could

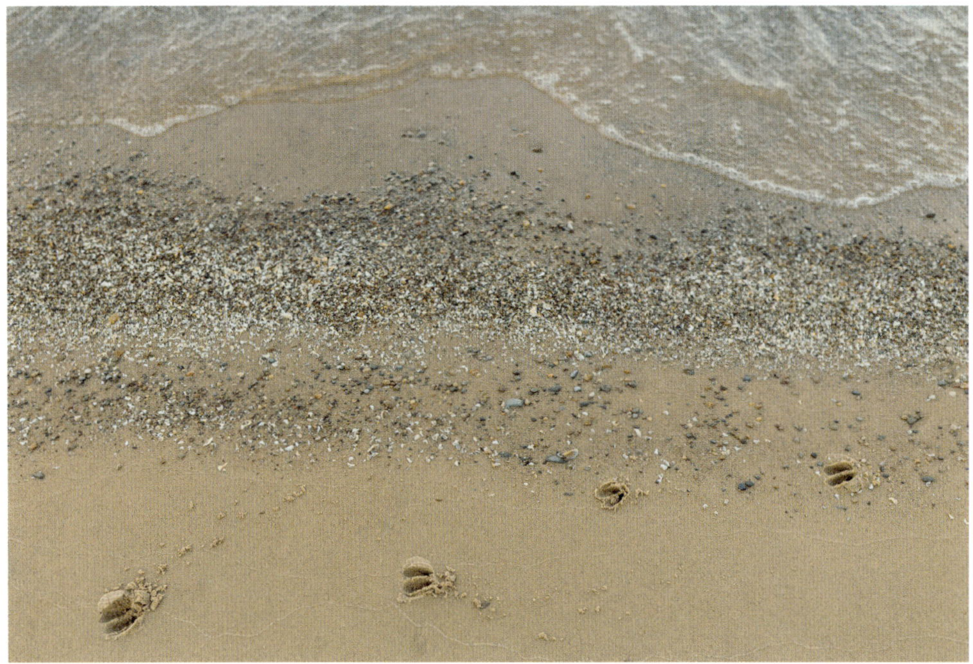

have gone anywhere. So it felt a little silly when we eventually decided to drive an hour to a small lake town for a staycation.

I'm learning that sometimes everything I'm looking for is just down the road. It requires less than one tank of gas. It's right where the lake meets the sky.

We checked into the Lake Shore Resort in Saugatuck, a lovely boutique hotel set on a bluff overlooking Lake Michigan, and we had such an amazing time, so much so that I often had déjà vu. The hot sunny days spent alternating between the cold waves and the shade of colorful sun umbrellas called to mind previous tropical vacations. The quaint village with live music, art galleries, and candlelit dinners had whispers of my favorite European memories. The wild roaming deer, unending shoreline, and remarkable nightly sunsets watched from the wooden dock with a bottle of wine filled me with the same awe and wonder I've felt in faraway places.

This trip felt just as special, delightful, and memorable as many of my foreign travels even though I was mere miles from my driveway. Every day felt extraordinary, and yet I was minutes from where I grew up, where I've lived my whole life. If anything, the more I travel the world, the more I appreciate my home.

The Great Lakes, my own little ocean, free of salt and sharks and hurricanes.

The laid-back lake life and Midwest friendliness.

The mild Michigan summers with the greenest greens and bluest blues and deer tracks in the sand.

Not only do I love this region, but I also love my zip code. My cozy neighborhood and tiny village with my favorite local restaurant where the waiter knows my name

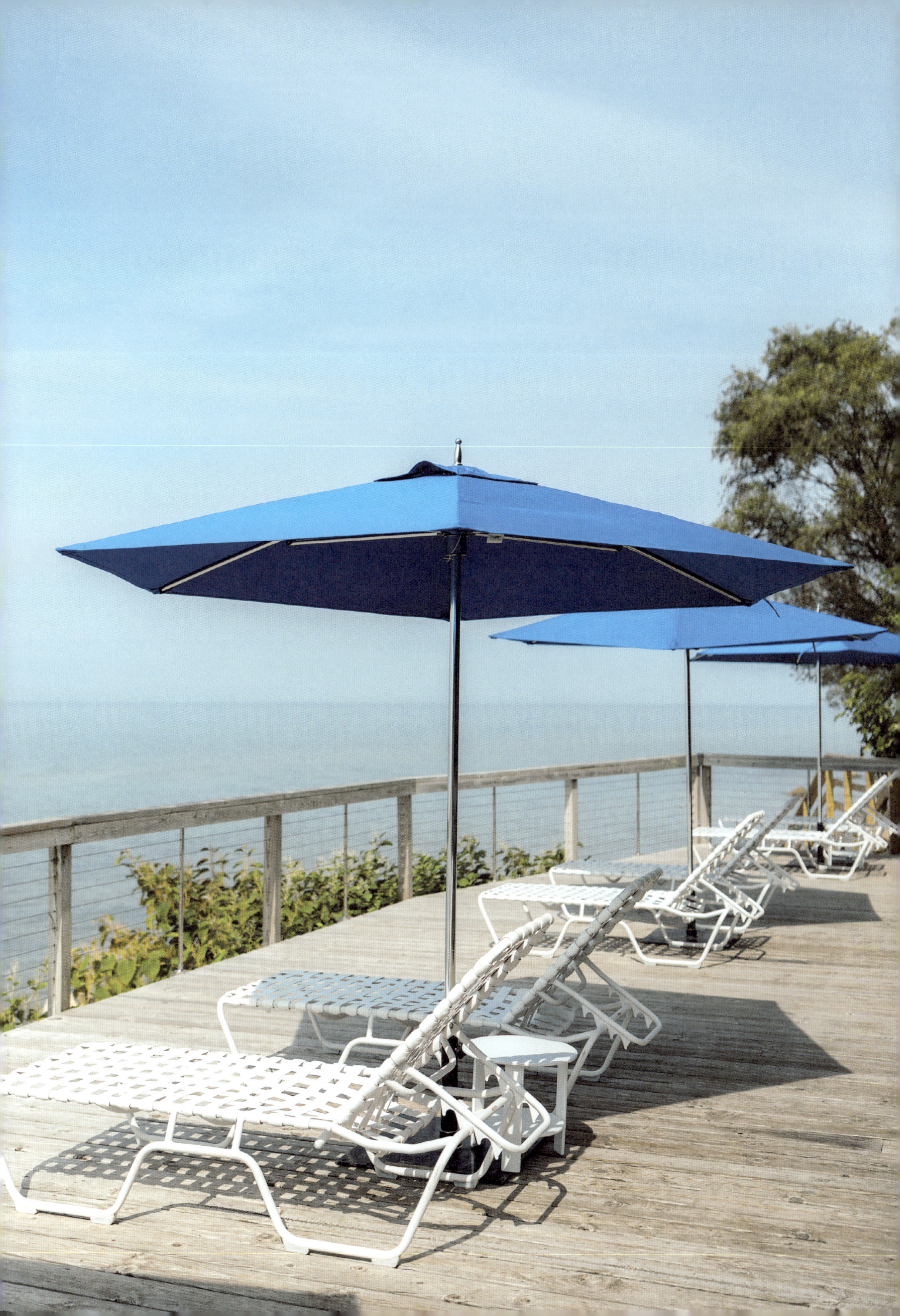

I'm learning that sometimes everything I'm looking for is just down the road. It requires less than one tank of gas. It's right where the lake meets the sky.

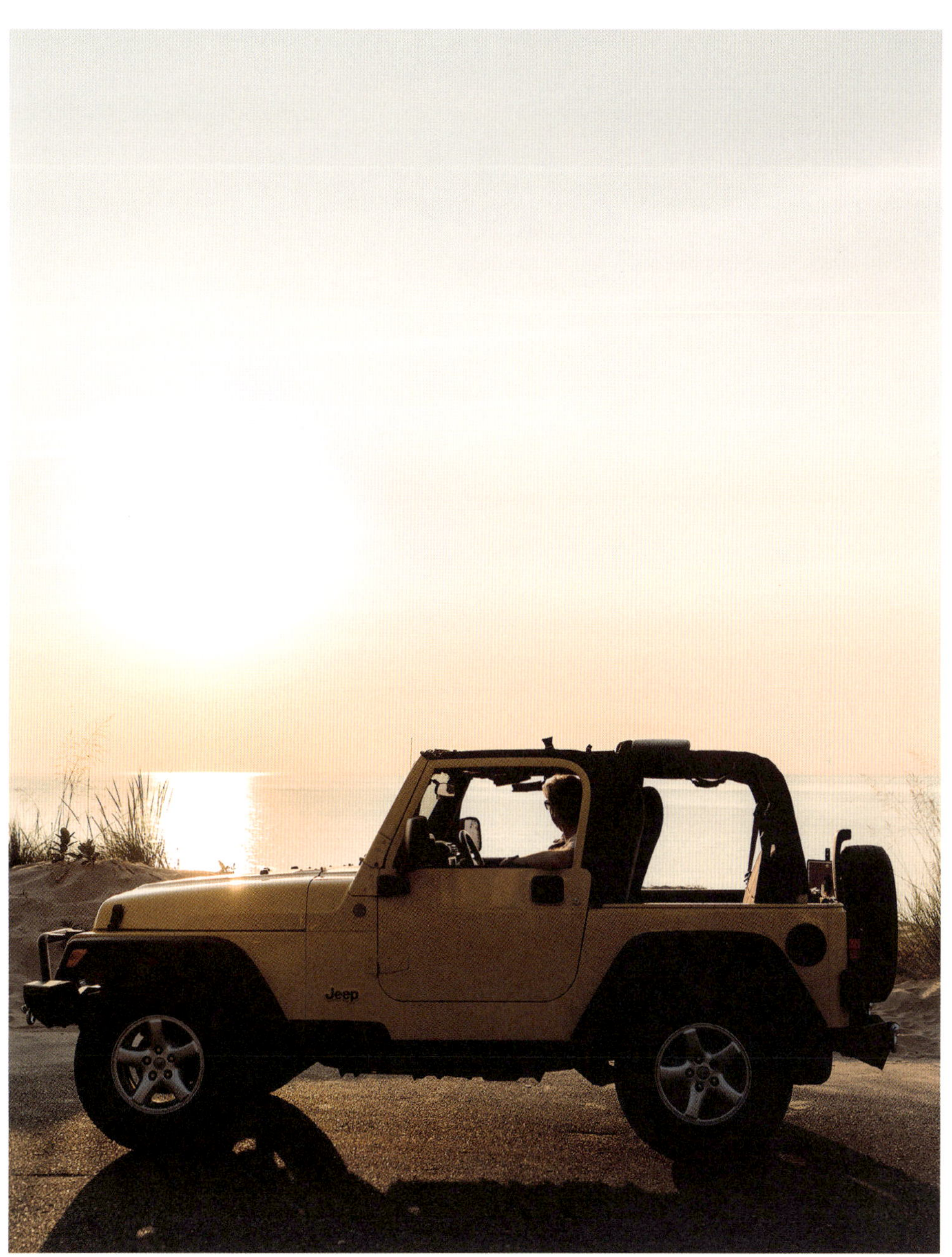
Jeep

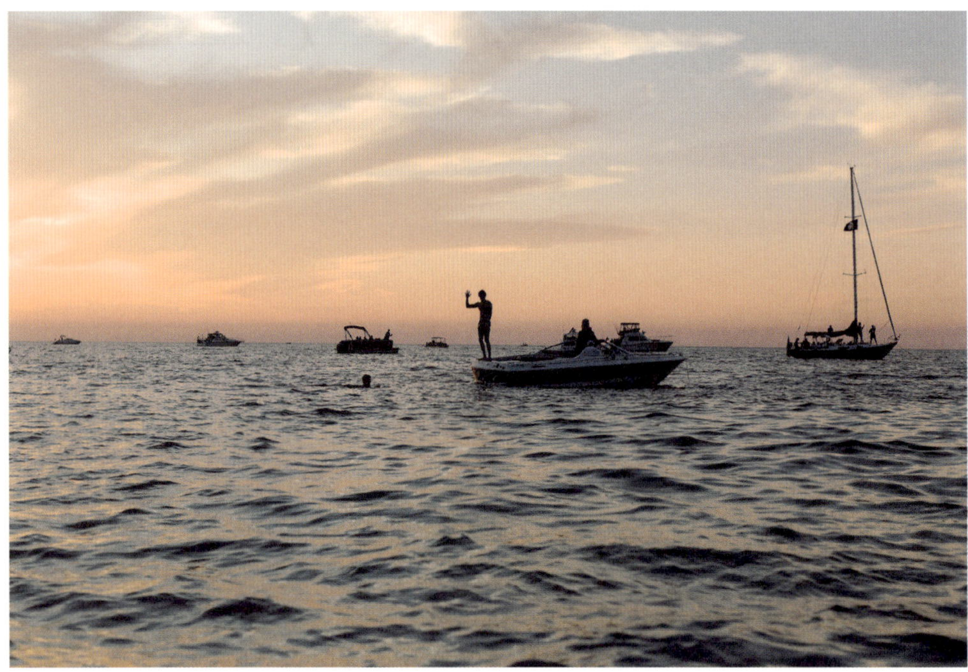

and my order: an olive burger with a side of truffle fries. The sounds of mopeds whizzing by, ice cream trucks jingling street by street, kids playing, and dogs barking.

Not only do I love my zip code, but I also love my house. The physical, tangible bones of my home. The creaky hardwood floors, the natural light in my kitchen, my bathtub and oversized couch and whimsical backyard, weeds and all.

I still love to travel, but this staycation was a pleasant reminder that I don't always have to go very far to find what I'm looking for. Plus, I love knowing that at the end of every trip, this is what I'll always return to.

As you plan your summer travels, try booking a staycation instead of a grand vacation. Cruise the lakeshore instead of international waters. Check into a local hotel and see the town with fresh eyes. Take a walk through your city, your neighborhood, your house, and try to articulate every little thing you love about it. Start a gratitude list and at the very top put your home address, your street name, your favorite park, your favorite lake.

It turns out you don't always need a passport, a time change, or a culture shock to feel wonder and experience beauty.

You just need a state park pass, a beach bag, and a tank of gas.

A swimsuit, snacks, and a good book.

An old wooden dock, a bottle of wine, and the sky.

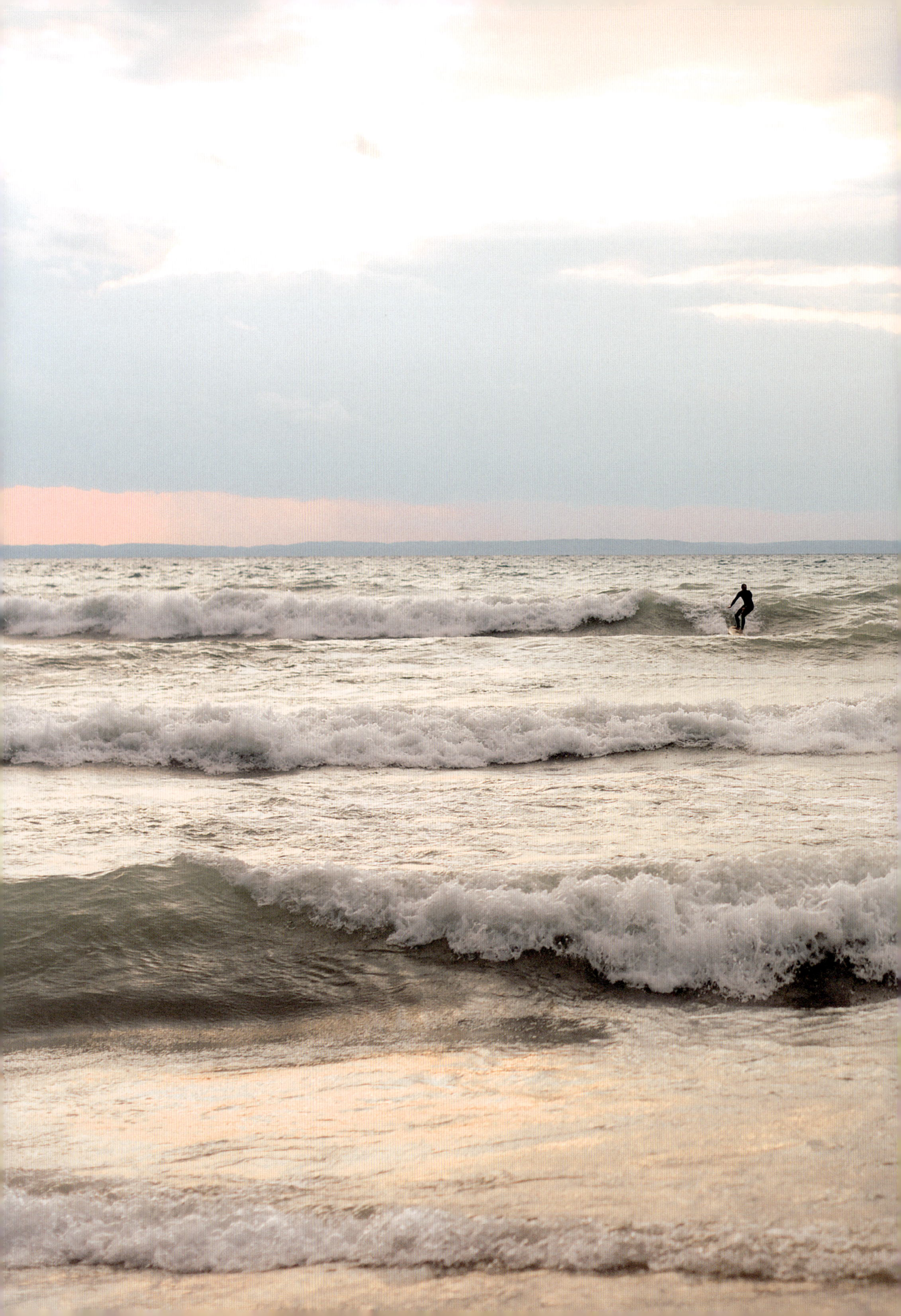

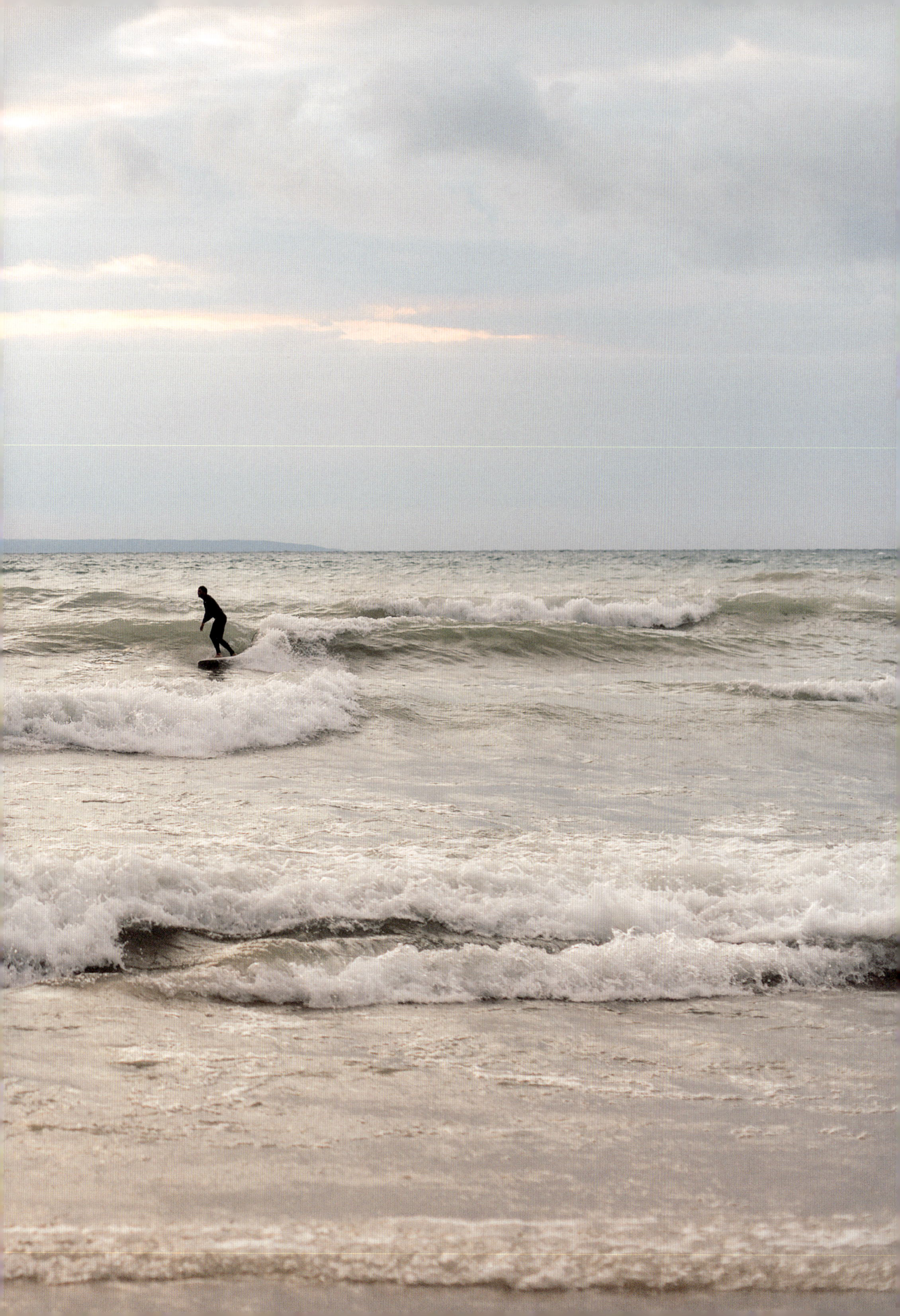

trading international travels for midwest adventures:

- Instead of tropical cruising, book a Great Lakes cruise. Several cruise lines offer trips with varying durations and destinations throughout the region. You can even find voyages that will take you through all five Great Lakes!
- Tuck away your international passport for a summer and get a Lighthouse Passport instead. Over seven hundred participating lighthouses across the United States offer stamps that you can collect. Visit the United States Lighthouse Society website for more information.
- Consider purchasing a state park pass for unlimited access to all the beaches, forests, and boating sites in your home state. Look into the park pass details in your own state and set yourself up for a summer at the lake.
- If you're interested in visiting several national parks, consider purchasing an America the Beautiful Pass. This grants you unlimited access to any national parks across the United States for one year. In Canada, the Parks Canada Discovery Pass offers the equivalent yearlong access to national parks and historic sites, making it a great option for exploring the Canadian side of the Great Lakes.
- Find a boutique hotel in your area and book a staycation. You can simultaneously support a local business and enjoy immersing yourself in the luxuries of your hometown or state.

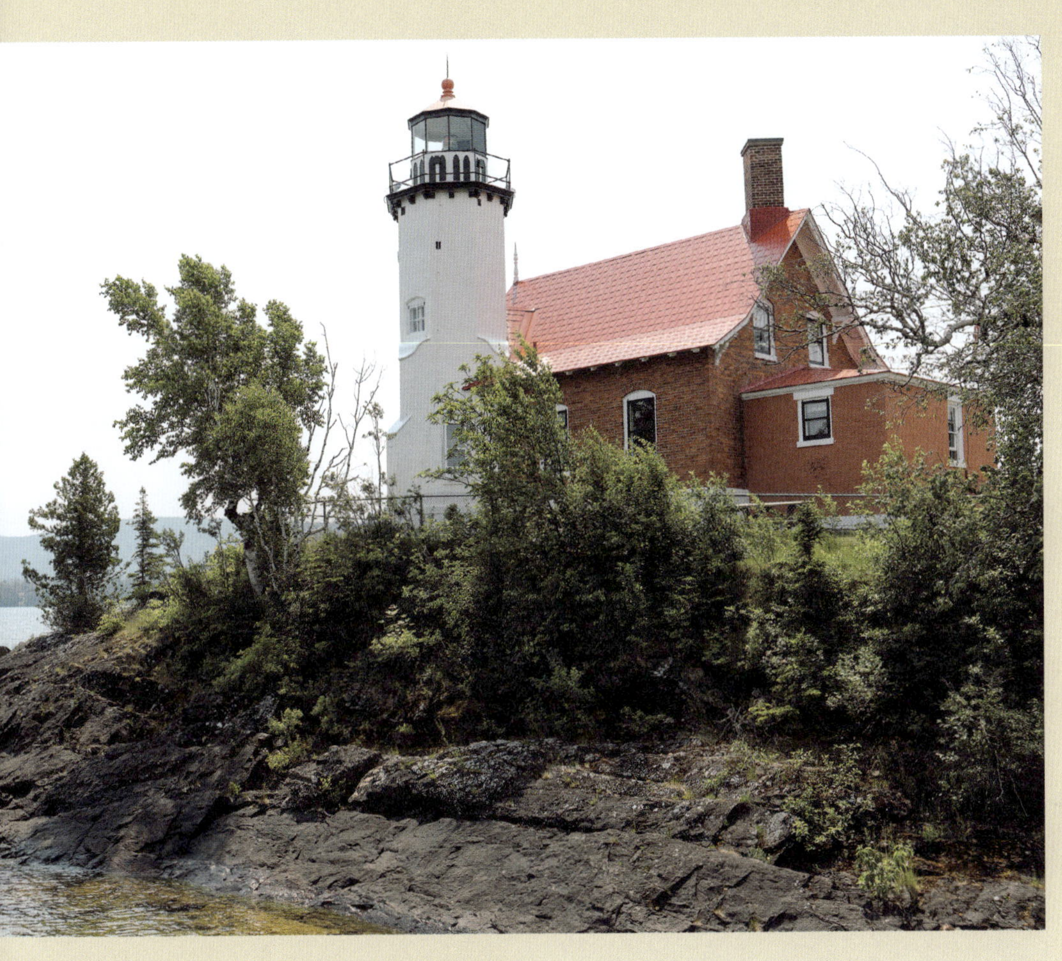

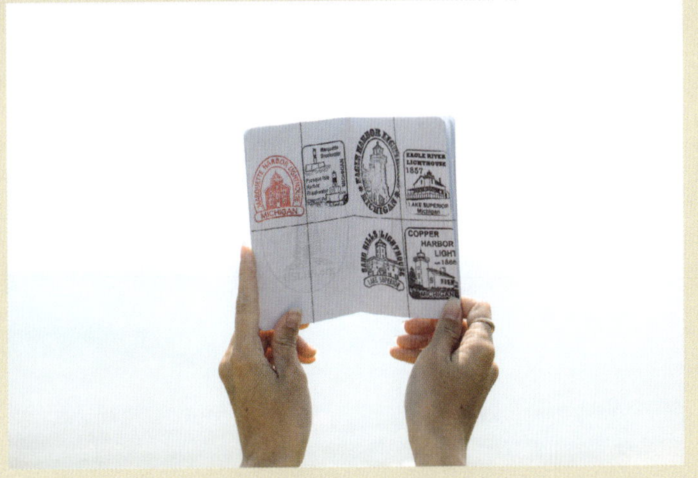
MICHIGAN
EAGLE RIVER
LIGHTHOUSE
1857
LAKE SUPERIOR
Michigan
MICHIGAN
SAND HILLS LIGHTHOUSE
LAKE SUPERIOR
COPPER
HARBOR
LIGHT
MICHIGAN

sunset supper in the sand

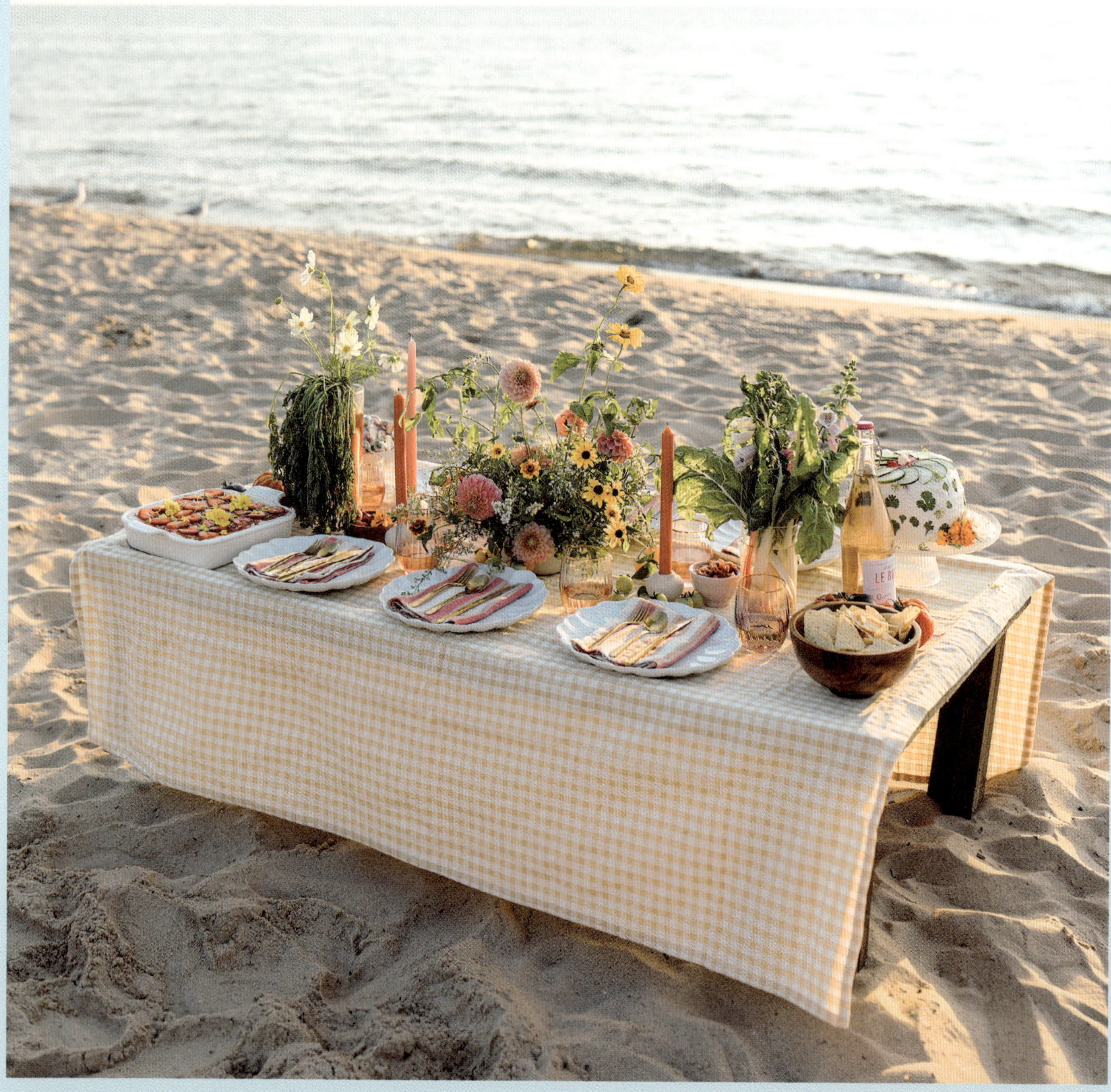

SETTING THE SUMMER TABLE:

- Cover a coffee table with a summery tablecloth for a picnic supper.
- Gather some colorful farmers' market produce: radishes, carrots, rhubarb, and rainbow Swiss chard, for example. Keep the stems and foliage attached, then arrange them in glass vases with water. Include a few flowers to create a delightful centerpiece.
- Choose a sunset color palette—pink, red, orange, and yellow—for your linens, candles, flowers, drinks, and foods.

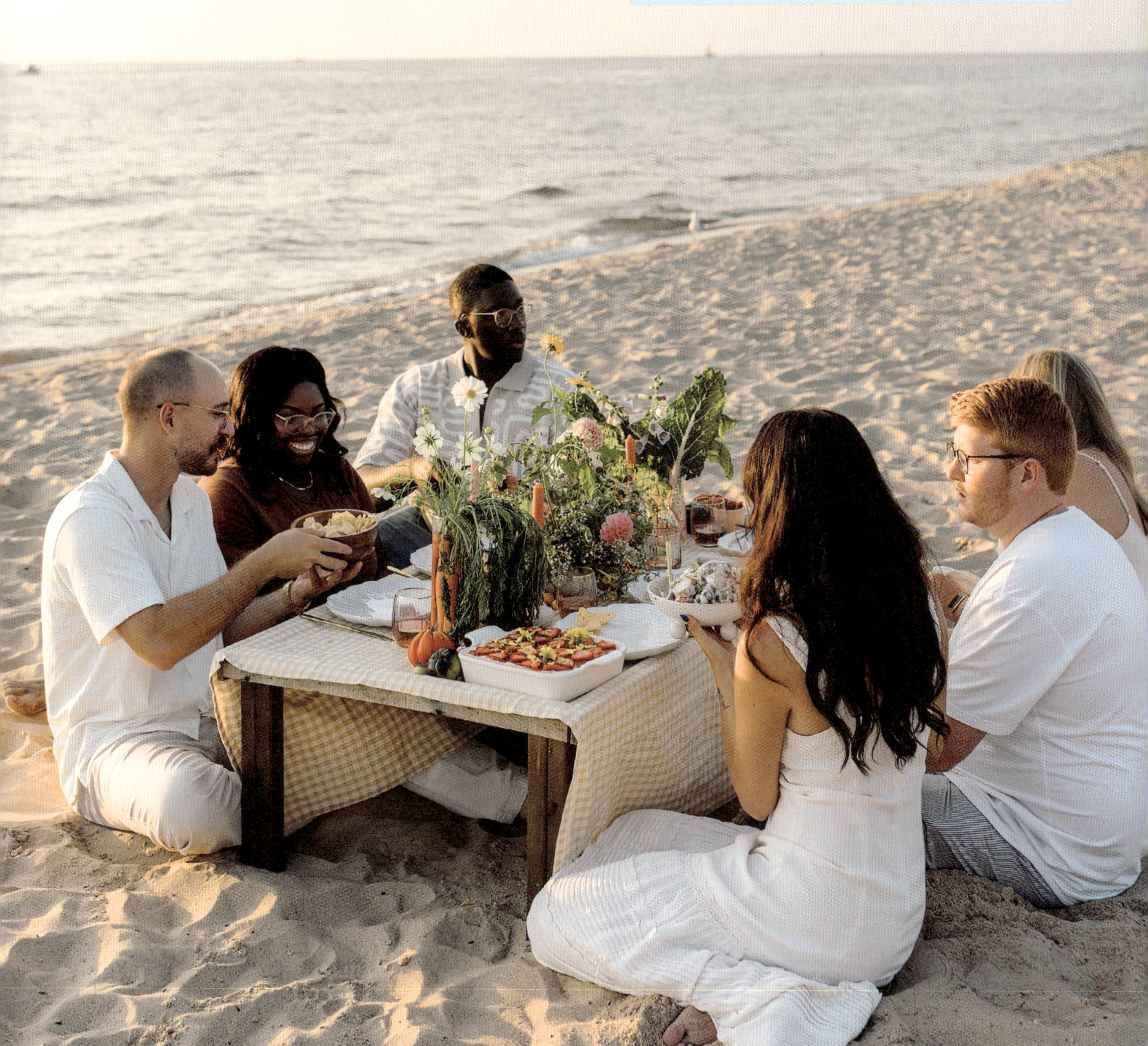

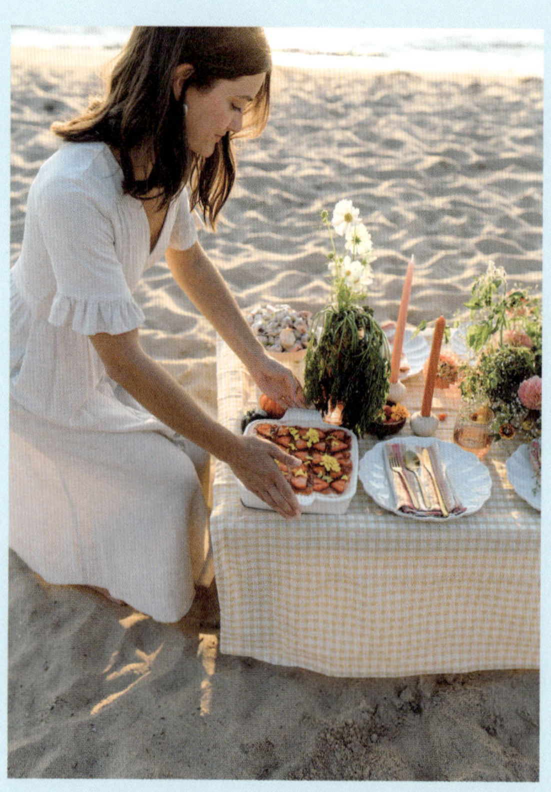

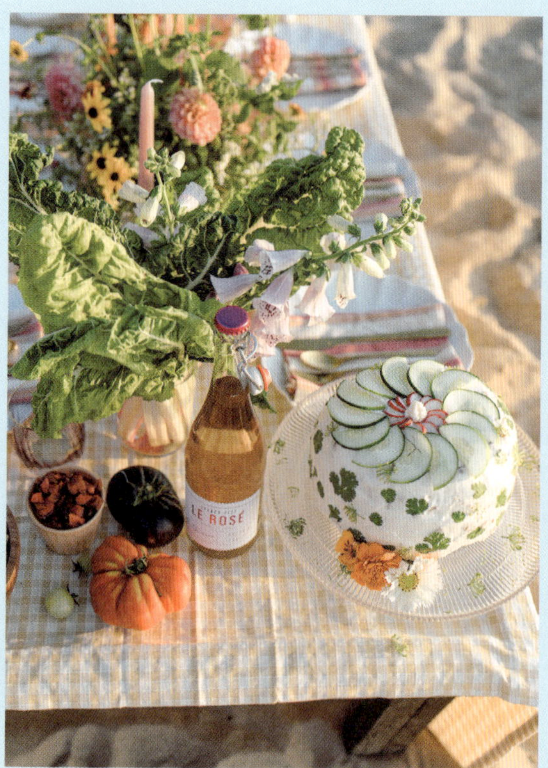

SERVING SUMMER FLAVORS

I grew up baking with both of my grandmas. One used the back of a knife to perfectly flatten every measuring cup of sugar and flour before placing it in the mixing bowl. The other didn't use measuring cups; she used her hands and her heart to measure, her fingers to toss and taste. In the kitchen, I take after the latter.

The recipes in this book are meant to be easy and unfussy. They are simple and straightforward with a focus on what's in season that month, the flavors of summer at the lake, plus ingredients that you likely already have in the pantry. They are family and friend recipes that I have modified and tweaked for preference along the way, so feel free to modify to your own preferences, too. Most important, they require minimal time in the kitchen—so you can be at the lake.

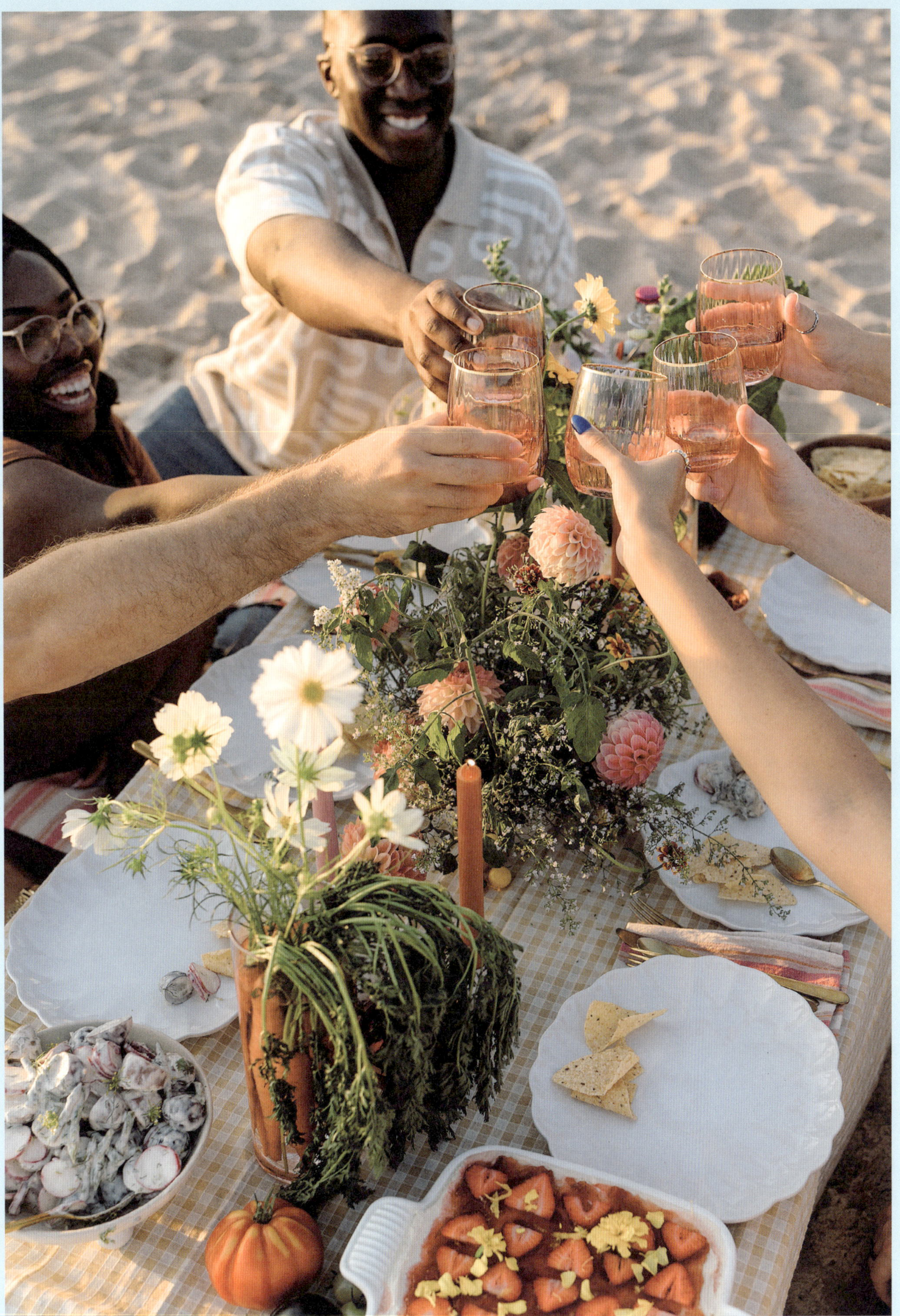

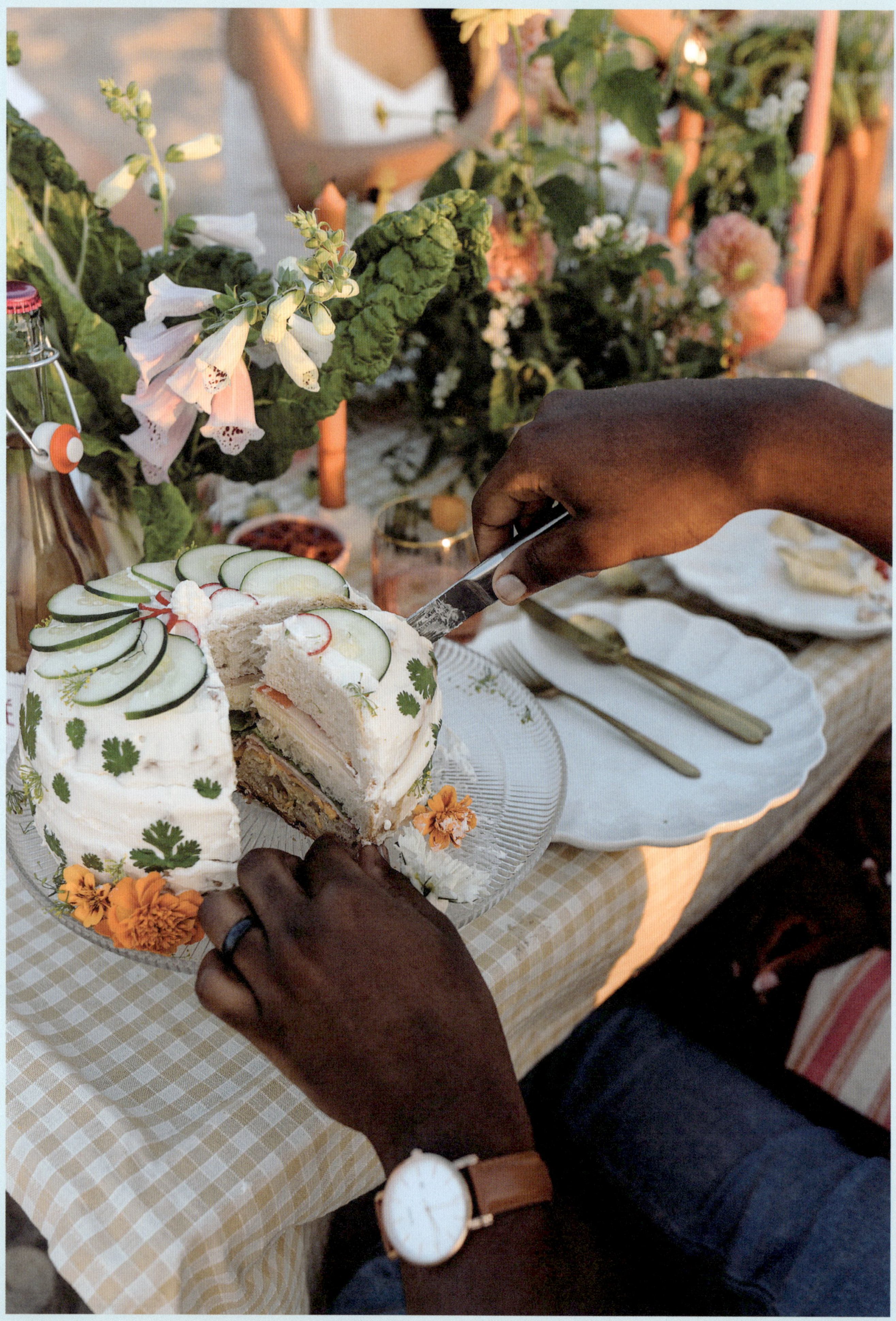

Sandwich Cake

SERVES 6 TO 8

This fun and impressive dish is great for any casual picnic, tea party, or garden lunch. Feel free to get creative and make your own variation with different fillings and toppings.

FOR THE SANDWICH

1 round loaf of soft bread (country loaf, boule, or sourdough), sliced horizontally into 3 equal layers
Dijon mustard
2 or 3 slices cheddar cheese
3 or 4 lettuce leaves, rinsed and dried
½ pound sliced deli ham
Mayonnaise, for spreading
2 or 3 slices provolone cheese
1 medium tomato, thinly sliced
½ pound sliced deli turkey

FOR THE ICING

1 (8-ounce/225 g) package cream cheese, at room temperature
1 cup (240 ml) mayonnaise

FOR THE TOPPINGS

1 cucumber, thinly sliced
4 radishes, thinly sliced (about 1 cup/115 g)
Fresh herbs, microgreens, and edible flowers

Make the sandwich: Set the bottom layer of bread on a serving platter or cake stand. Spread a thin layer of mustard over the top of the bread. Layer the cheddar, lettuce, and ham over the mustard. Spread a thin layer of mustard over the bottom of the middle layer of bread, then set it on top of the ham. Spread a thin layer of mayonnaise over the middle layer of bread, then layer the provolone, tomato, and turkey on top. Spread a light layer of mustard over the bottom of the final bread layer and place it on top of the turkey.

Make the icing: Place the cream cheese and mayonnaise in a medium bowl and beat with a handheld mixer to combine. Using a spatula, spread a thin layer of the cream cheese–mayo mixture over the top and sides of the sandwich cake. Chill the sandwich cake in the fridge for 30 minutes. Remove from the fridge and add another layer of icing around the sides and top, spinning the platter or cake stand as you go to make the icing smooth. You can even use a piping bag to add the icing to make it look like a real cake!

Garnish the top and sides of the cake with the cucumbers, radishes, herbs, microgreens, and edible flowers. Arrange the toppings in any way you like.

Store any leftovers in an airtight container in the refrigerator for up to 3 days.

Strawberry Lemon Summer Tiramisu

SERVES 9

The first time I made this tiramisu, I spent the afternoon driving around and hand-delivering it to my family members around town. It was too good to keep to myself! It's so yummy, so summery, and it doesn't require turning on the oven.

FOR THE LEMON SIMPLE SYRUP

1 cup (240 ml) water
1 cup (200 g) sugar
Zest and juice of 1 lemon

FOR THE TIRAMISU

16 ounces (455 g) mascarpone
½ cup (120 ml) heavy (whipping) cream
⅓ cup (80 ml) honey
1 teaspoon pure vanilla extract
24 ladyfingers (one 7-ounce/200 g package, gluten-free optional)
1 cup (240 ml) strawberry jam
1 cup (145 g) strawberries, sliced
Lemon peel spirals or edible marigold petals, for garnish (optional)

Make the lemon simple syrup: Combine the water, sugar, lemon zest, and lemon juice in a small saucepan and bring to a simmer over medium heat, stirring until the sugar is dissolved, about 5 minutes. Remove from the heat and let steep for 15 minutes until cooled. Strain out the zest and set the syrup aside in a shallow bowl.

Make the tiramisu: In a large bowl using a handheld mixer (or in the bowl of a stand mixer if you have one), beat the mascarpone, ¼ cup (60 ml) of the heavy cream, the honey, and the vanilla until lightly whipped, about 2 minutes. In a separate bowl, whip the remaining ¼ cup (60 ml) heavy cream (if using a stand mixer, use the whisk attachment) until soft peaks form, 2 to 5 minutes. Fold the whipped cream into the mascarpone-cream mixture to gently combine.

One at a time, dip the ladyfingers into the lemon syrup, quickly turning them to coat all sides (but don't dip them for too long or they'll get soggy), then arrange them over the bottom of an 8- or 9-inch (20 or 23 cm) square baking dish (you should have a layer of about 12 ladyfingers).

Spoon half the mascarpone cream on top of the ladyfinger layer. Then spread half the strawberry jam over the mascarpone cream. Arrange about half the strawberries in a layer over the jam. Repeat to make a second layer of ladyfingers, mascarpone cream, and jam, finishing with the remaining strawberries on top.

Chill in the fridge until ready to serve. Garnish with lemon peel spirals or marigold petals, if desired. Store leftovers in an airtight container in the refrigerator and enjoy within 3 days.

P.S. Keep any leftover lemon simple syrup in a jar in the fridge for up to 2 weeks and use it in lemon lattes in the morning or lemon gin and tonics in the evening!

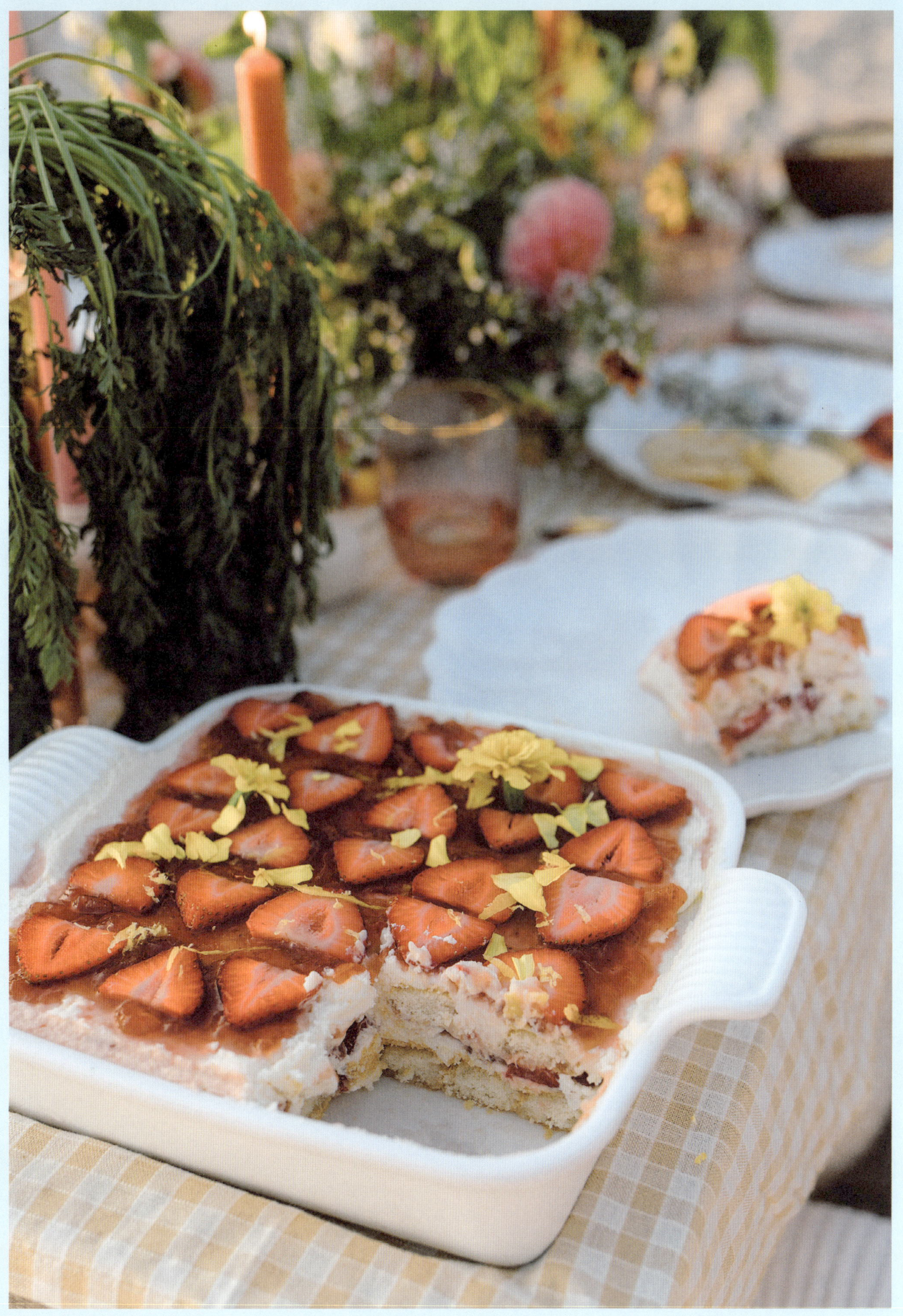

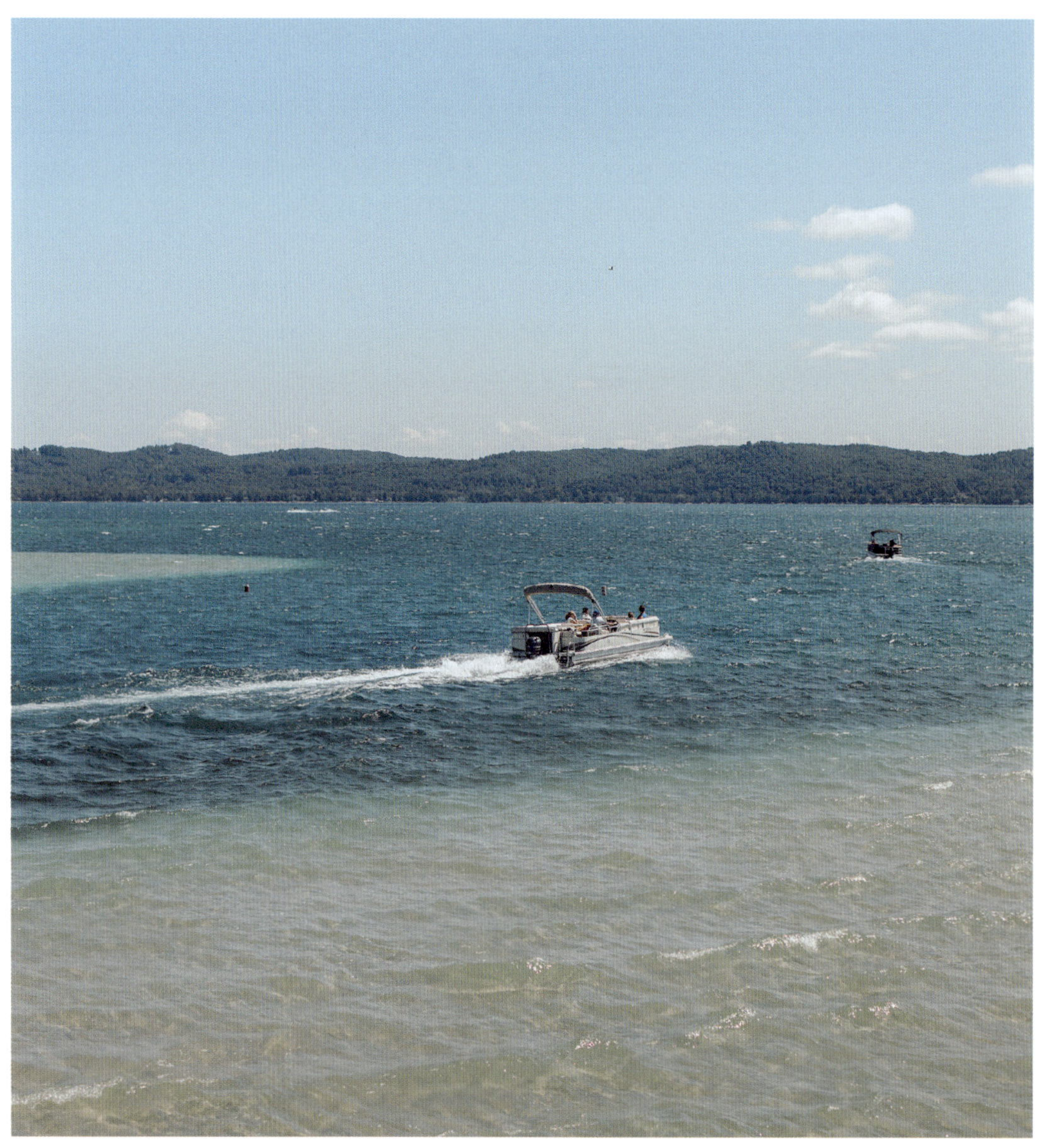

July

July at the lake is pure celebration, the peak of summer. We gather at cottages and campgrounds for frivolous fireworks shows and family reunions, barbecues and bonfires, county fairs and carnival rides. Days are filled with lemonade and watermelon, Popsicles and fishing poles, baseball hats and bikinis. We leave rings of condensation on Adirondack arms, and flip-flops on the front porch. The lake is in a constant choppy commotion from the wake of countless boats, with kids of all ages getting pulled through the waves, collecting sunshine on shoulders and mouthfuls of lake water. Tan lines are now defined, and freckles have made their annual appearance. Butterflies dance through the sky in July, and fireflies come out to disco at night, joining in on the summer fun. Searing July afternoons require a swim to cool off, a float on the tube, an anchor at the sand bar, a sun umbrella for shade, a race across the hot sand before it burns your feet. Warm July evenings smell like campfire smoke and citronella candles; they sound like bullfrogs and crickets serenading the sun as it sets; they look like starry skies and warm fireside chats carrying long into the night, faces lit by the flames. July is when we realize that our current moments are core memories in the making. In July, the good ole days are today.

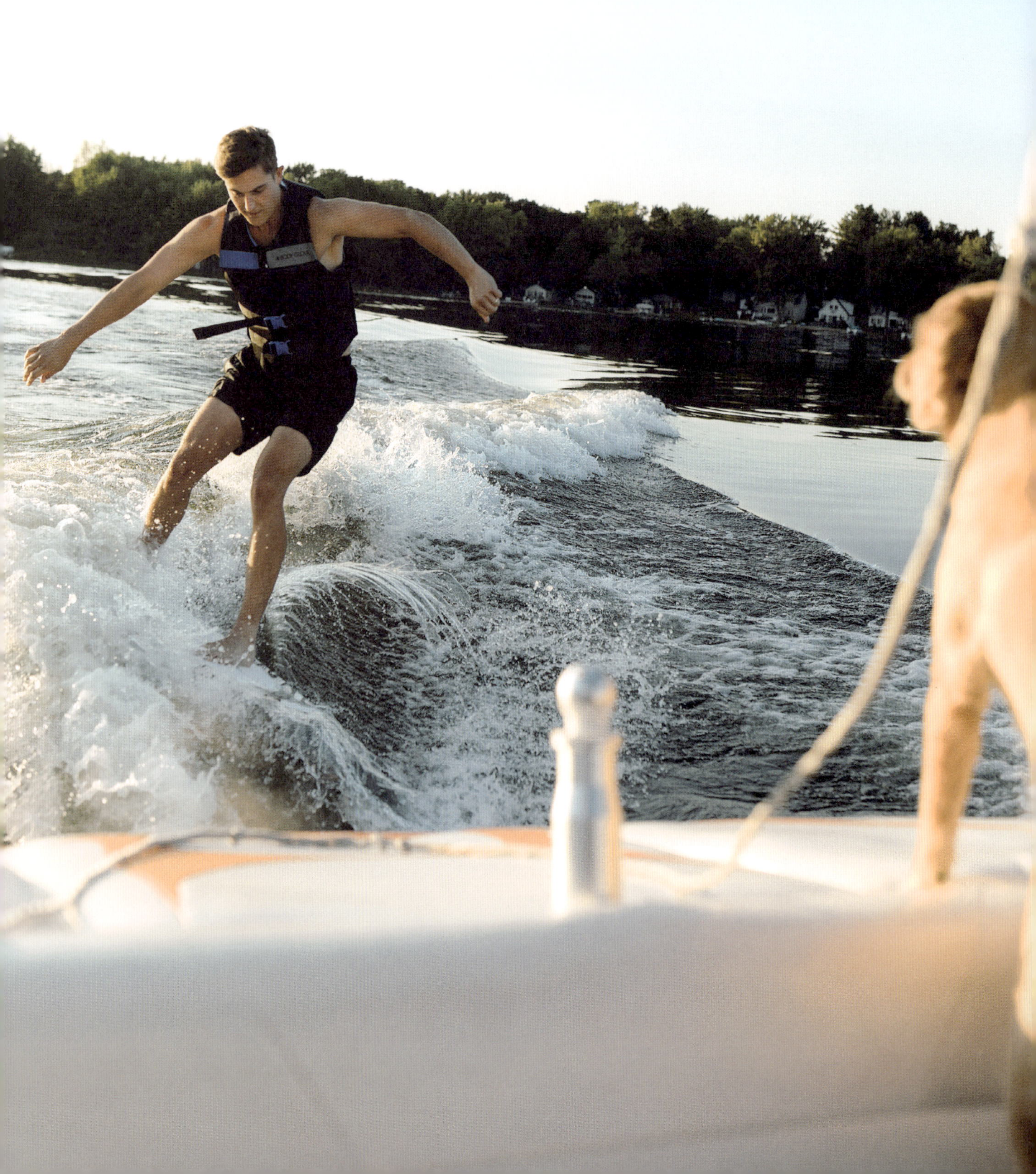

Lake Olympics

WHAT HAPPENS AT THE LAKE

The first time I attended my husband's family reunion, I didn't know what I was getting myself into. His extended family gathers at a lakeside cottage each summer, and every year they do the Lake Olympics—a wild competition that starts on the first day and lasts for the duration of the reunion.

As everyone arrives and unpacks their cars, two teams are assigned: a red team and a blue team. Then an opening ceremony commences the start of the tournament; usually it involves blaring a song on the speakers while revealing that year's trophy and prizes.

After that point, any game played over the course of the weekend counts toward the ongoing team scores. Whether it's a card game, board game, yard game, sport game, water game...every challenge requires players from opposing red-blue teams and a scorekeeper as a witness. The winners get to add a tally mark to their team's overall score, but not until their formal score sheet is signed by the witness (apparently at prior reunions things got a little too competitive and hearsay).

That first year, I remember thinking it was crazy. There were endless rounds of euchre, Bananagrams, Spikeball, cornhole, Frisbee golf, volleyball...the games and challenges and shouting and friendly competition were happening at all hours of the day and night. I also distinctly remember a mandatory full-group relay race that involved wearing a life jacket like a diaper, one of Grandma's shoes and one of Grandpa's shoes on each foot, and running down to the lake to fill a bucket of water using a sponge. This was not the welcome-to-the-family that I was anticipating.

The Lake Olympics are chaotic and intense and all-around goofy. But that's what makes the reunion so memorable.

It's the only time and place each year that we do these kinds of activities with these extended family members, and as silly as it is, I appreciate how much thought and intentionality my in-laws put into making lasting memories.

Sometimes meaningful moments require prior planning; they don't just happen organically. But all it takes is one person to coordinate something out of the ordinary for everyone to reap the most memorable benefits.

Find a way to make your lake days unforgettable. Maybe it's a certain meal that you only cook once per year, at the lake. Or a special flavor of ice cream that you only buy at the cottage. Or a certain kind of music that you only listen to on the boat. Or a wild, silly game that you only play at the reunion, possibly involving your grandparents' shoes and a life jacket around your legs.

Designate a special activity to happen when and only when you're at the lake, in the summer, all together.

What happens at the lake stays at the lake.

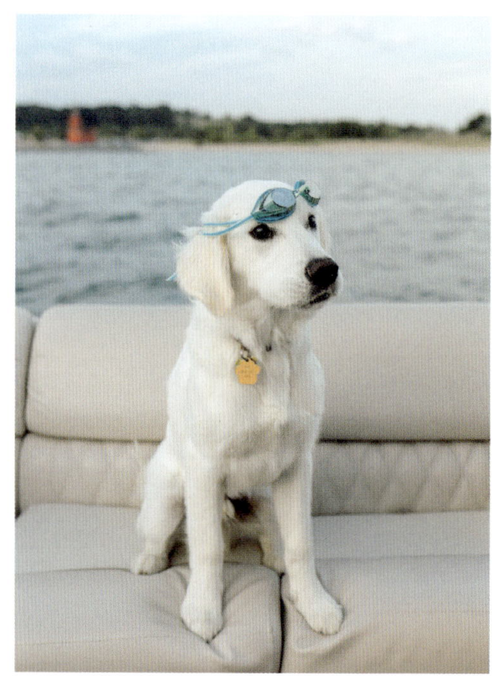

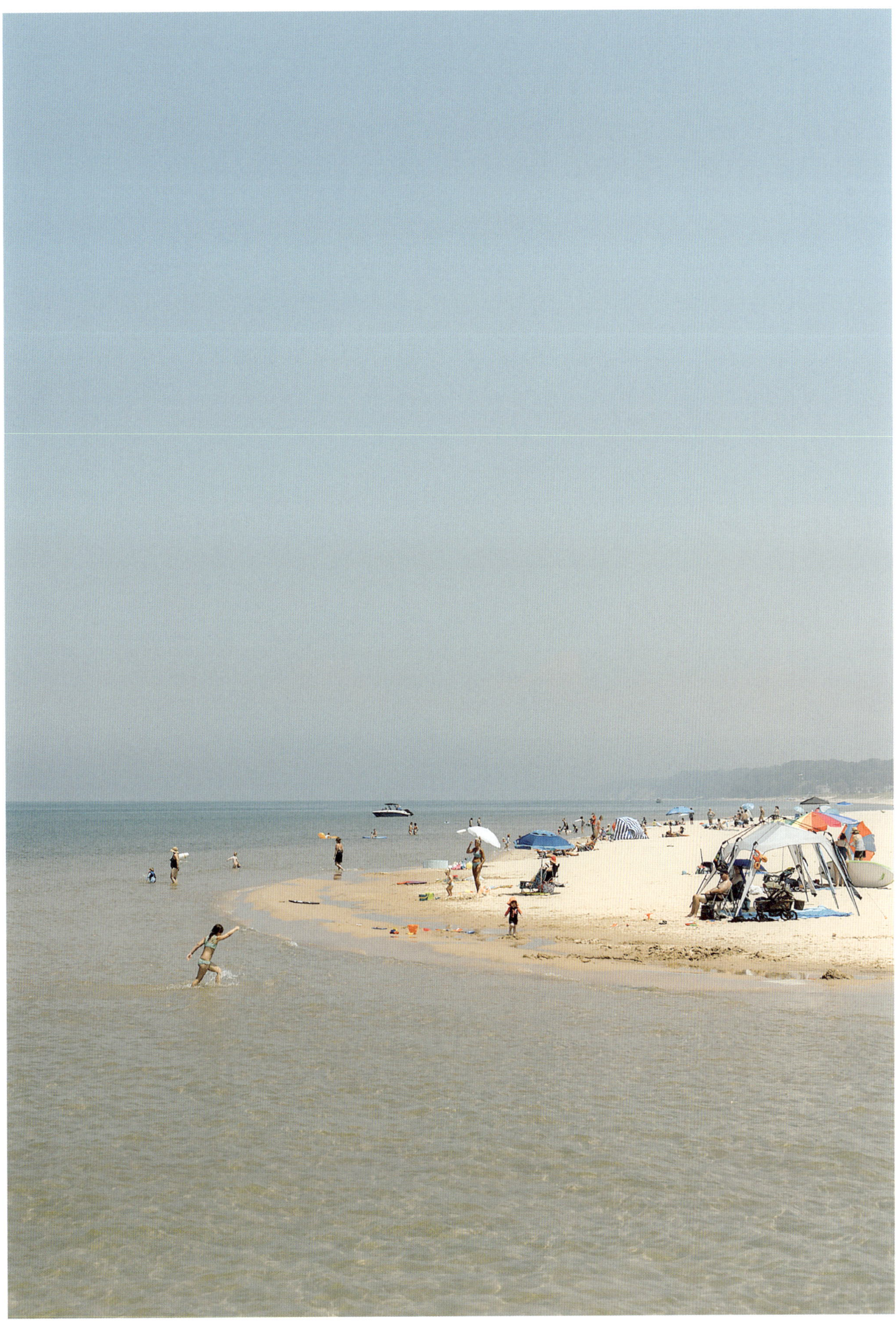

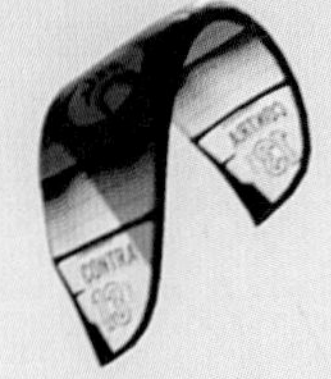
CONTRA

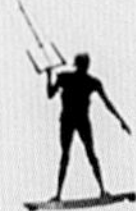

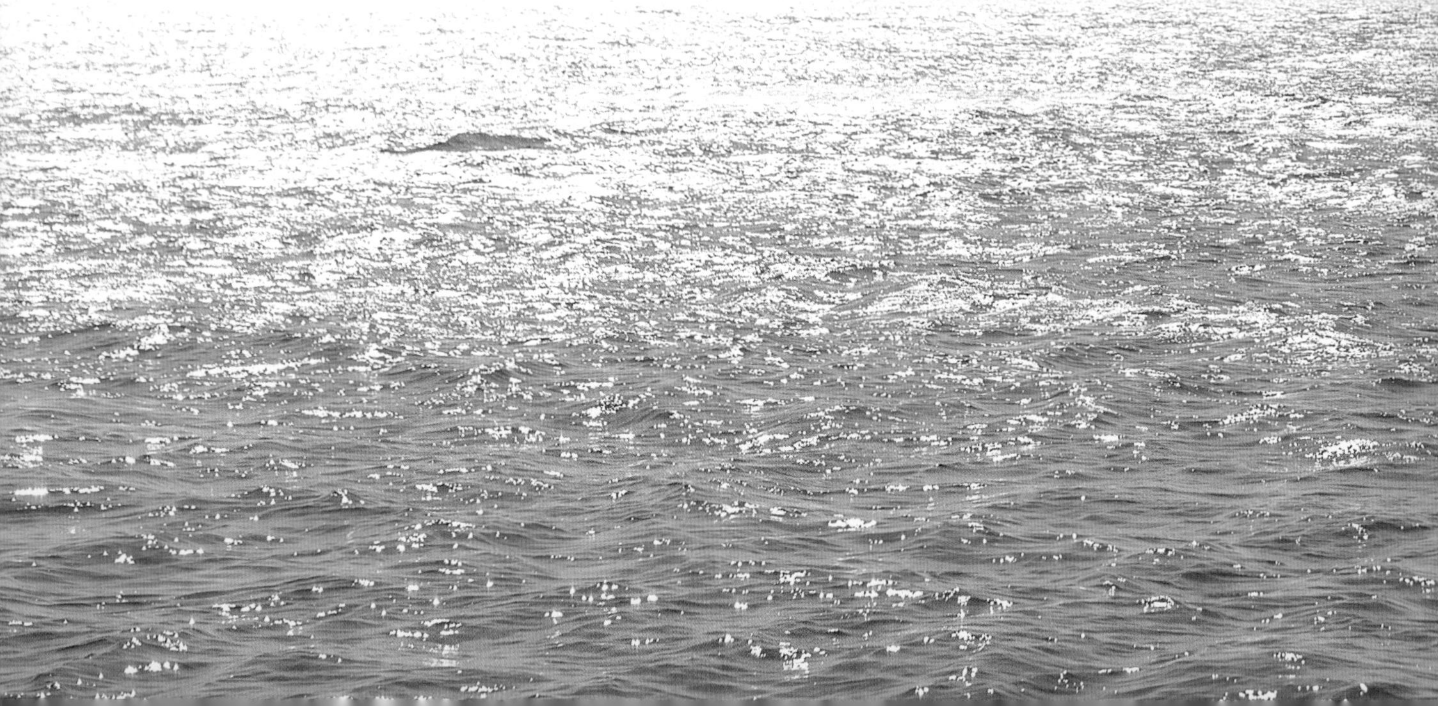

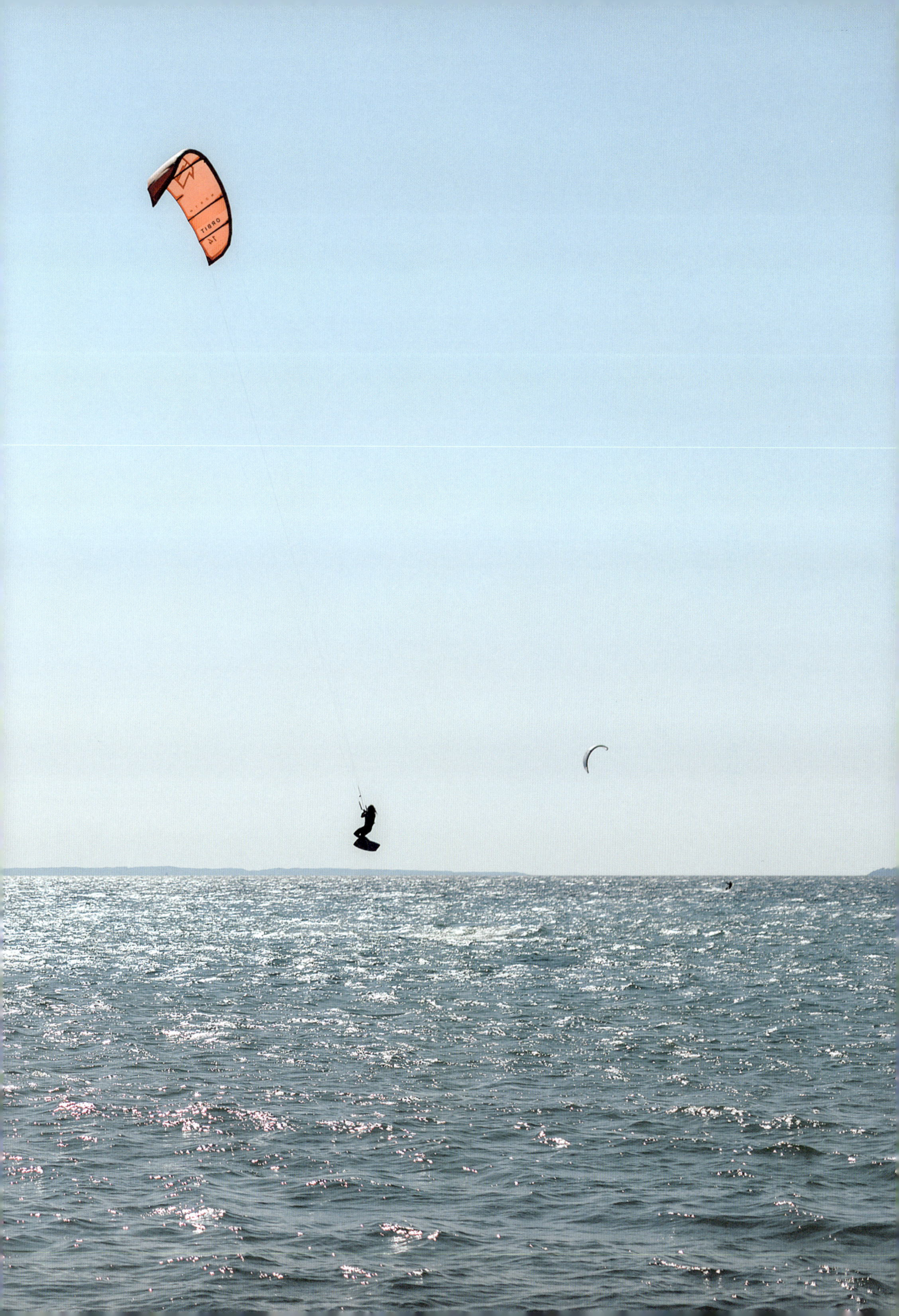

lake olympic activities:

If you want to host your own Lake Olympics, here are some fun challenges to coordinate. Have special prizes at stake so everyone gives it their all.

- Kayak or canoe race
- Diving competition off the dock
- Synchronized swimming performances
- Longest wake surf or water ski challenge
- Bravest belly flop contest
- Underwater handstand competition
- Fishing tournament for the biggest catch
- Swimming race to the other side of the lake

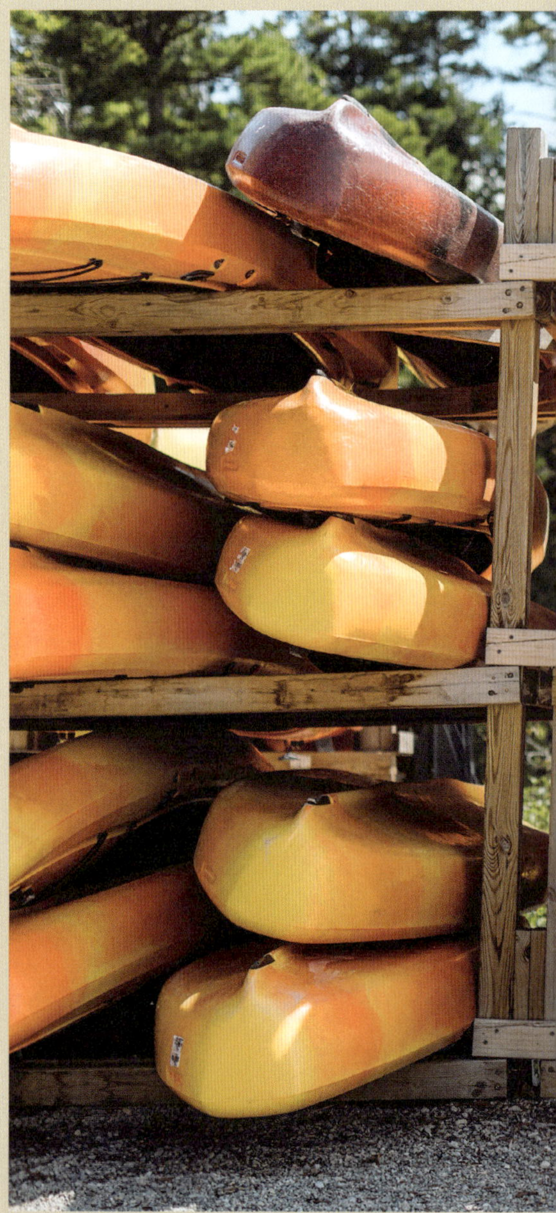

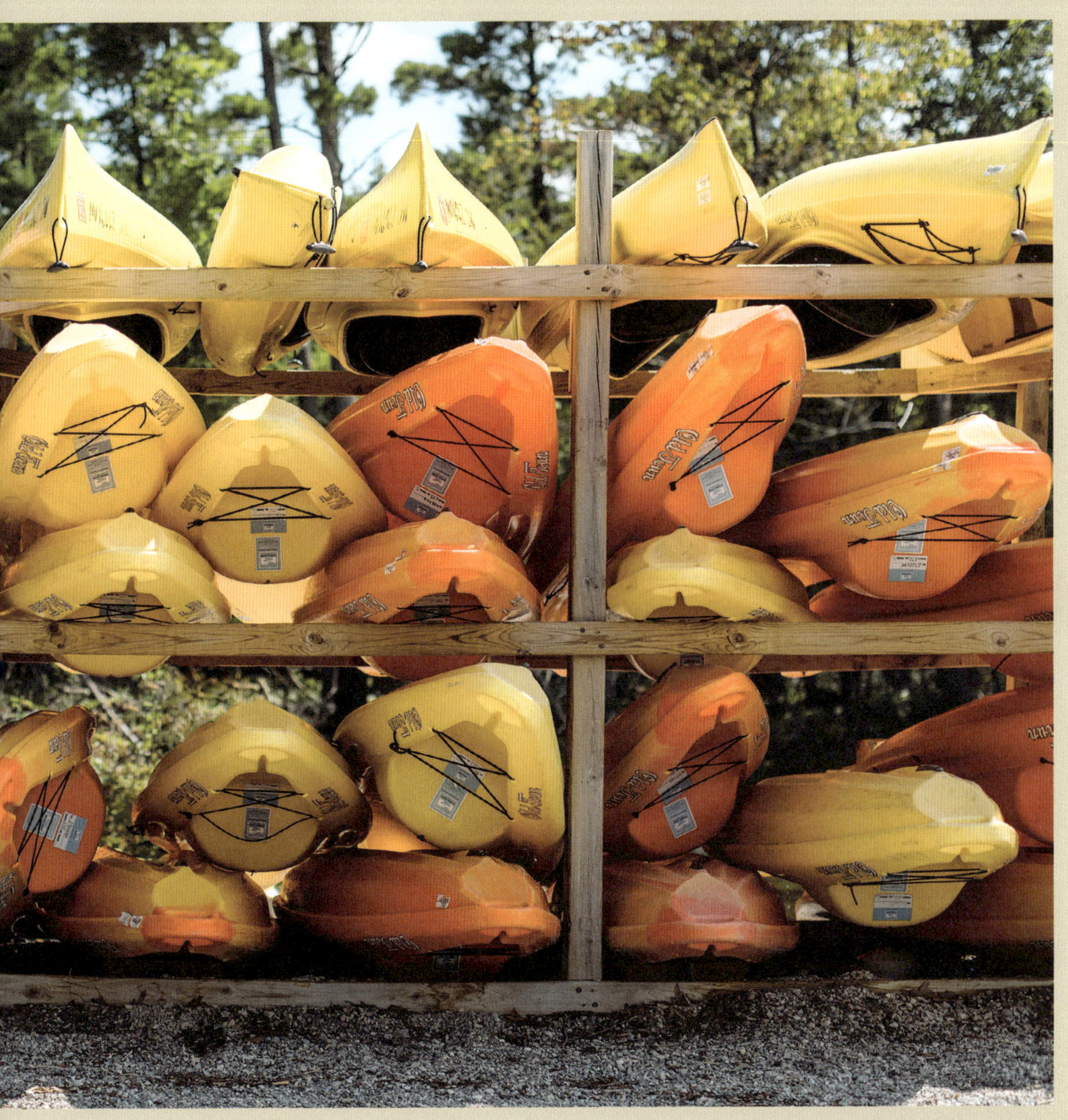

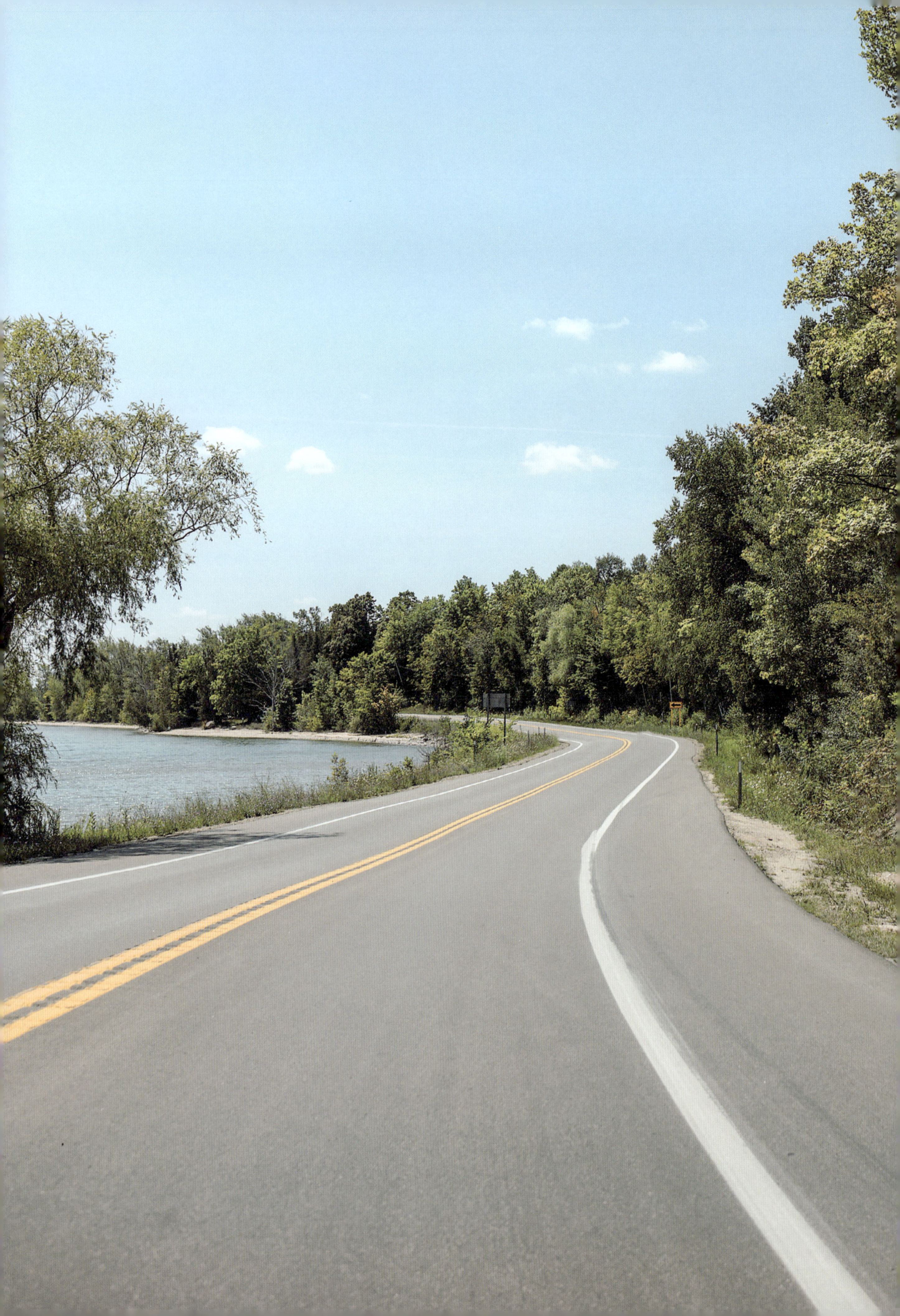

Up North

A SENTIMENTAL SUMMER RETREAT

"Up North" is a proper noun, a formal phrase in Midwest vocabulary. Its coordinates may vary from person to person, but its meaning is synonymous and its reverence is unanimous: escape, nature, nostalgia.

Driving Up North puts mental and physical distance between routines and responsibilities. With every mile the pine trees grow taller and thicker on each side of the highway. The lake water gets bluer, the air crisper, the land hillier. The speed limit gets higher, but the pace gets slower. Boutique hotels and lakeside inns still use vacancy/no vacancy signs. Towns are a touch more quaint, restaurants more rustic, and life more simplistic.

Everyone has their own version of Up North, a sentimental summer retreat. For some it's a short drive to a nearby state; for others it's a longer drive to where the peninsula ends. For some it requires a ferry ride to an island; for others it requires a four-wheel drive down a seasonal road. For some it's a generational family cottage on the big lake; for others it's a cherished campsite on a small lake. For me, it was our tiny cabin in Northern Michigan.

When I was young, my parents would pack us into the car on Friday afternoons and we'd happily settle into the back seat for the two-hour drive, knowing we were heading straight north. With my brothers and cousins, I spent days riding quads through the trails, building forts in the forest, catching frogs and fireflies and sometimes even salamanders, sitting around the campfire while Papa played the guitar and harmonica. I have so many sweet memories from those summer trips Up North.

Over the past few years, my husband and I have started finding our own places and forging our own traditions. We've made memories in our favorite lakeside towns for enough summers now that they feel like our Up North.

We've stayed in Traverse City, wading in the blue waves of the West Bay, picnicking on sandy beaches and playing cards, visiting Rove and Brys and Gilchrist, our favorite wineries.

We've cozied up in little Leland, getting coffees at Madcap, walking along the dam, eating sandwiches from Village Cheese Shanty, and swimming at Van's Beach.

We've spent weekends in Glen Arbor, sipping cappuccinos at The Mill, hiking the Sleeping Bear Dunes, and stopping in Cherry Republic for cherry salsa and cherry ice cream, because when you're on vacation Up North, visiting an ice cream shop is a daily ritual. Some days even two visits are necessary—one in the afternoon for something fruity and refreshing, and one after dinner for something chocolatey and rich. Up North is a place where everyone's happy, everyone's vacationing, and everyone orders the extra scoop.

Wherever Up North is for you, make a point to go there this summer and every summer after. Familiarize yourself with a particular place until returning is met with intense nostalgia. And if you don't have a cottage or cabin, you can always rent a vacation home and make it your own for the weekend. Or book a lakeside campsite and pitch a tent. Stay on a houseboat, or in an RV, or find a waterfront inn with vacancy.

It doesn't matter where it is or what it looks like; it just matters who you're with and how often you return. Simply get in the car and start driving north.

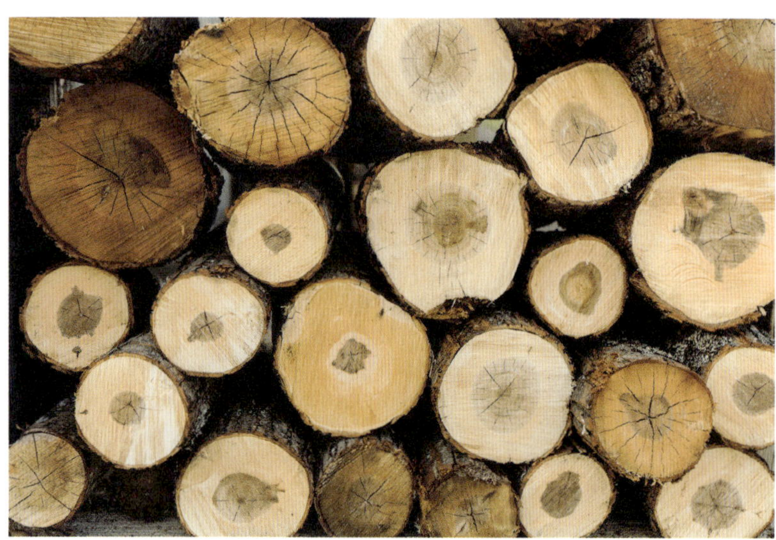

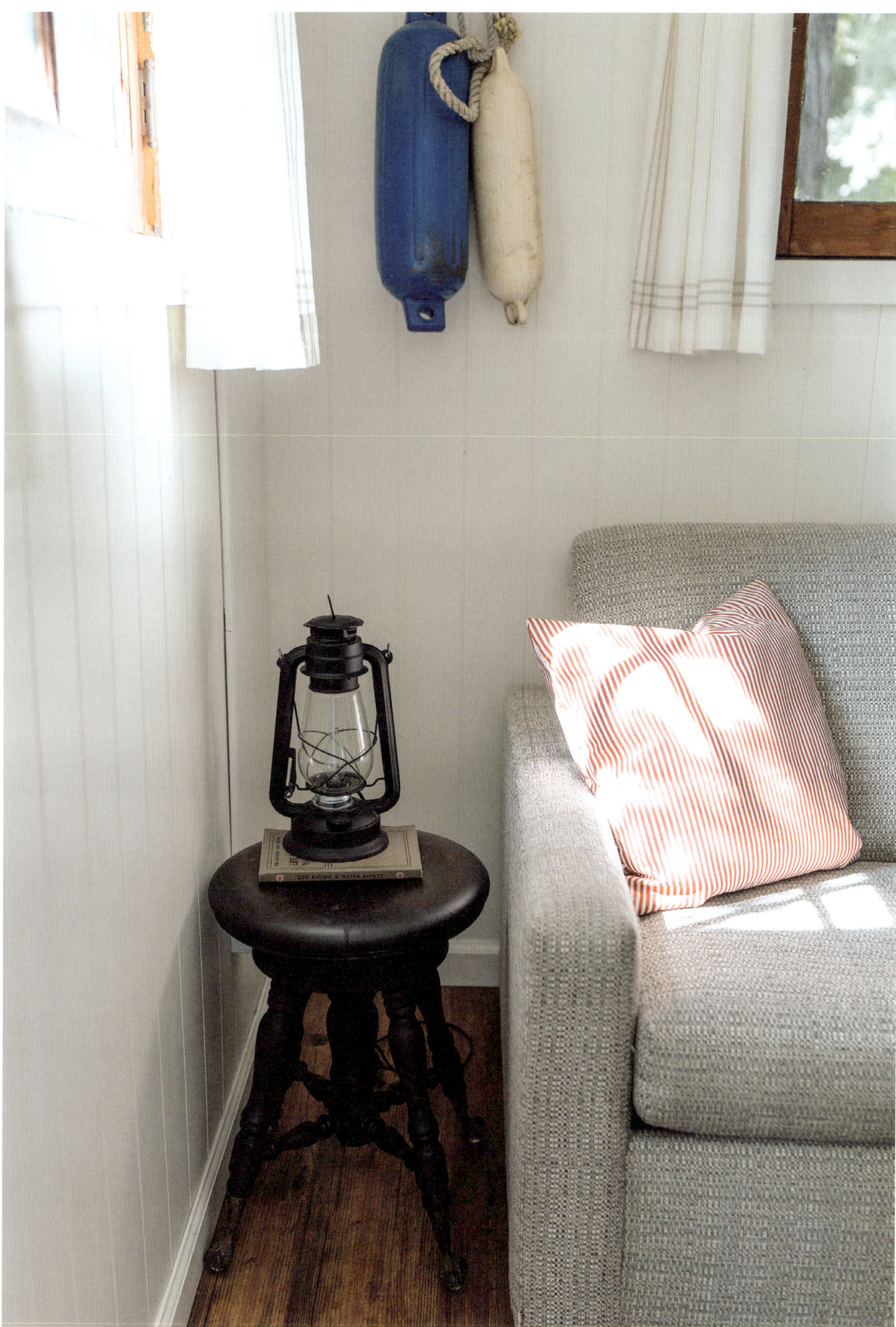
LIFE SAVING & WATER SAFETY

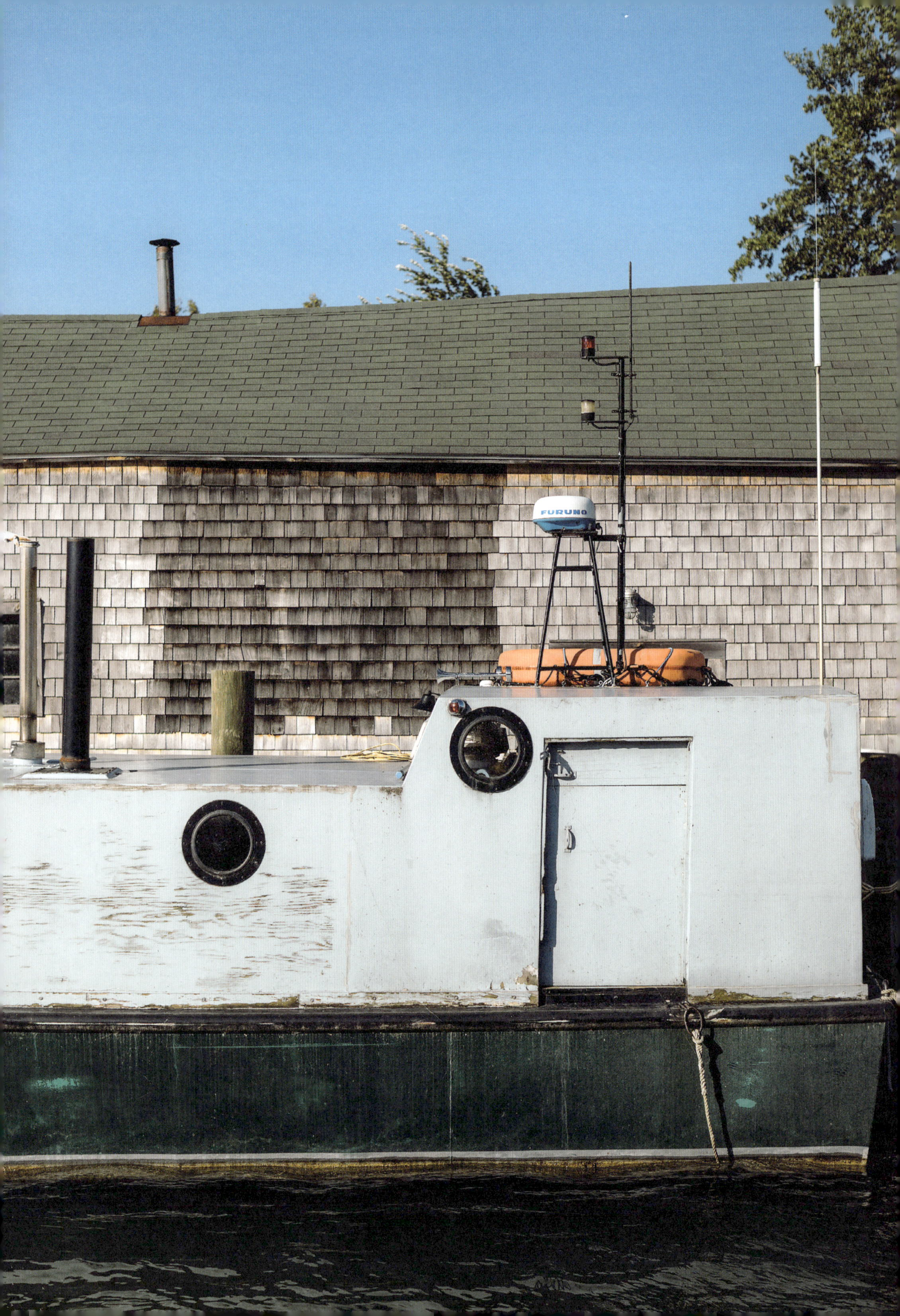
FURUNO

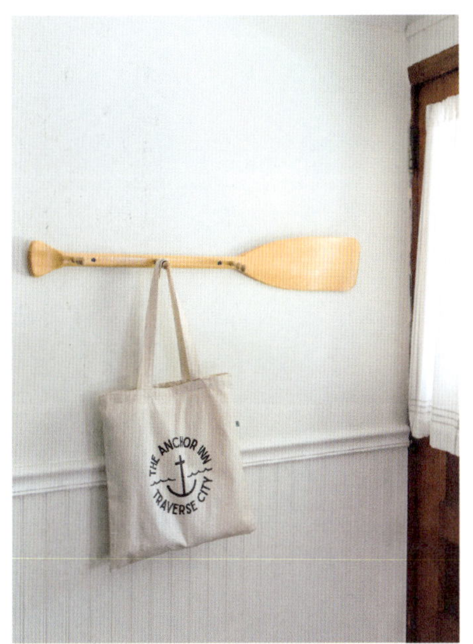
THE ANCHOR INN
TRAVERSE CITY

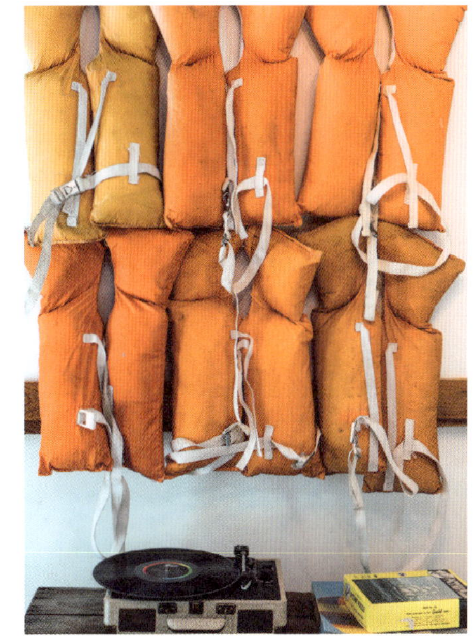

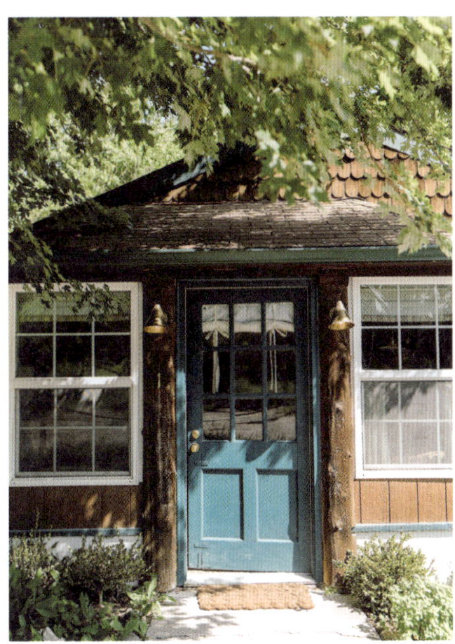

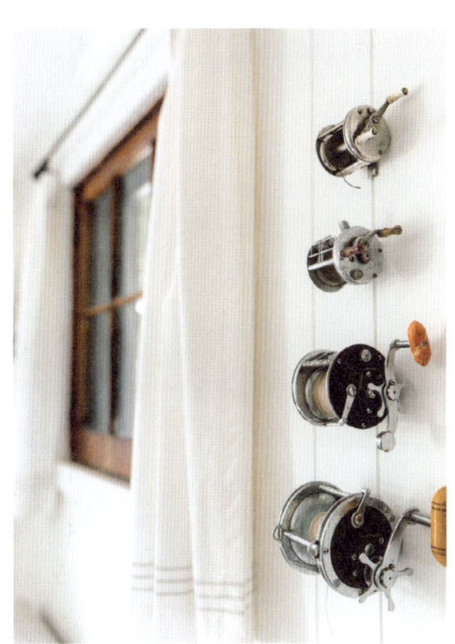

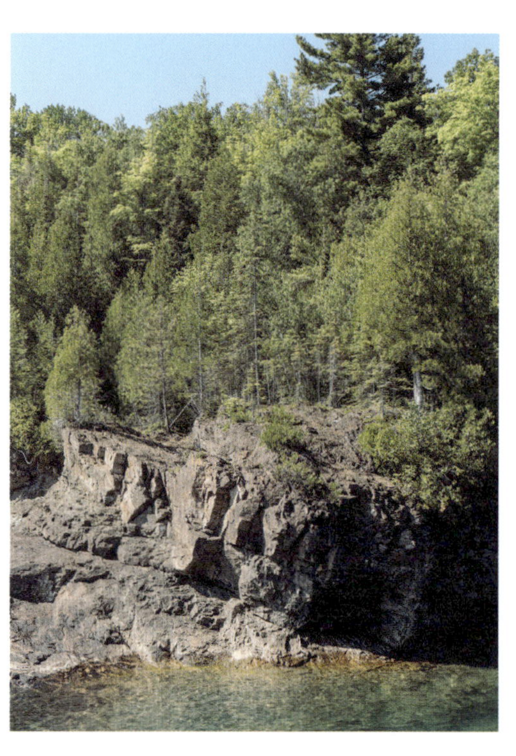
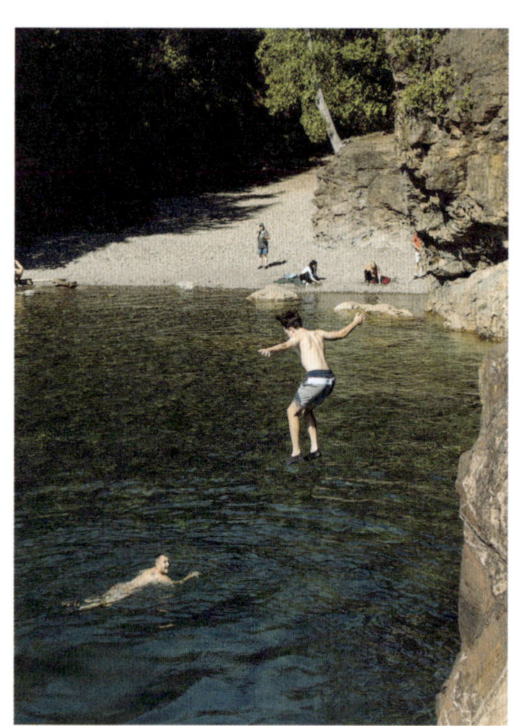

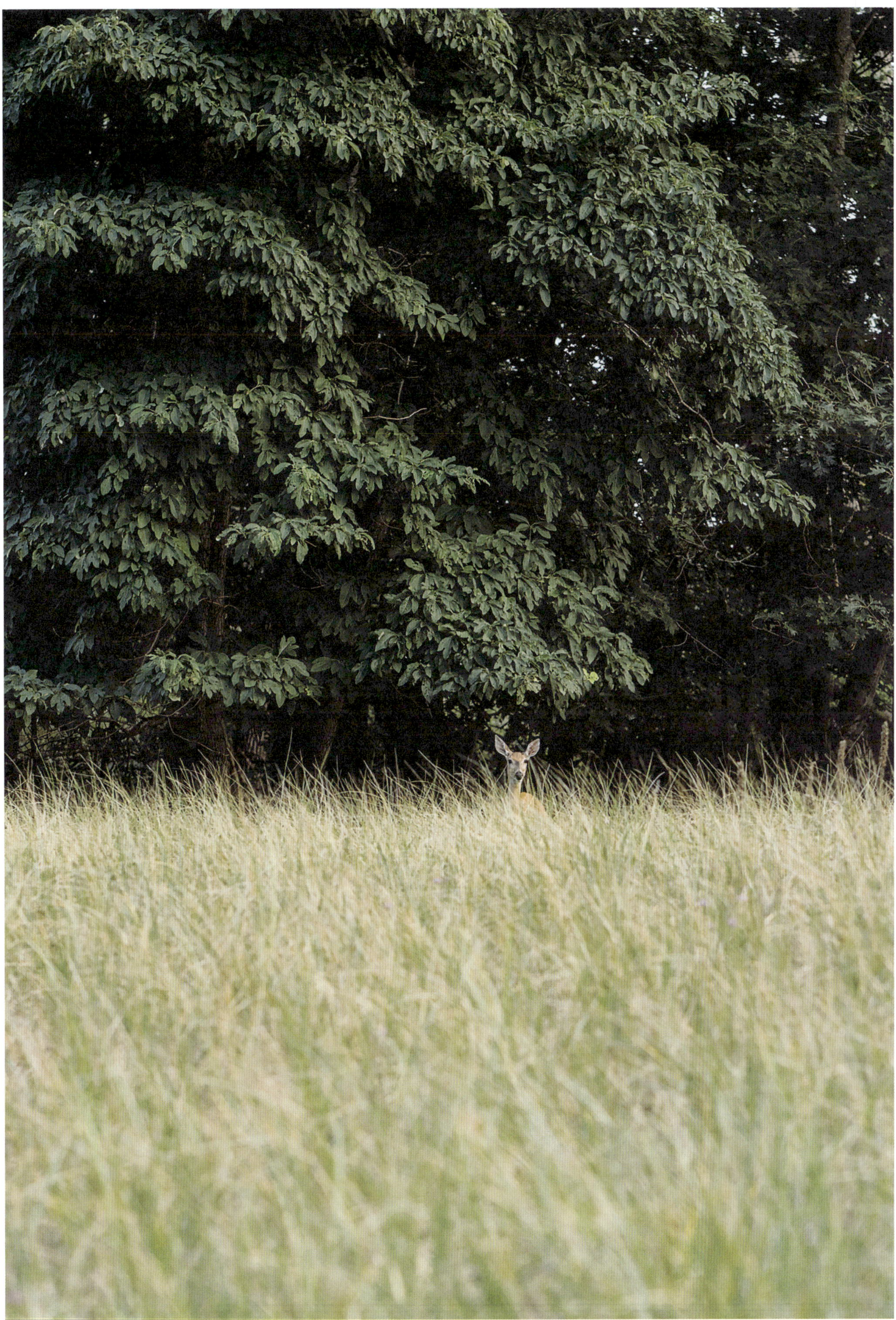

Leave Last

A COMMITMENT TO LINGER LONGER

In an effort to savor every last drop of summer, I'm making a commitment to be the last to leave. Allow me to explain.

I'm a type A person. I love waking up early and accomplishing half my to-do list by 10:00 a.m. I thrive when my house is clean and I'm living within my routines, sleeping in my own bed, and sticking to a schedule.

Because of this, I've found that I tend to be one of the first to leave. Whether it's an evening social event or a weekend getaway, I like to get back home, reset the house, wash my face, and unwind for a good night's sleep and productive morning.

But I'm starting to realize how much this desire to get ahead is holding me back.

My family has a Sunday night campfire tradition in the summer months. Every week, we gather at my brother's house, a central location for everyone, and it's generally an open invitation for whoever can make it that week. My dad and brothers, my aunts and uncles, always a handful of my cousins, and occasionally my grandparents. BYOB and BYOC (bring your own beverage and camp chair). We sit in a circle around the fire, and we just talk. Life updates from that week, church sermons from that morning, our jobs, the news, the latest thing my niece learned to say or do.

One week there were pop-up summer rain showers drizzling on and off all day, but this didn't stop us. We were so dedicated to conversation, to coexisting, to community, that we went through with it anyways. We sat around the fire with umbrellas that week.

It's the best summer Sundays ritual, and I look forward to it every single week. However, I started noticing that I was one of the first to leave.

If things were winding down, or if it was pushing my bedtime, I'd pack up my chair and say my goodbyes. I'd justify this because of the work I had on my to-do list for Monday morning, and because, out of

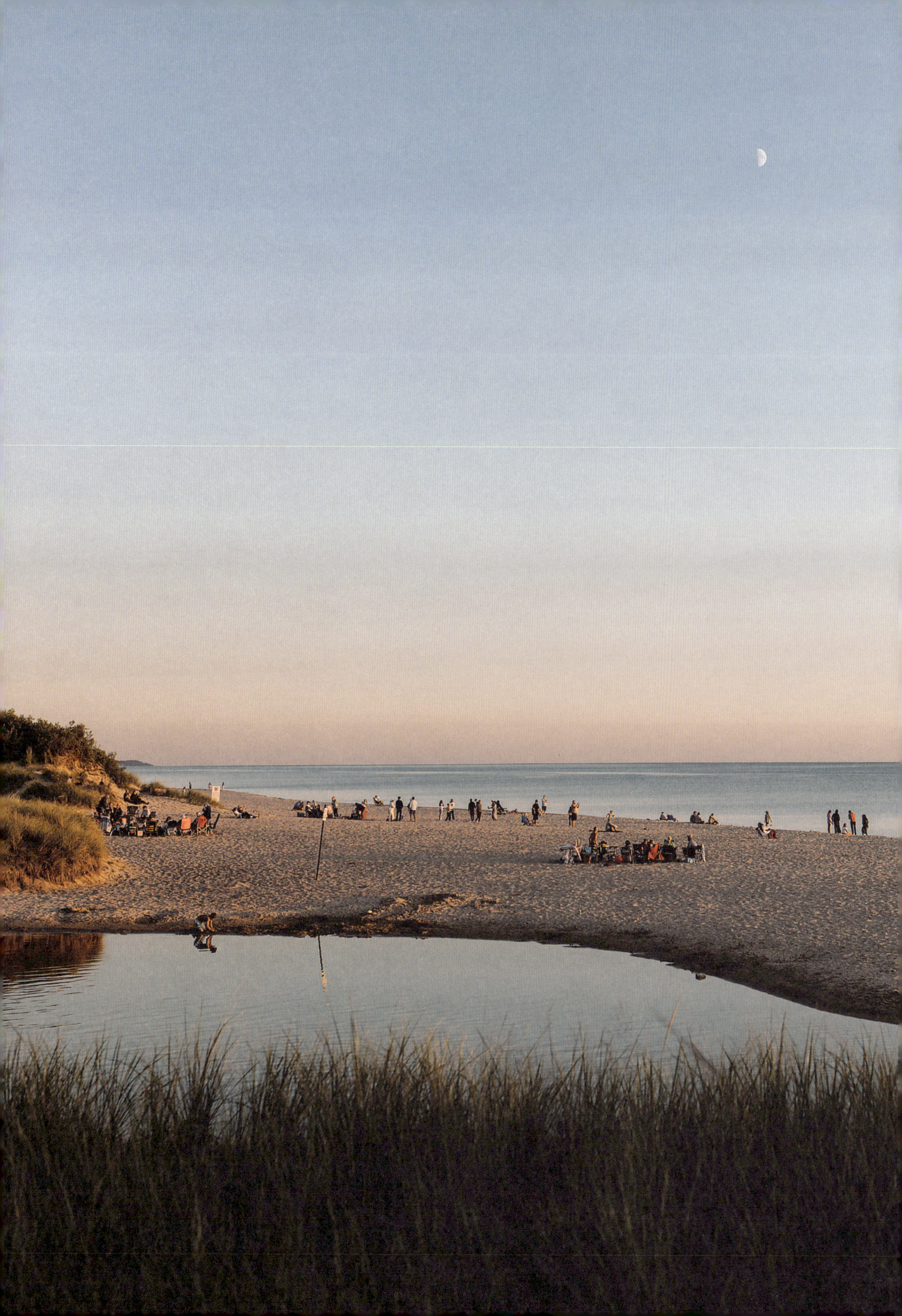

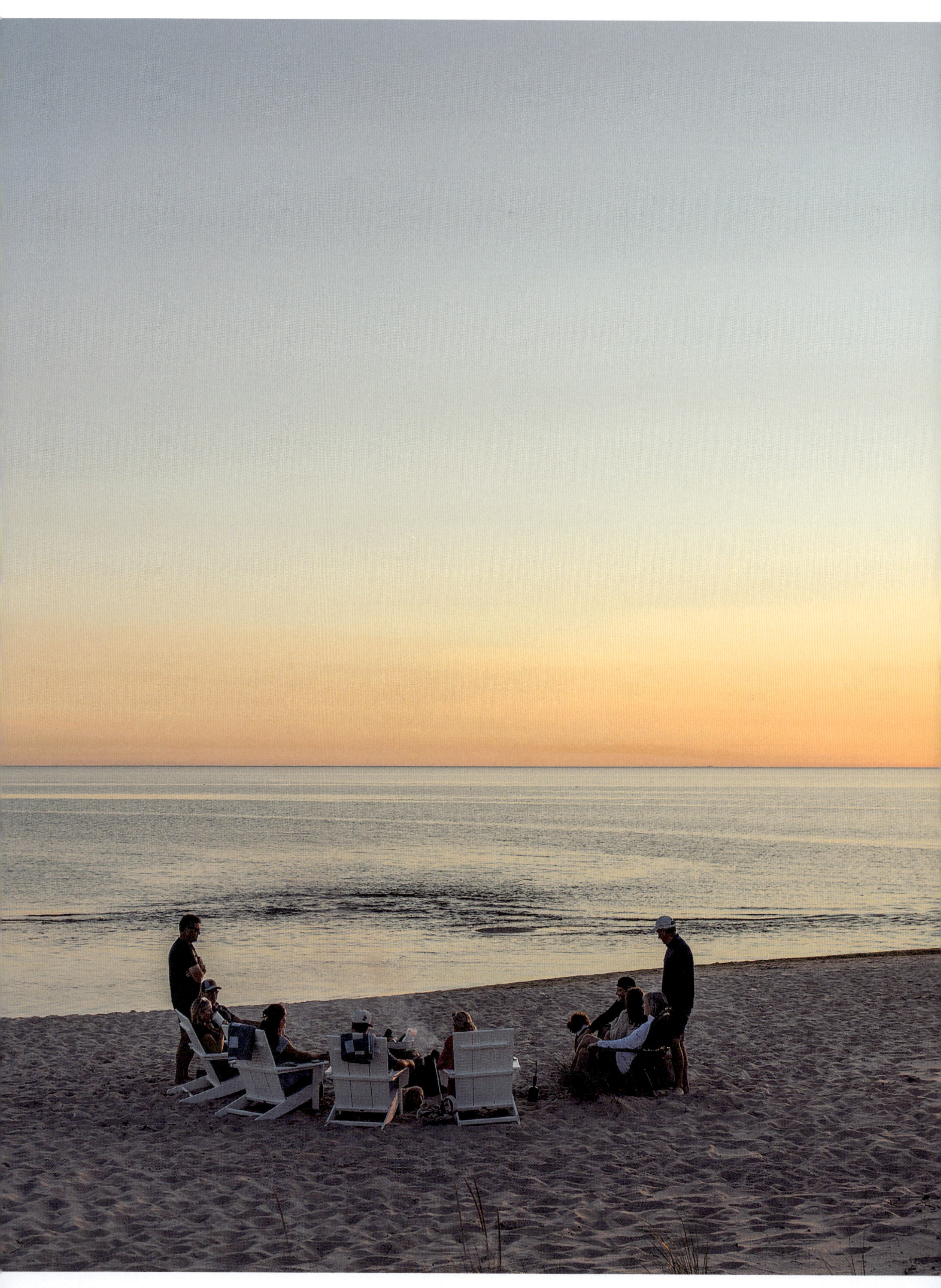

everyone around the fire, I have the longest drive back home.

But it's dawning on me just how fast summer is flying by. We're halfway through July and in just a matter of weeks the temperature will start to cool down, the sunset will creep up earlier and earlier into the evening, school will be back in session, and these campfires will be put to rest until next year.

Not only is this summer fleeting, but life is fleeting too, and these moments spent with family are truly sacred. We're not guaranteed next summer, we're not even guaranteed next Sunday. We're only guaranteed right now.

So I'm making a commitment: For the rest of the summer, I will be the last to leave.

I'm going to linger as others start trickling out, packing up their chairs and heading home.

I'm going to keep the conversation going and stay for the deep life chats that happen when only a few of us remain.

I'm going to watch the fireflies light up, hear the crickets start to sing, and be present for every last minute.

Because that is how you make the most of summer. You sacrifice some sleep, leave to-dos undone, forfeit routines, all for the sake of quality time and fresh air.

When I look back on this season, when I look back on my life, I want to know that I was fully there. I want to know that I was the first to arrive and the last to leave.

places to linger:

- Get a late checkout for your summer vacation reservations and utilize another day to play.
- When you're packing up the cottage, keep your swimsuits out and take one more dip in the lake before you leave, then drive home with the windows down to dry your hair.
- Be the last one left at the family reunion and hug every person goodbye.
- Extend dinners by serving each dish separately and slowly, maybe even use conversation starter prompts between each course, and linger at the table until the candles burn down.
- Stay on the dance floor at the wedding until the music stops.
- If you're going to the beach for the afternoon, plan ahead and pack sandwiches for dinner so you can stay all the way through until sunset.

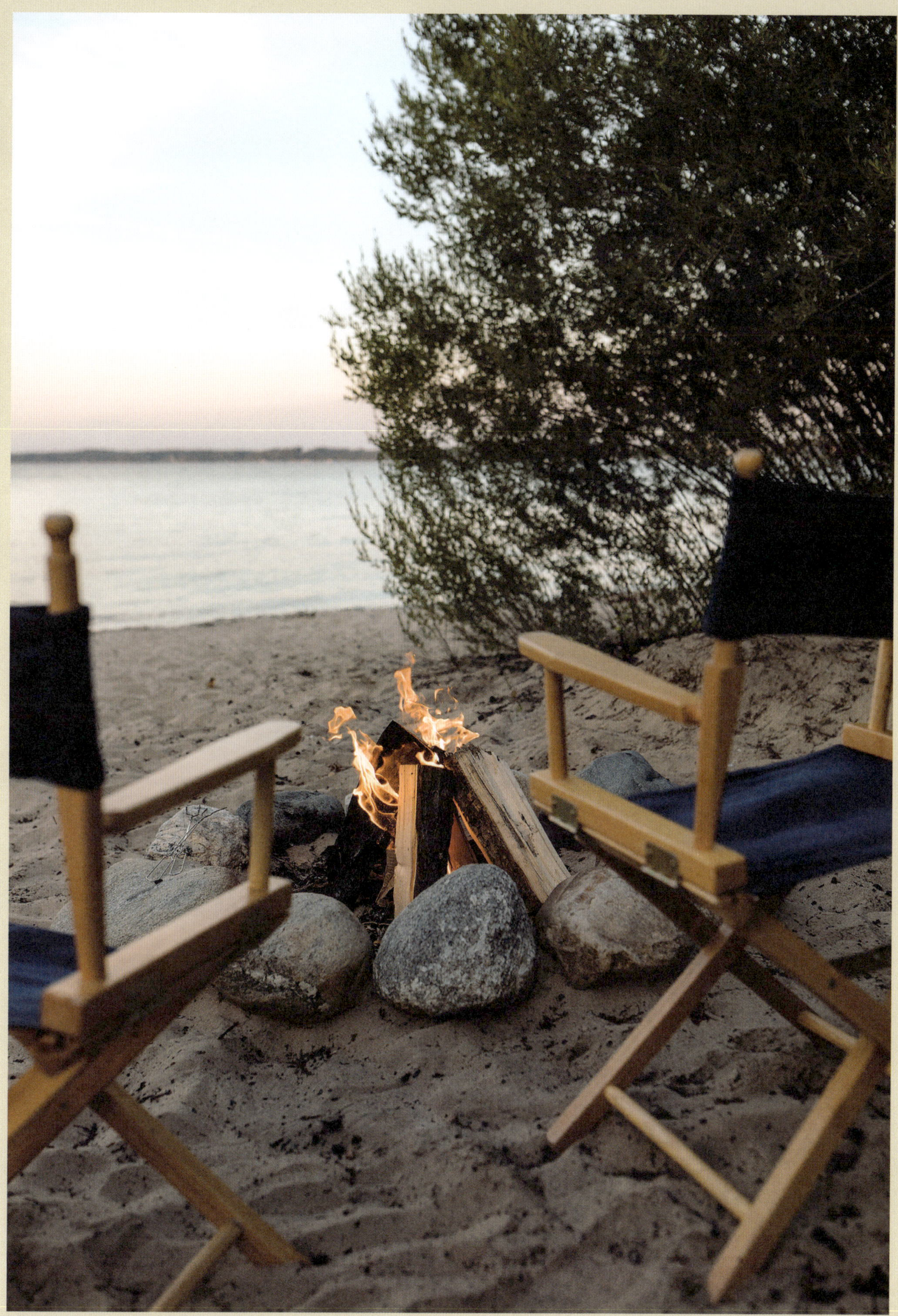

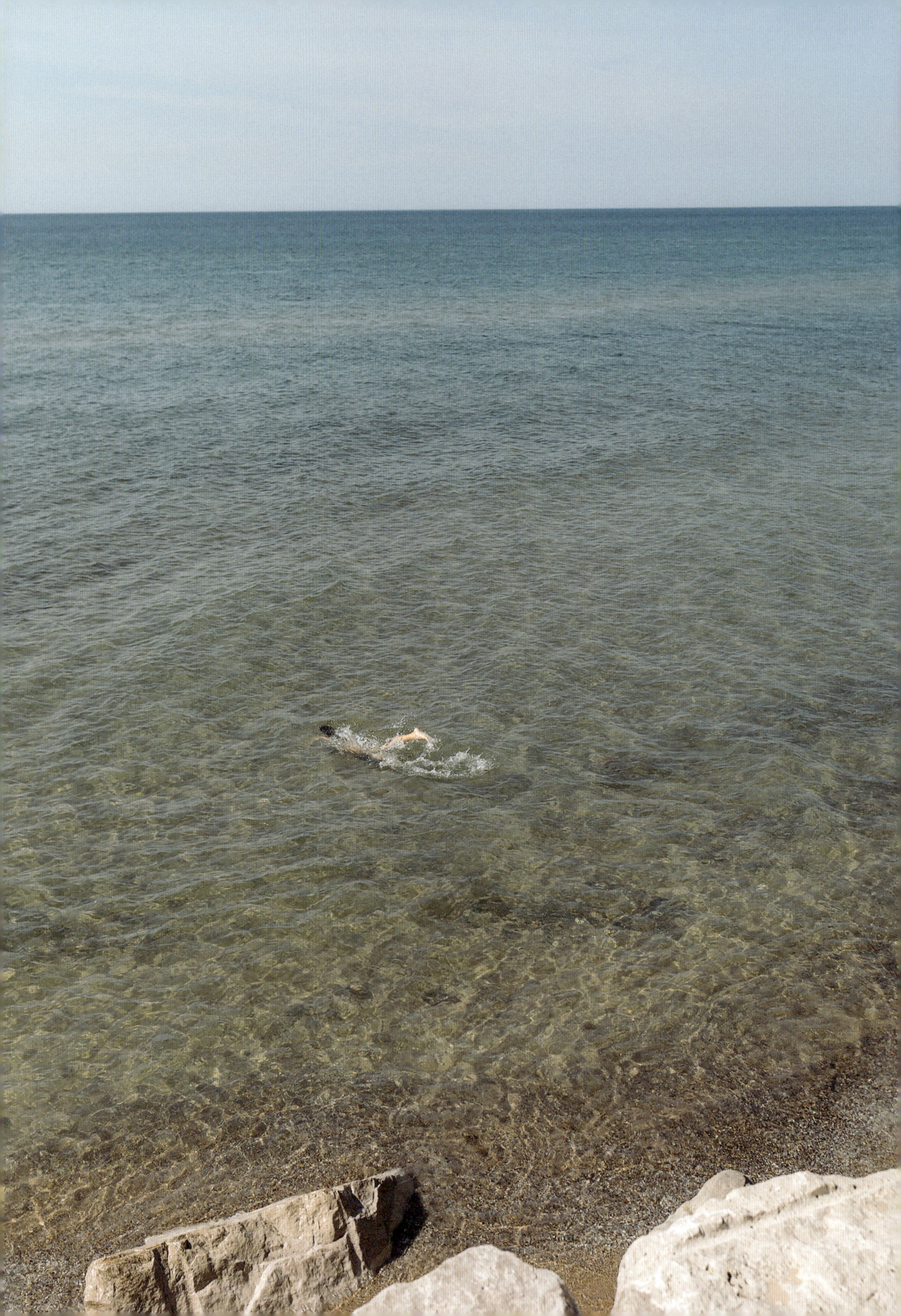

Swimming

THE OTHER SIDE OF COMFORT

For the longest time, swimming has felt inconvenient to me. Somewhere along the way, I traded the joy of jumping in and making a splash, floating on warm water and being gently rocked by waves, submerging in the most serene place and feeling held on all sides, for the convenience of preserving my mascara and saving myself another load of towels. Swimming started to feel childish, impractical, even a little bit gross if the lake appeared murky. It always seemed simpler to stay on the shore and in the boat, watching from a safe, dry distance while others took the plunge.

Until this summer. For whatever reason, I suddenly felt like I was the one missing out. I felt like I was more of a bystander than a participant in all the summer fun. So I made it my mission—this summer, I'm going to swim more. I'm going to actually get in the water, leave the beach, leave the boat, and leave all of my practical tendencies at the shore.

This may seem silly, but I think it's necessary to challenge our comfort zones every once in a while, because they might be keeping us from sheer delight.

Maybe the water's a little colder than you'd like, or there's too much seaweed tickling your legs. Maybe it seems too early in the day for a boat ride, or too late at night for another swim. Maybe the drive to the cottage feels too long, or the hike to the lighthouse too far. Maybe pulling that canoe out of storage feels too difficult or waiting in the long ice cream shop line too time consuming.

In moments where you're having an inner battle, debating if the potential fun outweighs the inconvenience, let this be your anthem: Some of life's greatest joys are right on the other side of comfort.

I'm so glad I challenged myself to swim more, because my fondest memories from this summer include moments when I was in the waves, fully drenched, with lake water dripping from my eyelashes.

On a cool calm morning in Traverse City, my mom and I got up with the sunrise and promptly walked over to the beach. Her motive was to rock hunt along the shore and see what had washed up overnight; my motive was to swim. At the edge of the dock, I gave myself multiple pep talks before I finally plunged into the still surface. I came up above the water feeling awake and alive, pleasantly surprised at how enjoyable it was to swim in the morning light.

Another day, Gavin and I had a date night at the beach. The plan was to just pick up dinner and picnic in the sand, but when we realized the water was warmer than the air we simply had to get in, so we watched the sunset while sipping wine in the waves.

Let this be a reminder for both you and for me that even though something feels cumbersome—driving home with a wet swimsuit, doing another load of laundry, staying out past bedtime, getting up early with the sunrise—some of your greatest summer memories might be waiting on the other side.

What's stopping you from jumping in and fully participating in the summer fun?

What's something you feel like you might love doing but it seems inconvenient to try?

What's keeping you ashore?

There's still time. Several precious weeks of summer remain. So shed the skepticism and schedule whatever it is in your calendar. On Saturday, let's go swimming.

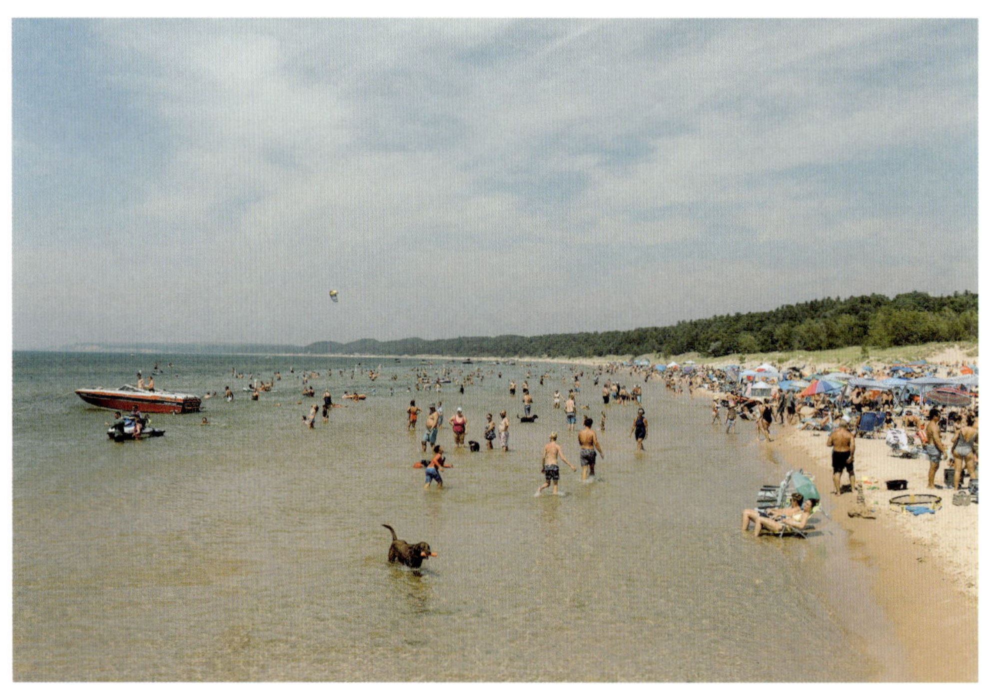

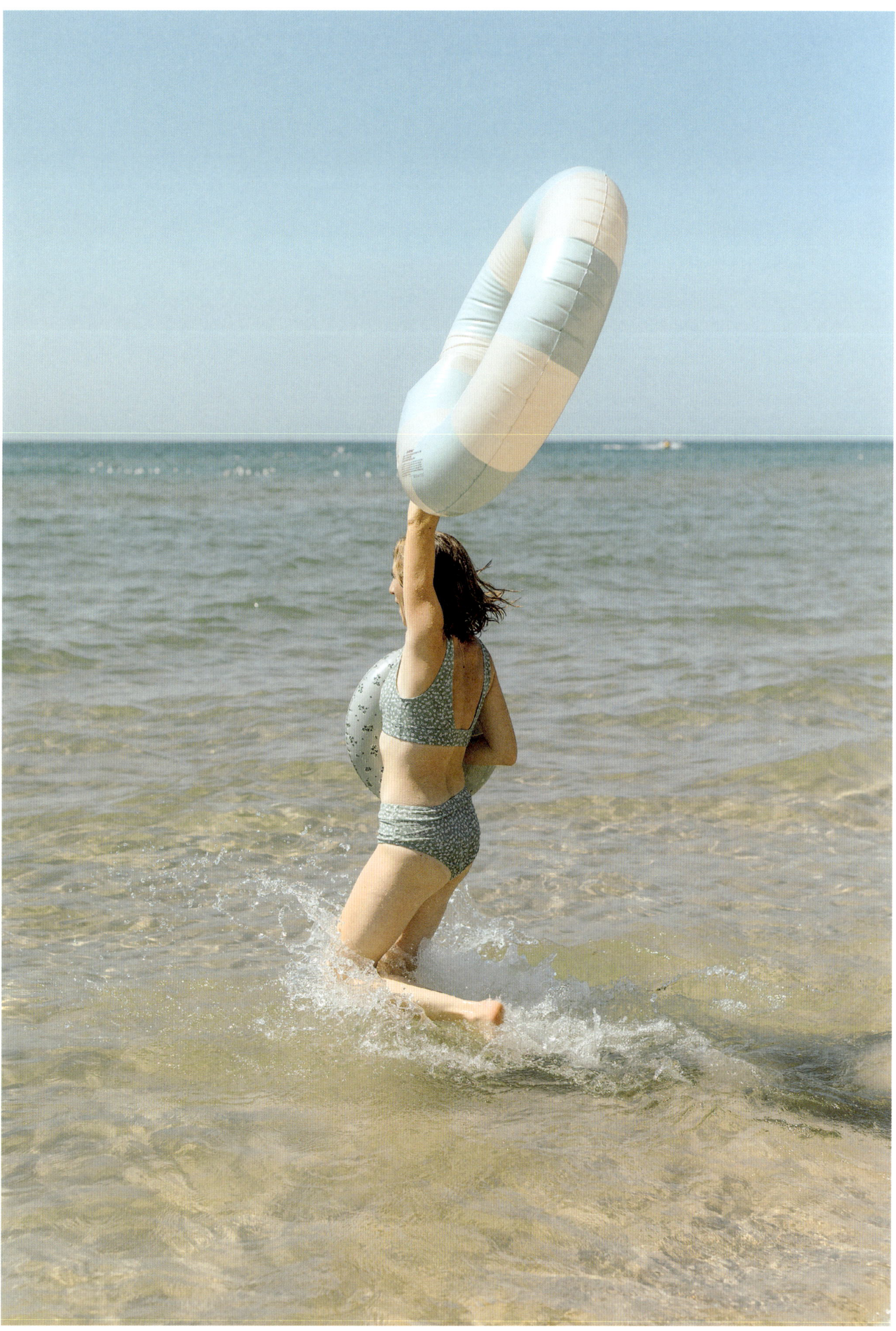

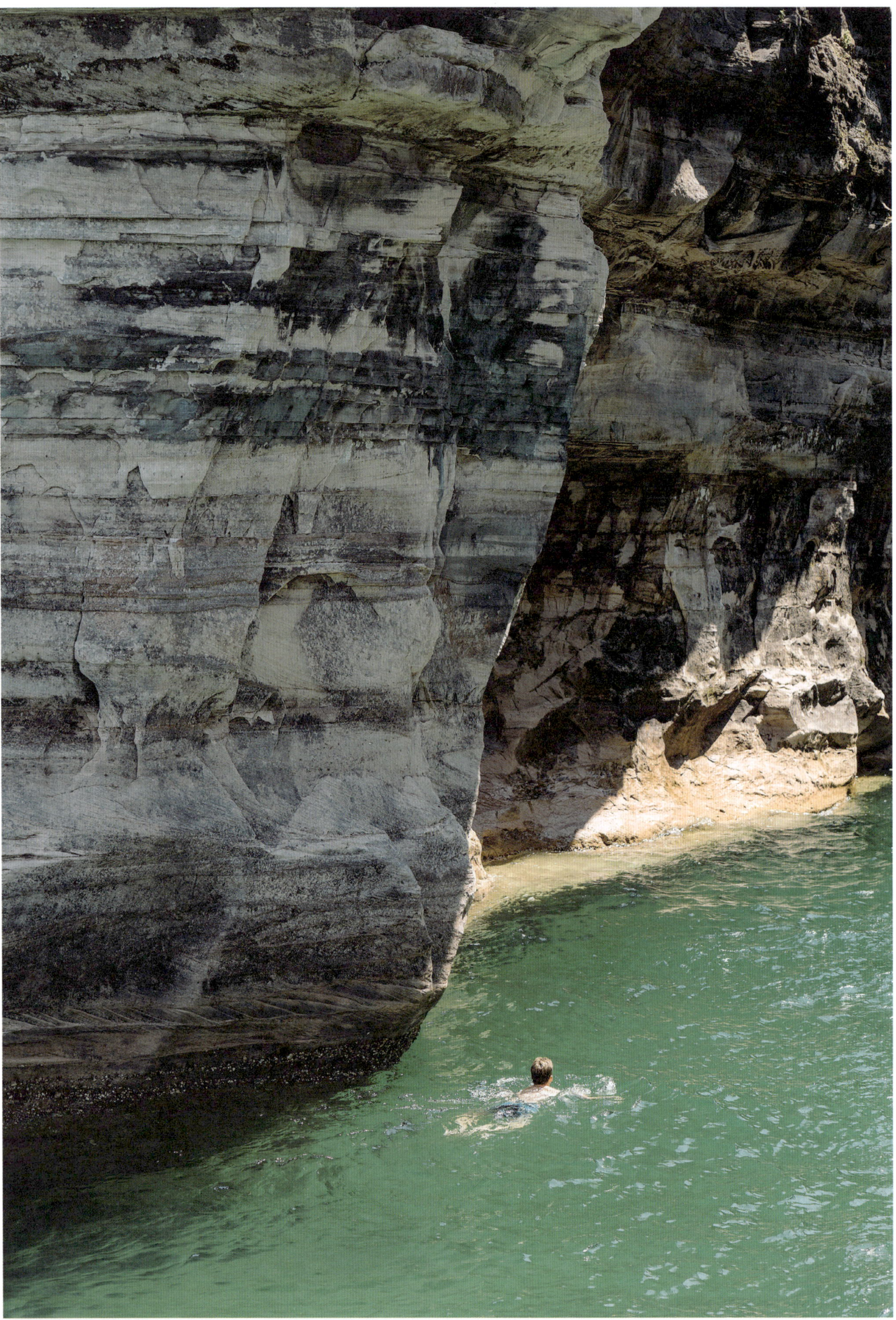

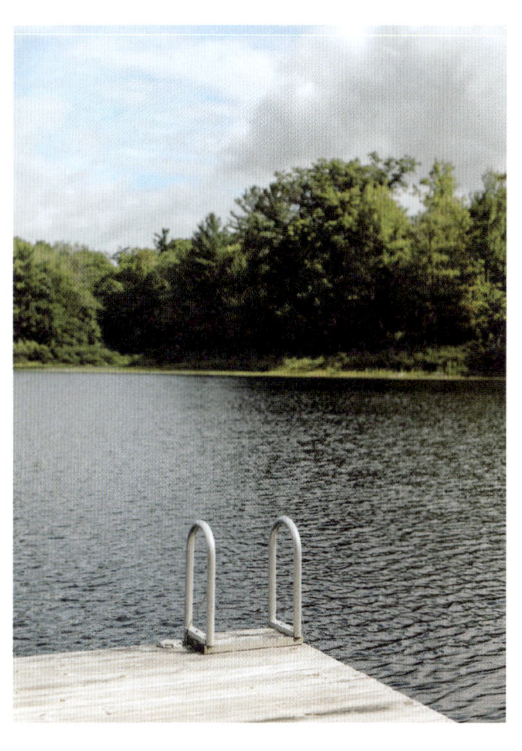

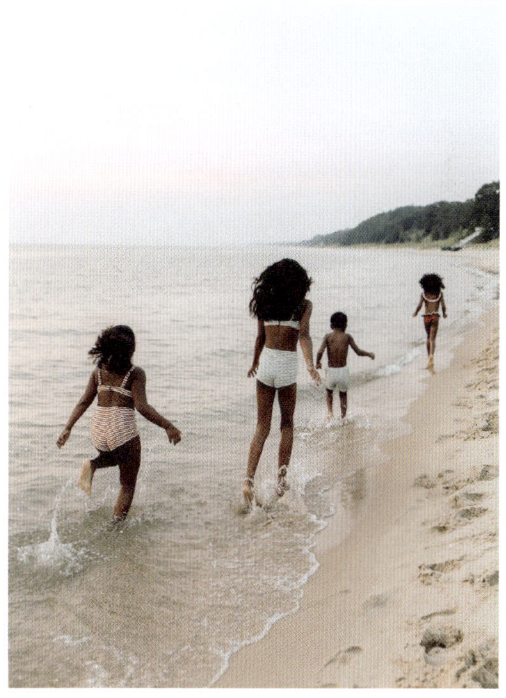

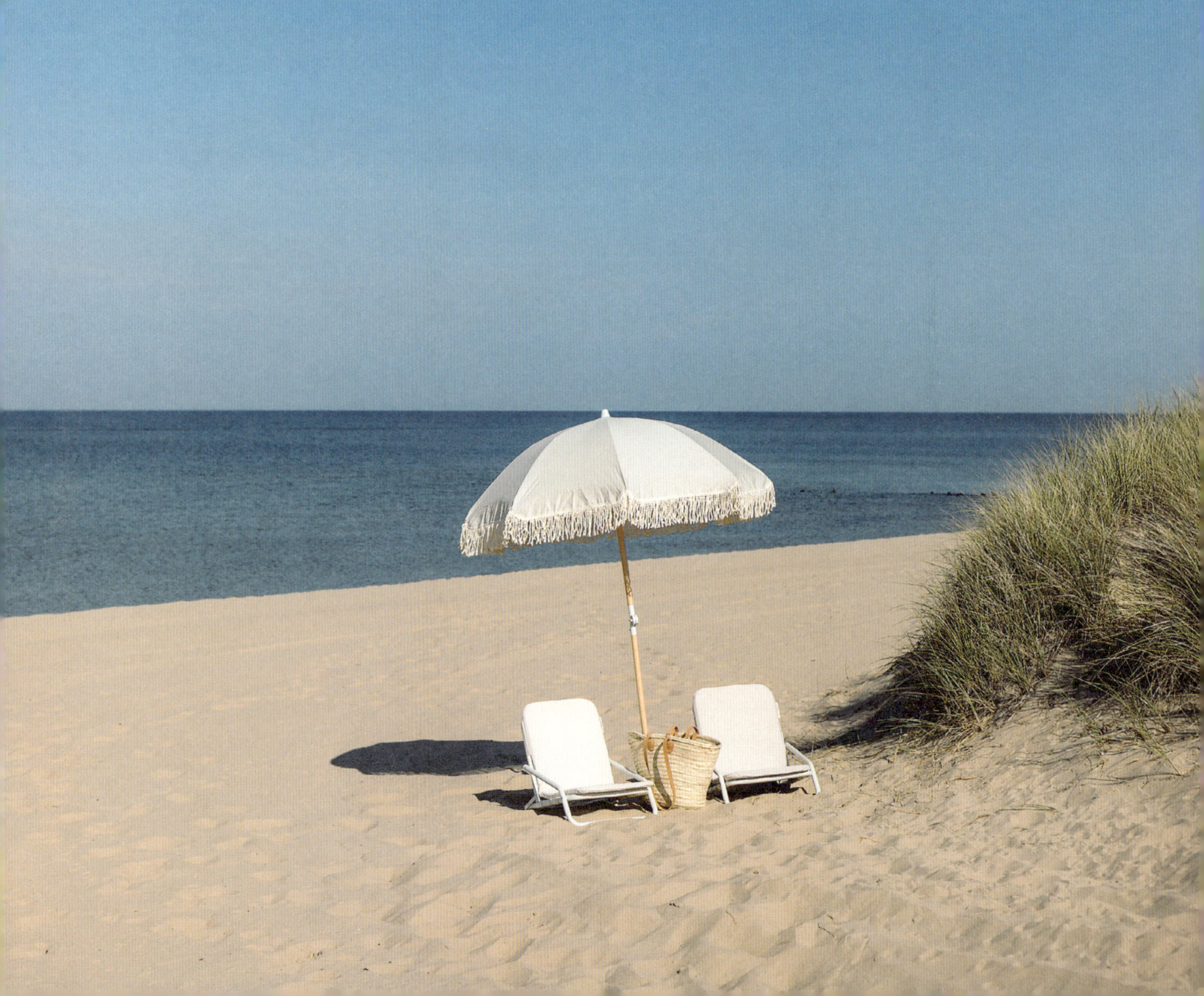

SOS

AN UNPLUGGED WEEKEND

I spent a weekend with family in Pentwater, a quaint town on Lake Michigan. Every morning we walked to grab coffees and breakfast burritos from Green Isaac's and wove in and out of boutique shops. We took Jeep rides with the top down to the marina and boat rides through the channel at sunset. We ate ice cream cones from the House of Flavors and taffy from the old-fashioned candy store. I bought a touristy sweatshirt, immediately ripped the tags off, and proceeded to wear it for three days straight. We grilled burgers and ate an entire watermelon and countless corn on the cob. We chased the sunset each night and watched it vanish right where the water meets the horizon.

We had the perfect getaway in a classic cozy lake town, and the whole time I had zero bars of service. My phone had an "SOS" icon in the top right corner all weekend long. At first it felt somewhat annoying, but it ended up being a blessing. Since my phone didn't work, I was able to be fully present.

I was free to hear the lake humming in the distance at all times, and I listened to the waves crescendo as we got closer and closer to the shore. I buried my toes in the sand and felt the soft, warm, loose earth get cooler and damper and heavier the further I dug down. I observed the way the sky looks immediately after the sun sets, like a vertical rainbow of pastels—pink orange yellow green blue indigo violet—from the surface of the water up to the heavens. I noticed so much more without the distraction of my phone.

That's one of the many things that I love about Lake Michigan—it forces me to disconnect. Most lakeside towns and beaches are off the grid, and while it can be bothersome, I now see it as an opportunity to be still.

Maybe your lake of choice has the same quirk; as you get closer to the lakeshore, service bars drop, and by the time your feet hit the water, they're gone completely. I find it ironic that while my phone says "SOS," my soul is being saved by the rhythm of the waves.

It's like the lake knows what we need—to hear the sounds of water, to feel the weight of sand, to admire the sunset and what comes after.

If you're in pursuit of an intentional life, if you're trying to be more present this summer, then it's essential to unplug. Fully committing to a slow-paced lifestyle during the summer months means silencing notifications and alerts, quieting our minds, and putting ourselves into places of stillness. And I love how the lake facilitates this for us, especially when we need it most.

As I drove home from Pentwater on Sunday afternoon, with my feet up on the dash, I felt rejuvenated and recharged. There's just something about a weekend spent in a quaint lake town. . . .

It's the sunsets and waffle cones.

It's the lighthouses and late nights.

It's the times where you reach for a deck of cards instead of your phones.

It's the hours spent watching the sky instead of a screen.

It's the moments you choose to fully attend instead of document.

It's the service, or lack thereof, and the way it saves our souls.

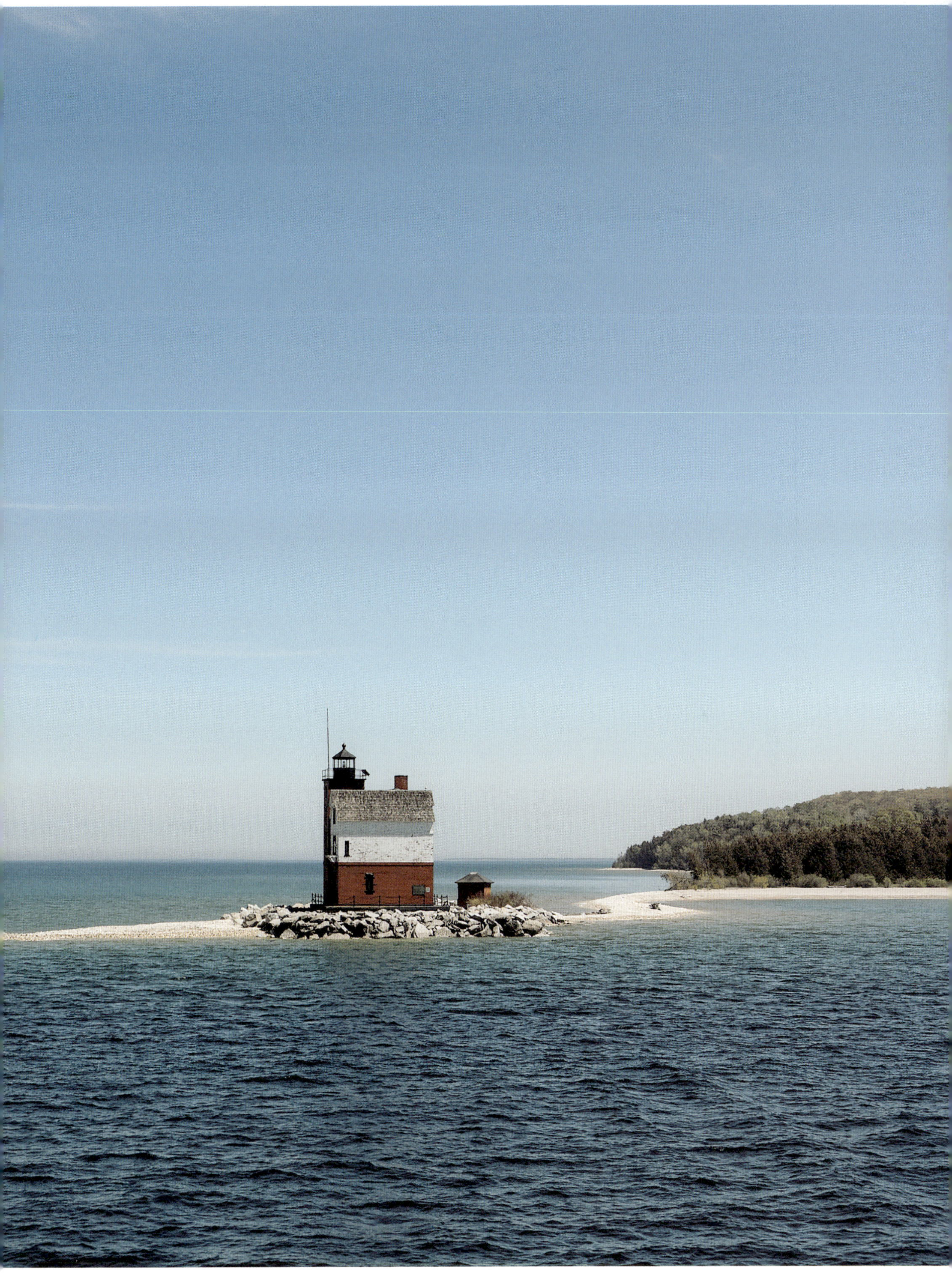

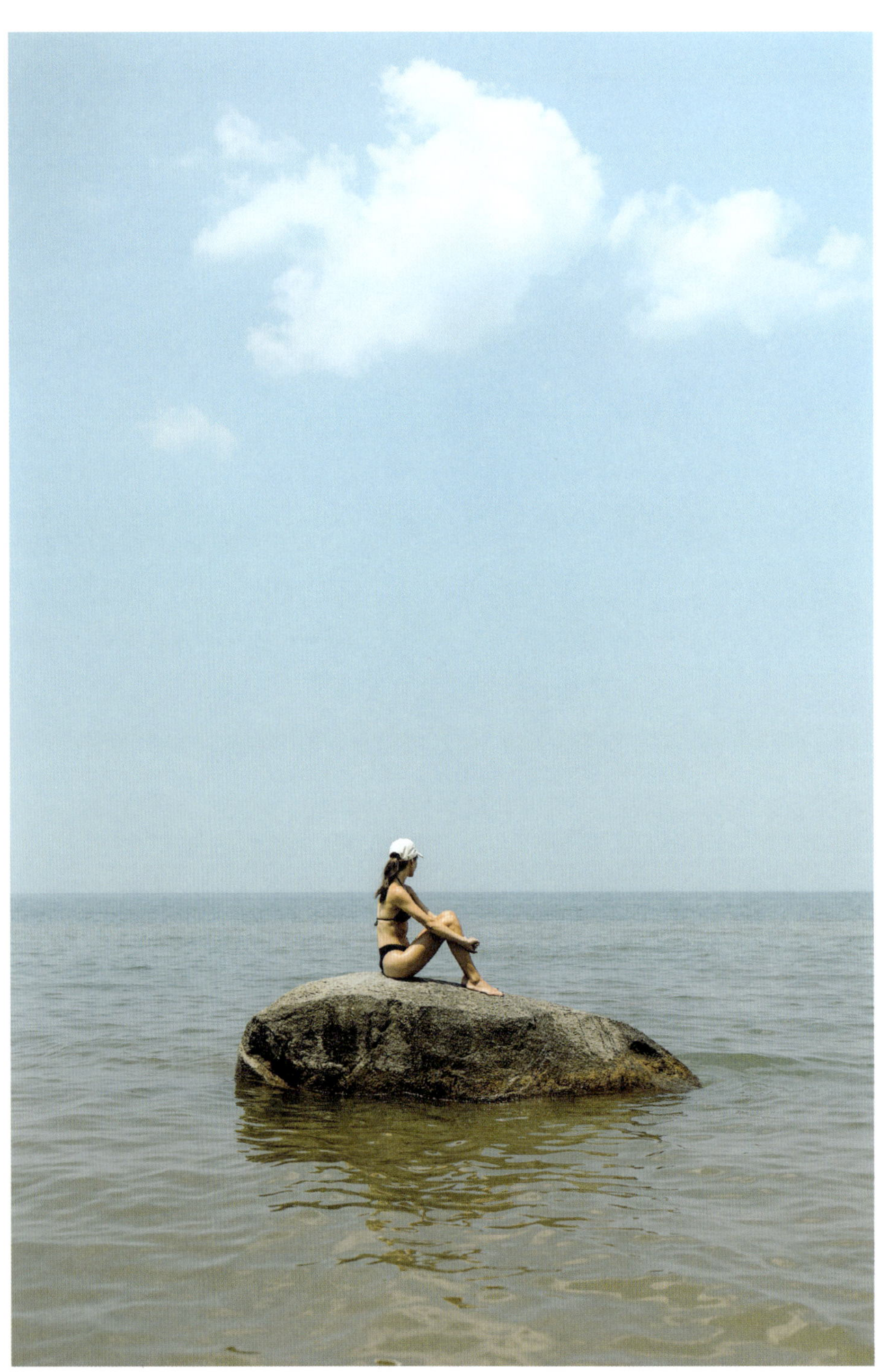

It's like the lake knows what we need—to hear the sounds of water, to feel the weight of sand, to admire the sunset and what comes after.

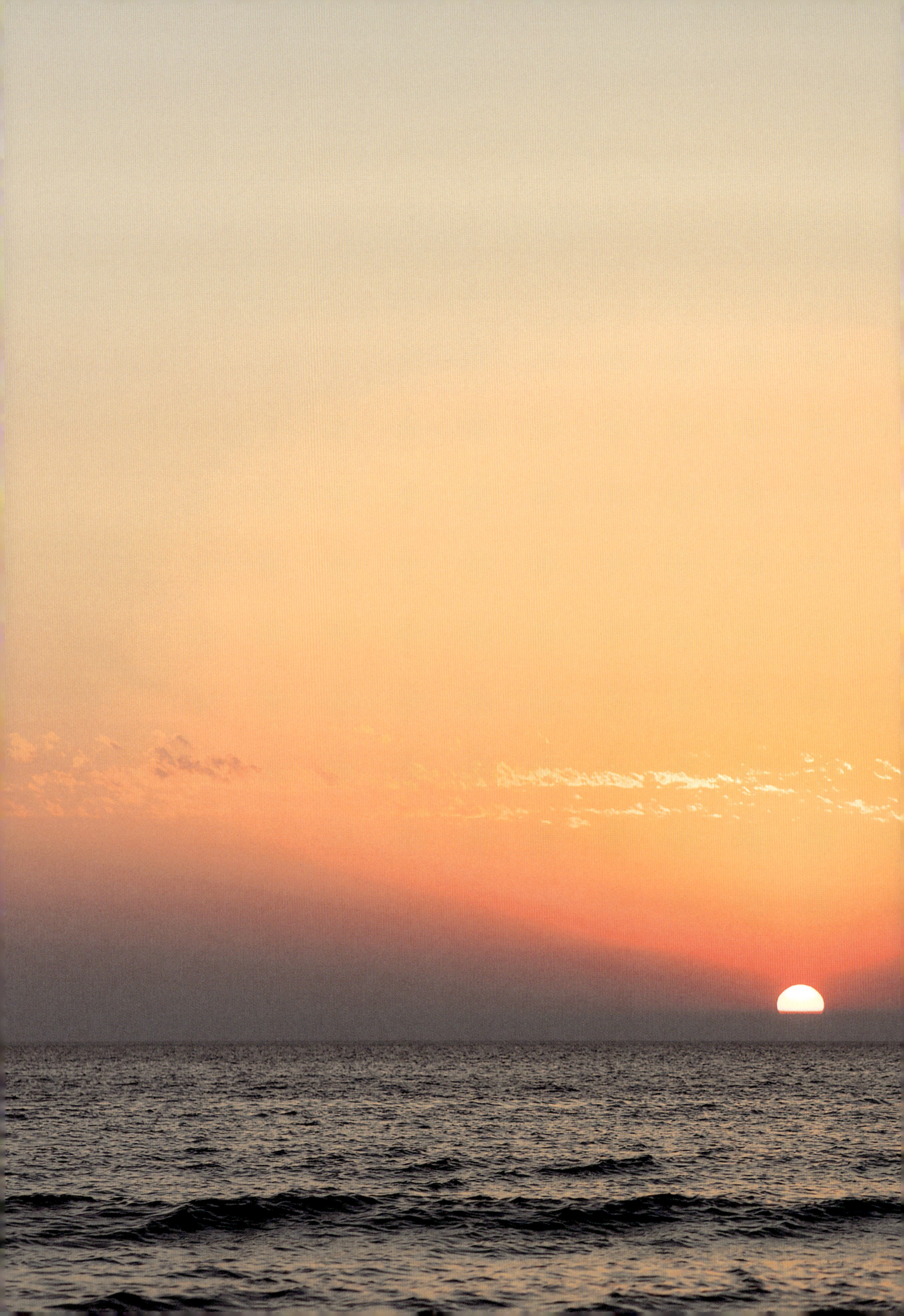

happy hour in the water

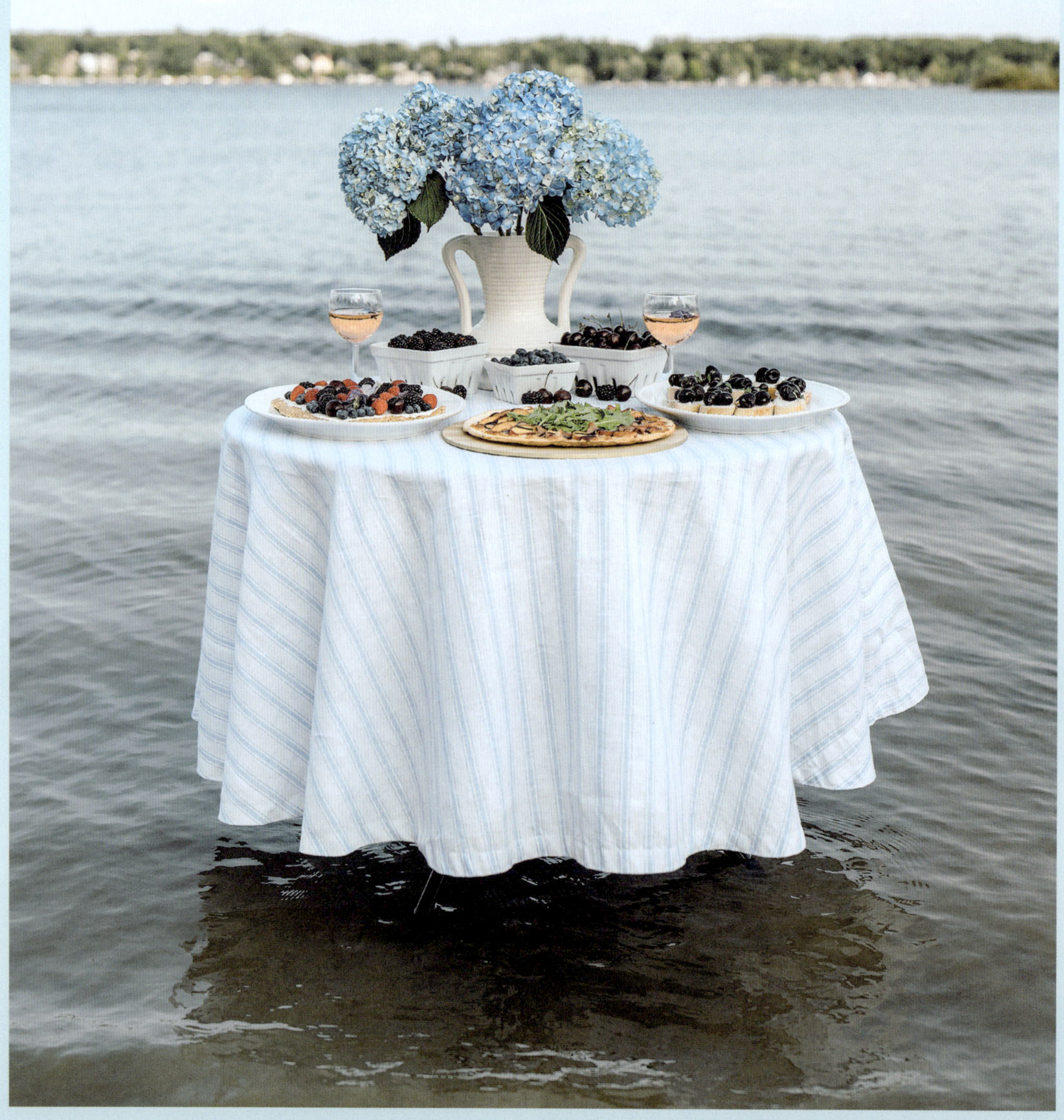

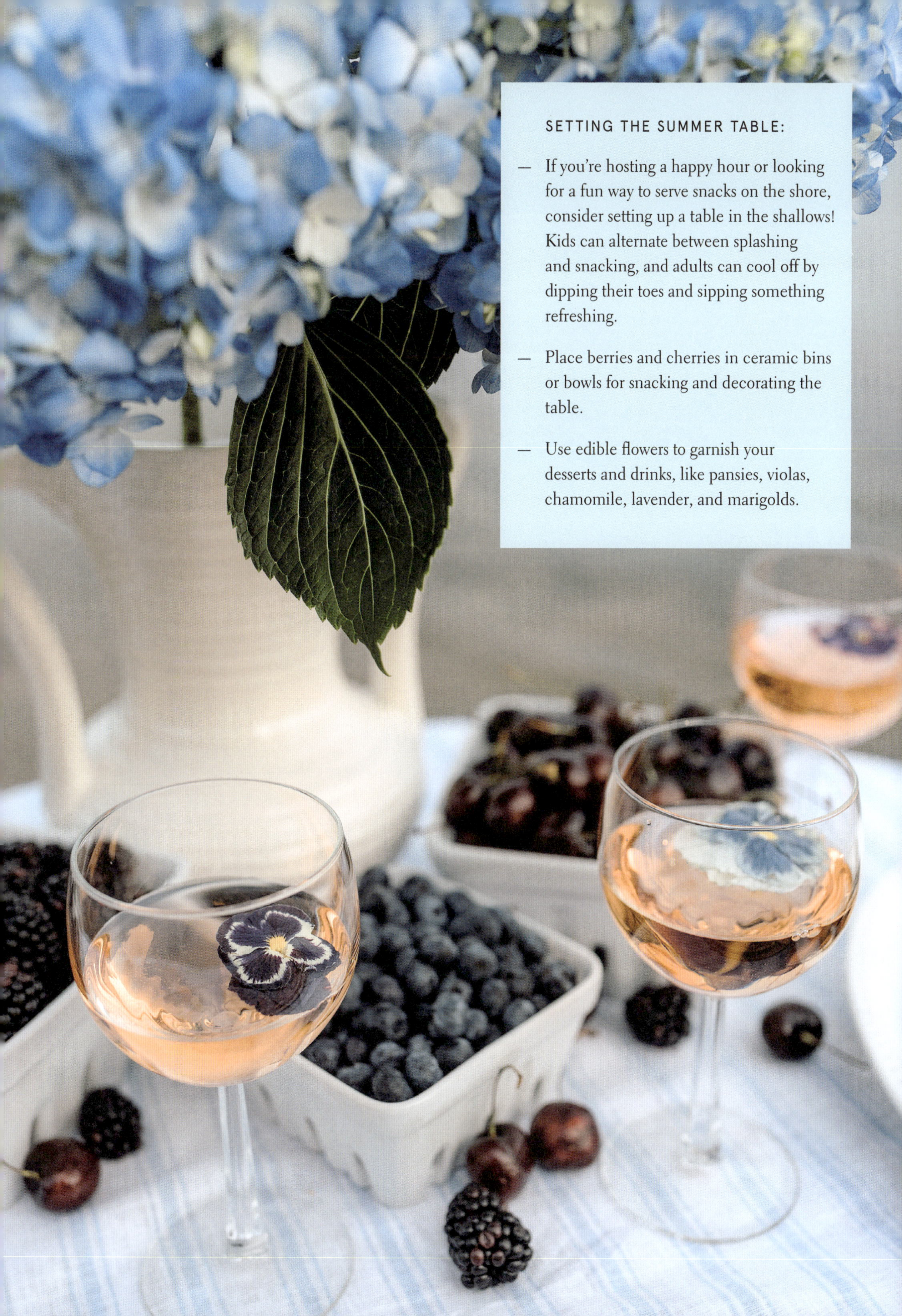

SETTING THE SUMMER TABLE:

- If you're hosting a happy hour or looking for a fun way to serve snacks on the shore, consider setting up a table in the shallows! Kids can alternate between splashing and snacking, and adults can cool off by dipping their toes and sipping something refreshing.
- Place berries and cherries in ceramic bins or bowls for snacking and decorating the table.
- Use edible flowers to garnish your desserts and drinks, like pansies, violas, chamomile, lavender, and marigolds.

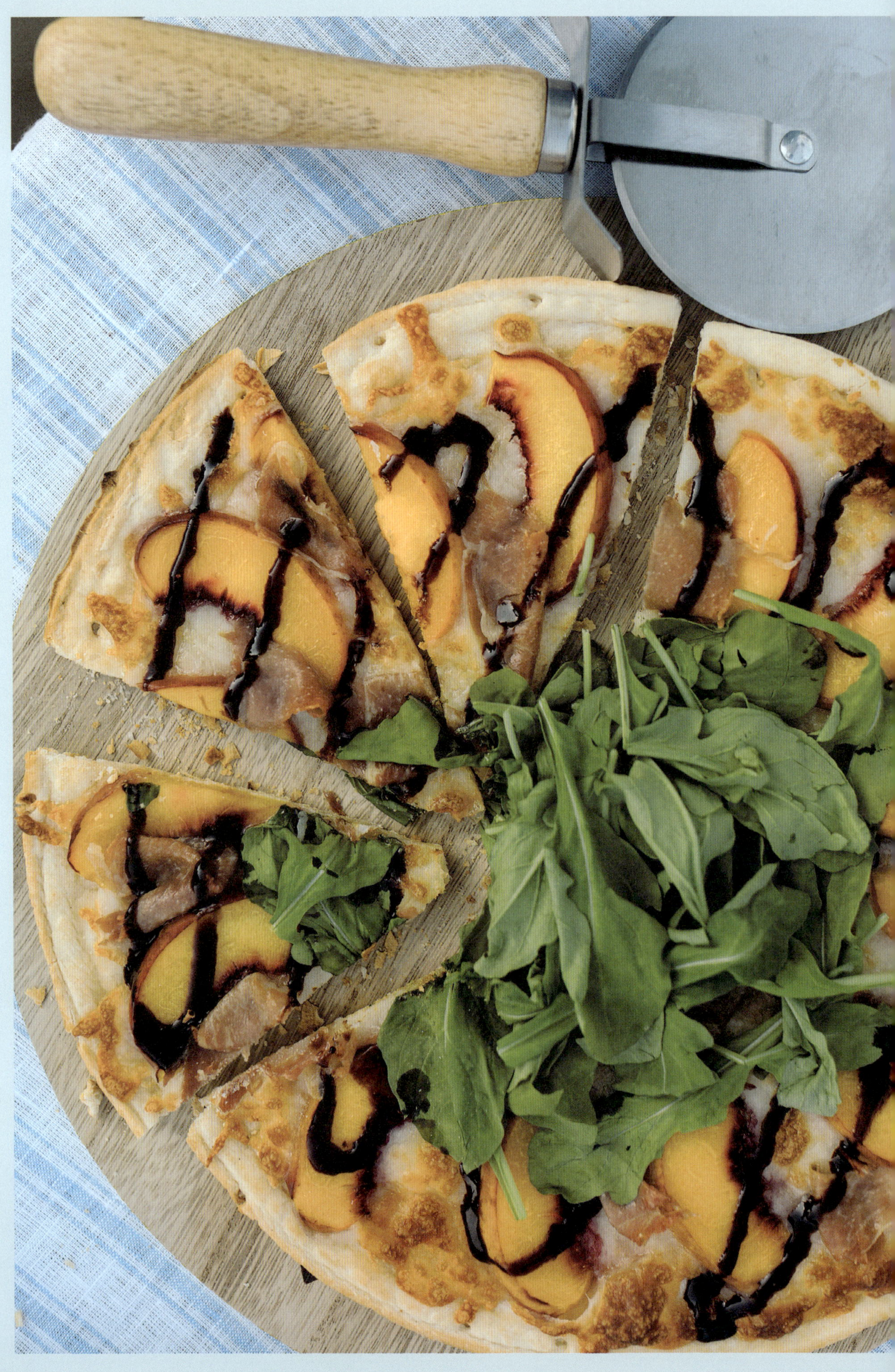

Peach and Prosciutto Pizza

MAKES 1 PIZZA

Peaches feel a little more frivolous than other fruits; they're so juicy and sweet and short-lived, and there's not too many practical things you can do with them other than pies and preserves . . . and pizza. Here's a fun way to enjoy these fuzzy stone fruits while they last.

1 pizza crust (frozen or fresh)
All-purpose flour (optional)
1 tablespoon olive oil
1 (8-ounce/225 g) package shredded mozzarella cheese
1 ripe peach, pitted and thinly sliced
1 (3-ounce/85 g) package prosciutto, chopped into bite-size pieces
Balsamic glaze, for drizzling
Handful of arugula

Preheat the oven and prepare the crust according to the directions on the package. If the crust needs to be rolled out, place the dough on a lightly floured surface and roll it out to the desired size and thickness. Place the crust on a pizza stone or perforated pizza pan and drizzle with the olive oil. Sprinkle the cheese over the oil, covering the entire surface of the dough. Arrange the peach slices and prosciutto over the cheese. Bake according to the package directions, or until the cheese is melted and the crust is golden. Transfer the pizza to a cutting board or plate and let cool, then drizzle with balsamic glaze and sprinkle with the arugula. Slice and serve.

Summer Berry Tart

SERVES 6 TO 9

This dessert is perfect any time you're craving a sweet treat. It's a quick and simple no-bake snack, and an ideal way to utilize your summer berry haul. It can easily be made gluten-free and dairy-free.

FOR THE CRUST

2 cups (240 g) crushed graham crackers (gluten-free optional)
½ cup (1 stick/115 g) unsalted butter, melted
¼ cup (60 ml) honey, plus more if needed

FOR THE TOPPING

1 (8-ounce/225 g) package cream cheese (dairy-free optional), at room temperature
2 cups (300 g) fresh summer berries (such as blueberries, raspberries, blackberries, pitted dark cherries, strawberries)
Edible flowers, for garnish (optional)

Make the crust: Line a baking sheet with parchment paper. In a medium bowl, combine the graham crackers, melted butter, and honey. Transfer the mixture to the prepared baking sheet and press it together with your hands to form a roughly 10-inch (25 cm) square crust. If the mixture is not holding together, add a little more honey. Place the crust in the freezer to chill for at least 1 hour, or until you're ready to serve it.

Make the topping: In a medium bowl using a handheld mixer (or in the bowl of a stand mixer fitted with the paddle attachment), beat the cream cheese until fluffy and creamy, then spread it over the crust. Top with the berries of your choice. Garnish with edible flowers, if desired. Serve chilled.

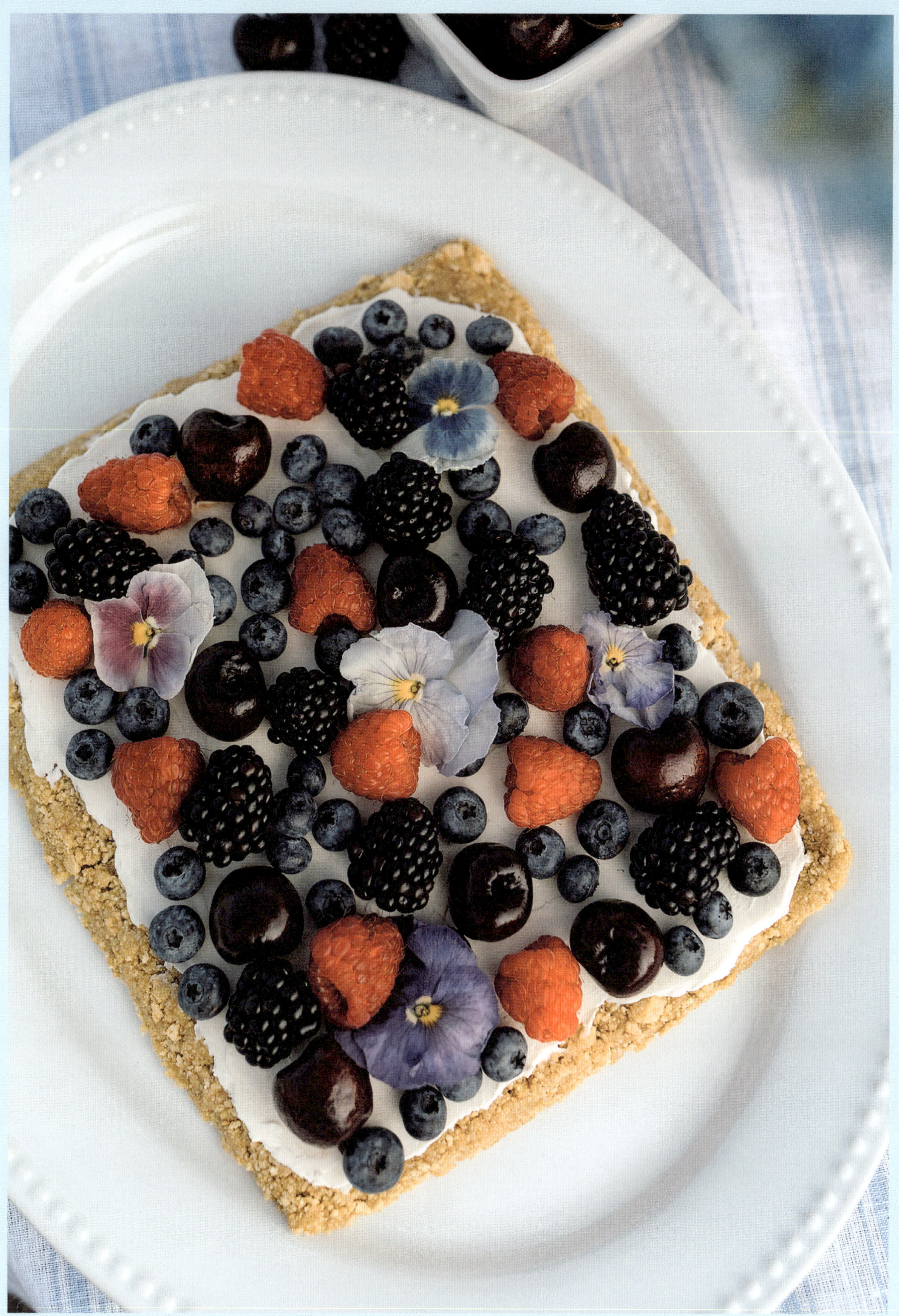

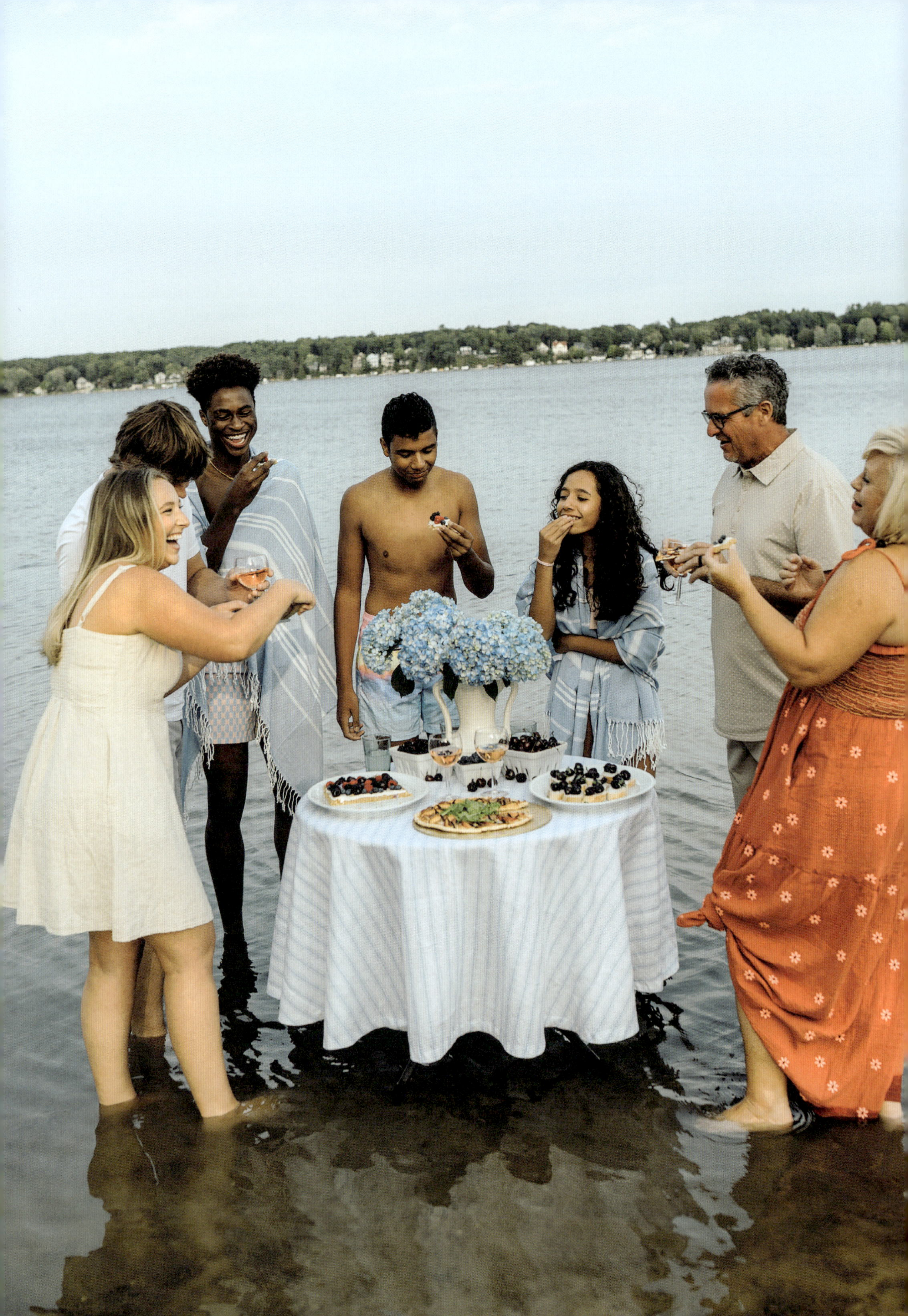

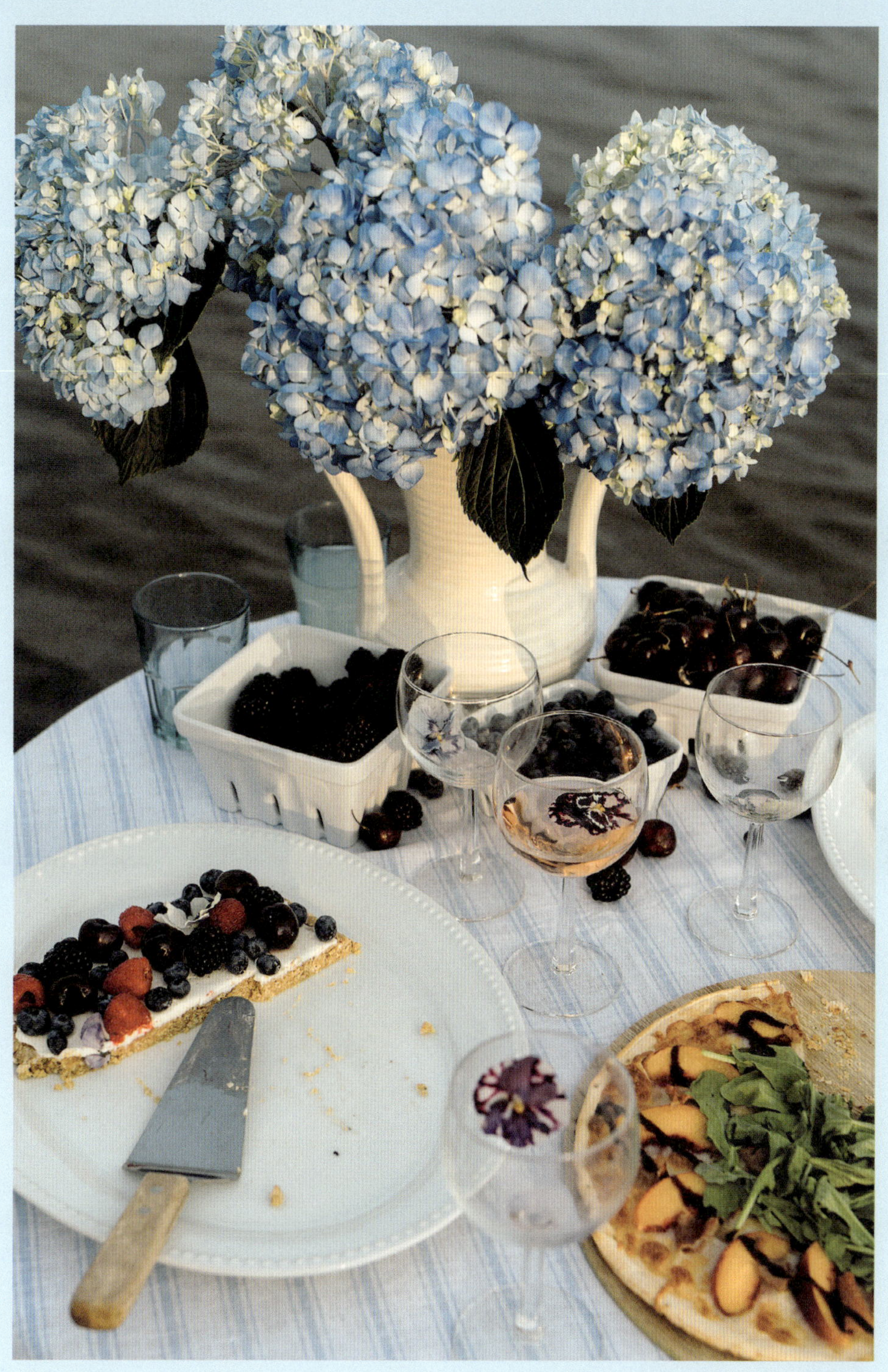

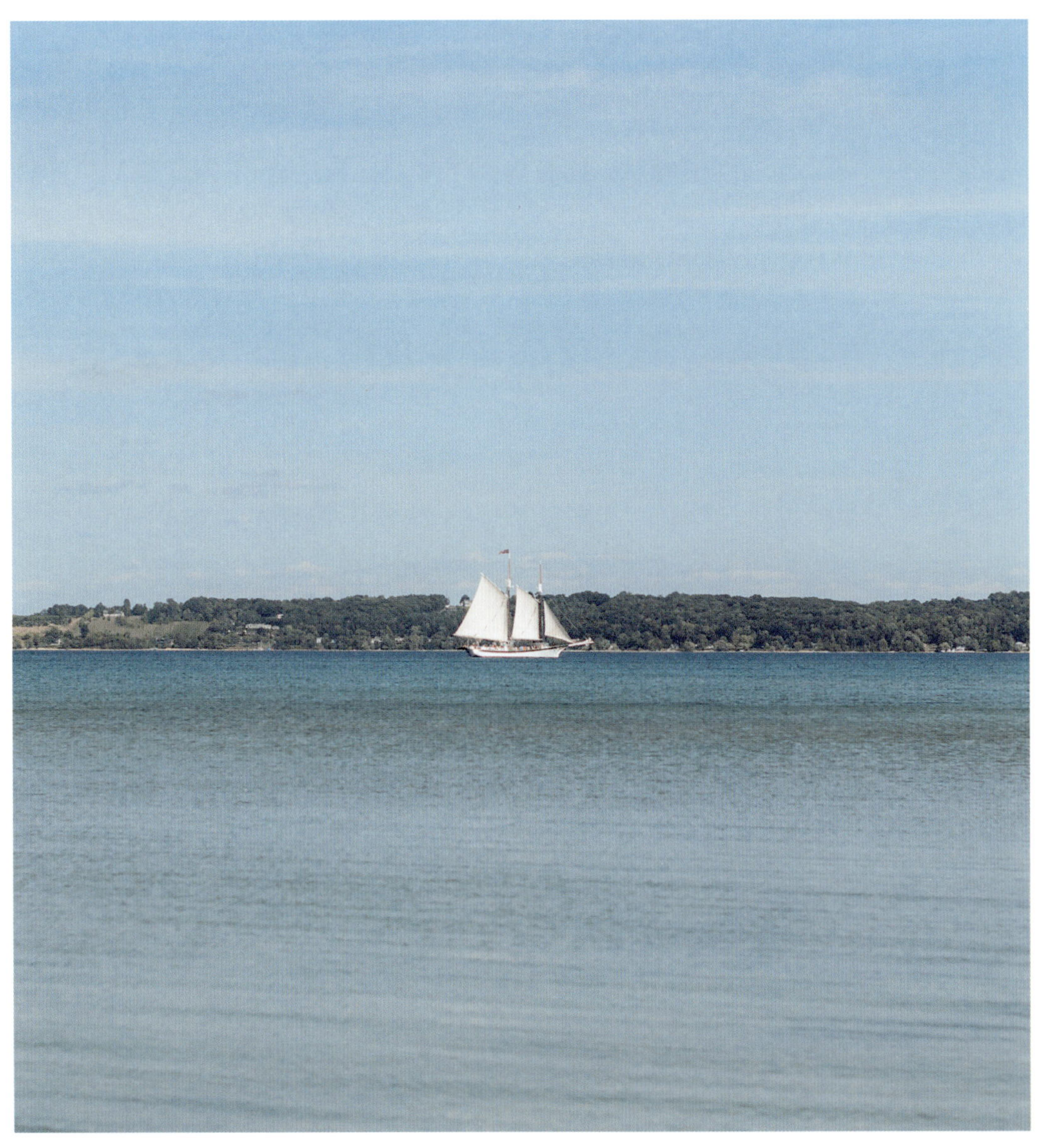

August

August is the most abundant month at the lake. Everything is in full swing, full force, and full bloom. The porch is permanently draped with wet towels and drying swimsuits, hanging in anticipation of another round. The lullaby of the ice cream truck is now a familiar tune, and street corners in August are a symphony of for-sale signs: fresh eggs and local honey, garage sales and garden produce, firewood bundles and fresh-picked flowers. Summer weather gains momentum in August; humidity raises the temperature even higher, thunderstorms and the occasional tornado siren beckon us toward the basement. Farmers' markets display a rainbow of produce: piles of sweet corn, peaches and blueberries, cucumbers and green beans. August brings an abundance of wildflowers too, so vivid and diverse, like confetti fell from the sky. But August also brings goldenrod. This sunshine-colored perennial blankets fields and borders lakes; it lines country roads and frames forests. I hear my dad's voice whenever I see it: "When the goldenrod turns golden, six weeks till the killin' frost." It's an indicator of change on the horizon, an admonition to embrace the final glimmering moments of summer, a reminder that August is a bittersweet grand finale. Ladybugs and mosquito bites. Blueberries and back to school. Ice cream truck lullabies and tornado sirens. Wildflowers and goldenrod.

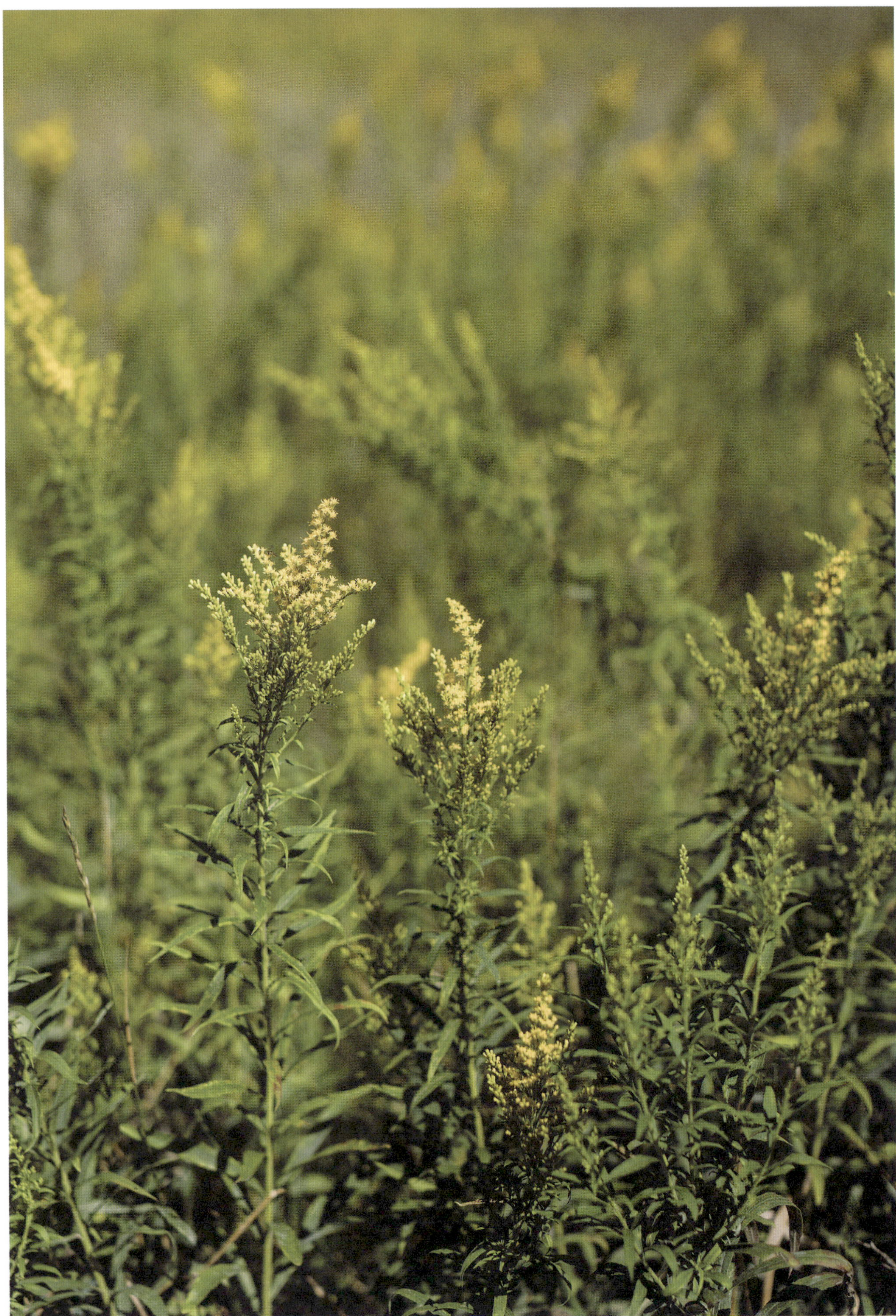

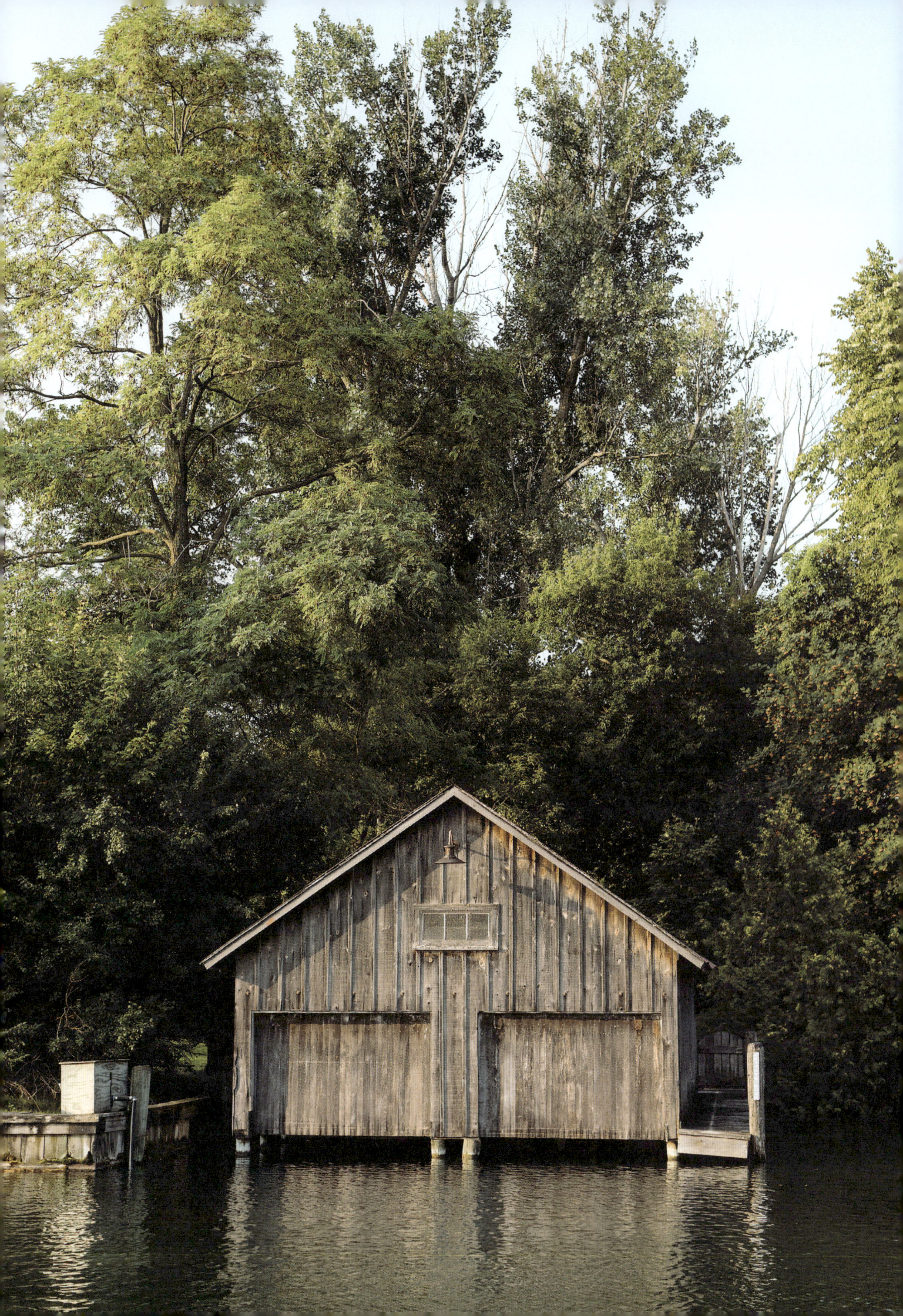

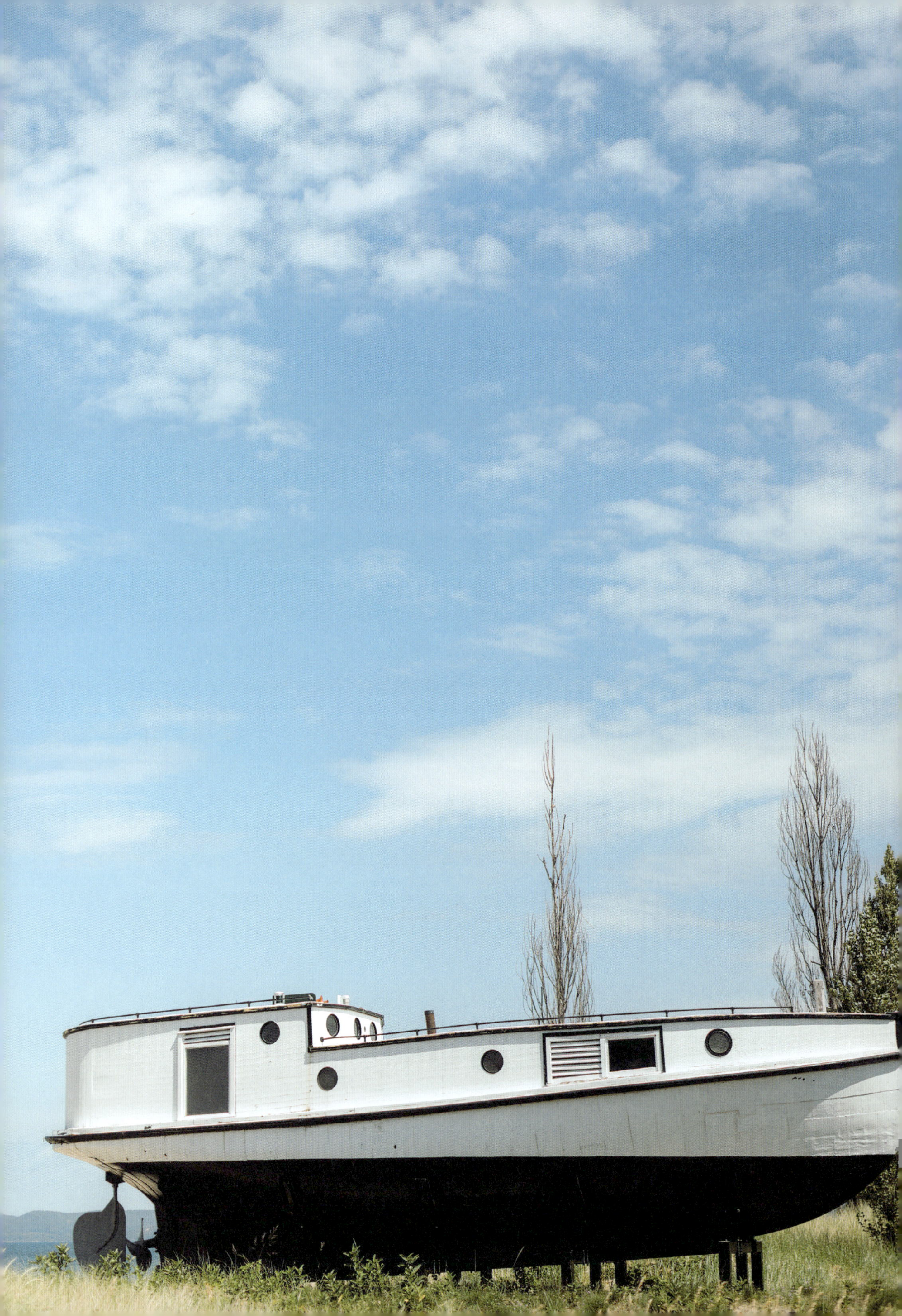

Grounding

SUMMER IN ALL FIVE SENSES

By now, the busyness of summer is weighing heavily. By August, we've had numerous pool parties and cookouts and weddings and weekend getaways. We've logged countless miles in the car, hours in the boat, days on the lake. We can't remember the last time we had a free weekend, a free day, or even a free evening. The fast pace and whirlwind and wildness of it all might be catching up to you, like it always does for me around this time of year.

Some nights, I lay in bed with a list of things to do racing through my mind: find a dress to wear to that wedding, plan group activities and stock the prize basket for my family reunion, recharge my camera batteries, add more sunscreen and s'mores supplies to the grocery list.

Some days, I wake up with my whole body feeling sore and I have no idea why. It could've been that intense game of beach volleyball with my cousins, or multiple rounds of pickleball with my friends, or the long sunset walk around the lake.

Summer is so full of movement and play that it can be hard on us physically and mentally. The longer days, late nights, and missed sleep can wear on us from our minds down to our bones.

Meanwhile, the pressure to still make the most of summer creeps in. My friend describes it as impending doom, the feeling that summer is slipping away paired with the lack of stamina to keep summering. Although we feel exhausted, we also crave the energy to keep doing the spontaneous lake days, to stay up for one more round of our favorite game, to go blueberry picking instead of ordering a plastic pint and doing curbside pickup.

One of my favorite ways to slow down and rejuvenate in the summertime is through grounding. In the simplest terms, grounding is doing something outdoors that reconnects you to the earth and its elements. It's pausing all the hustle long enough to actually smell the air you're

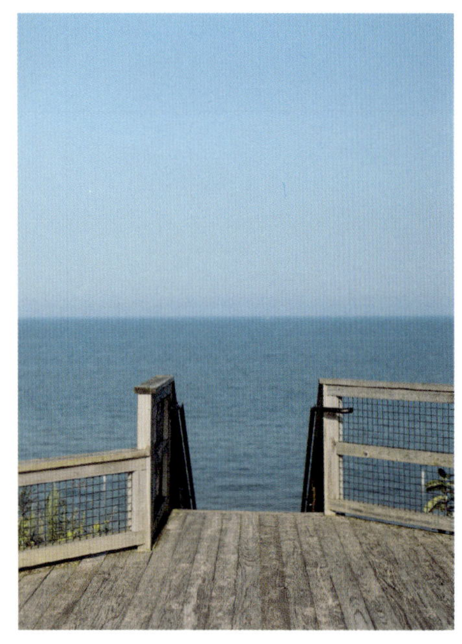
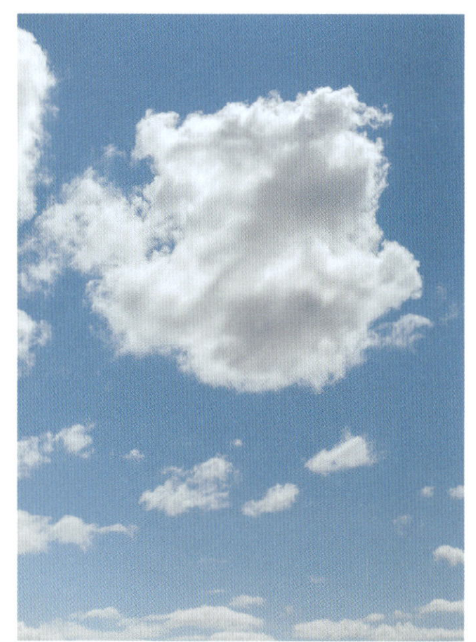
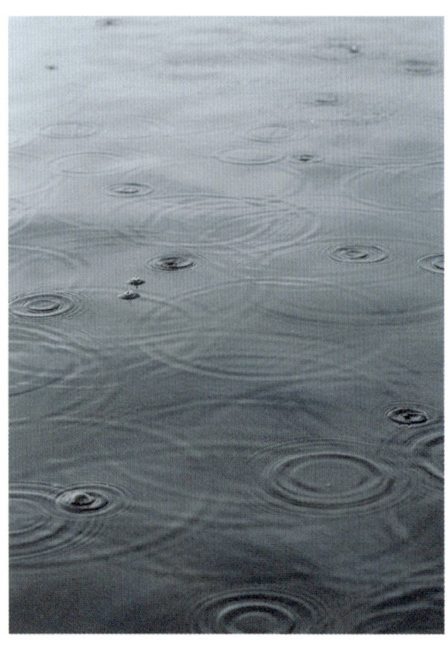
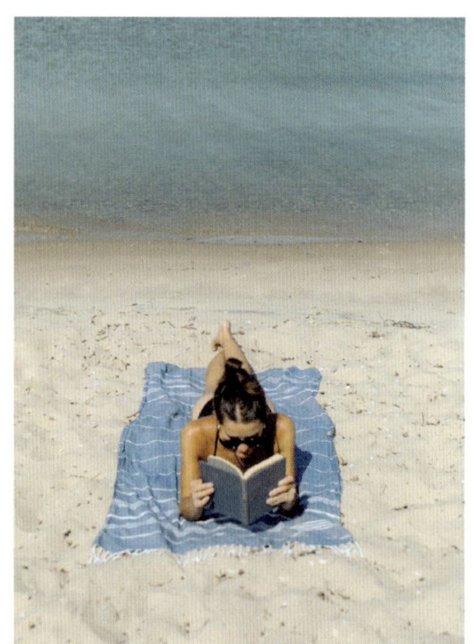

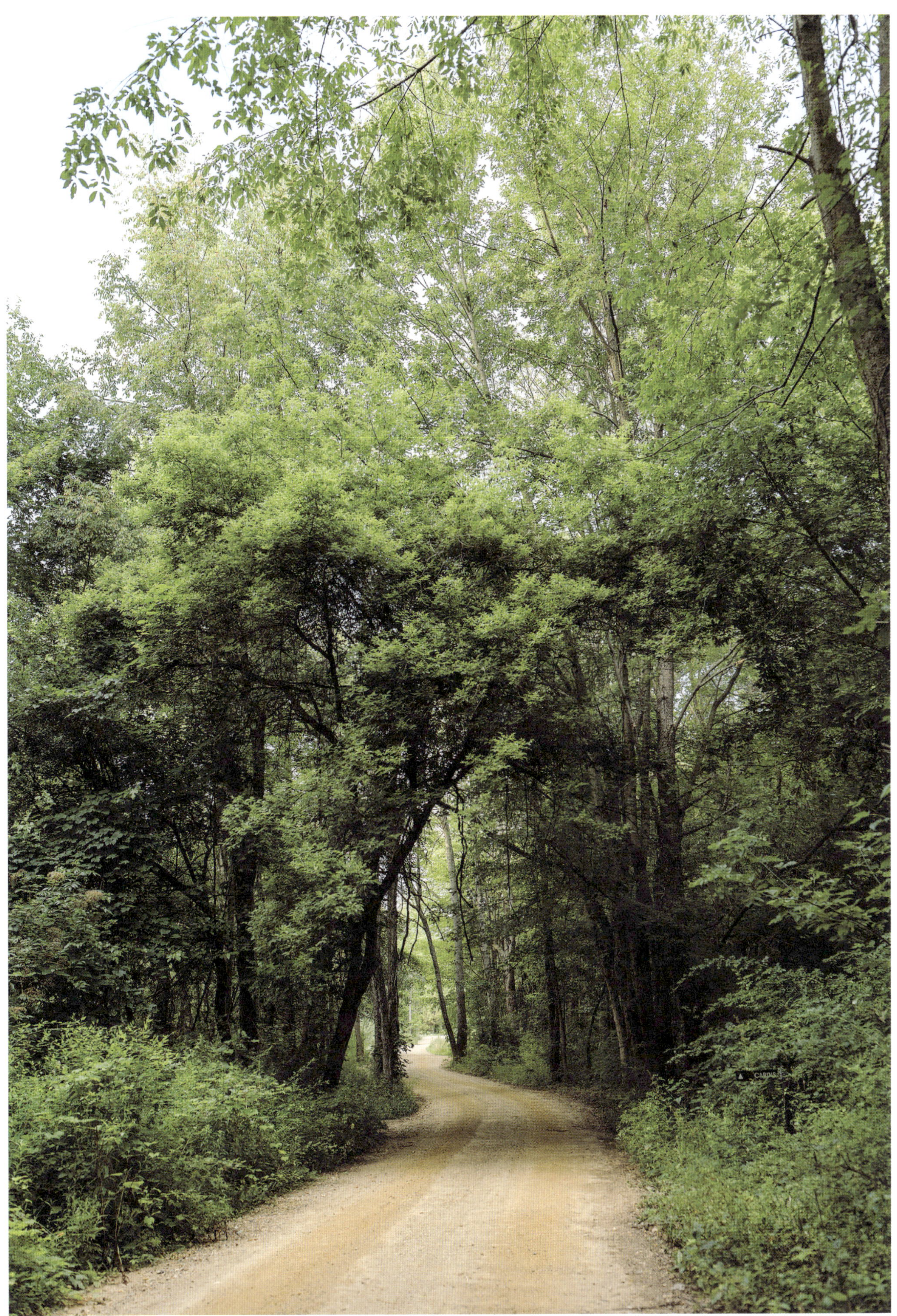
CABINS

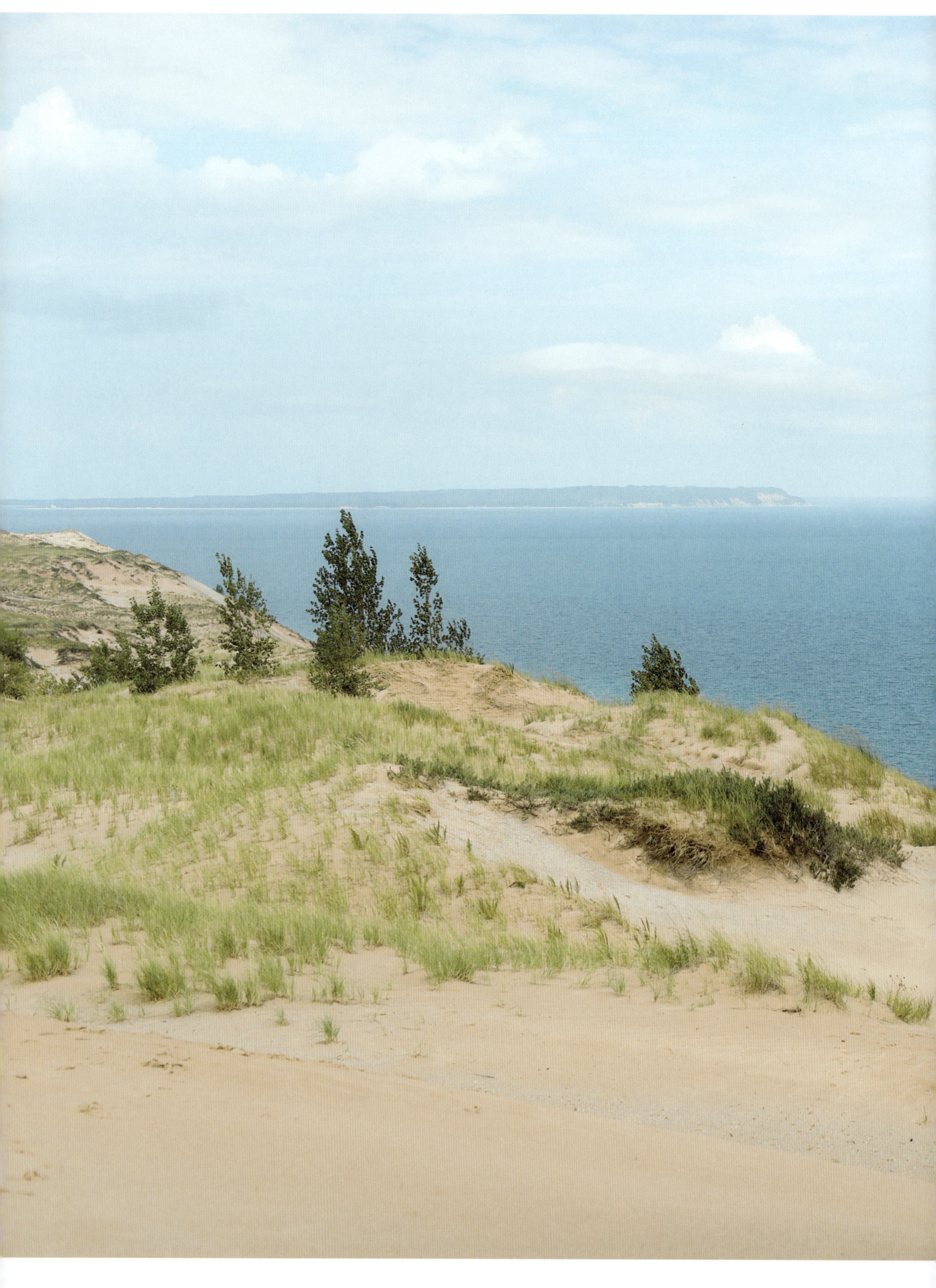

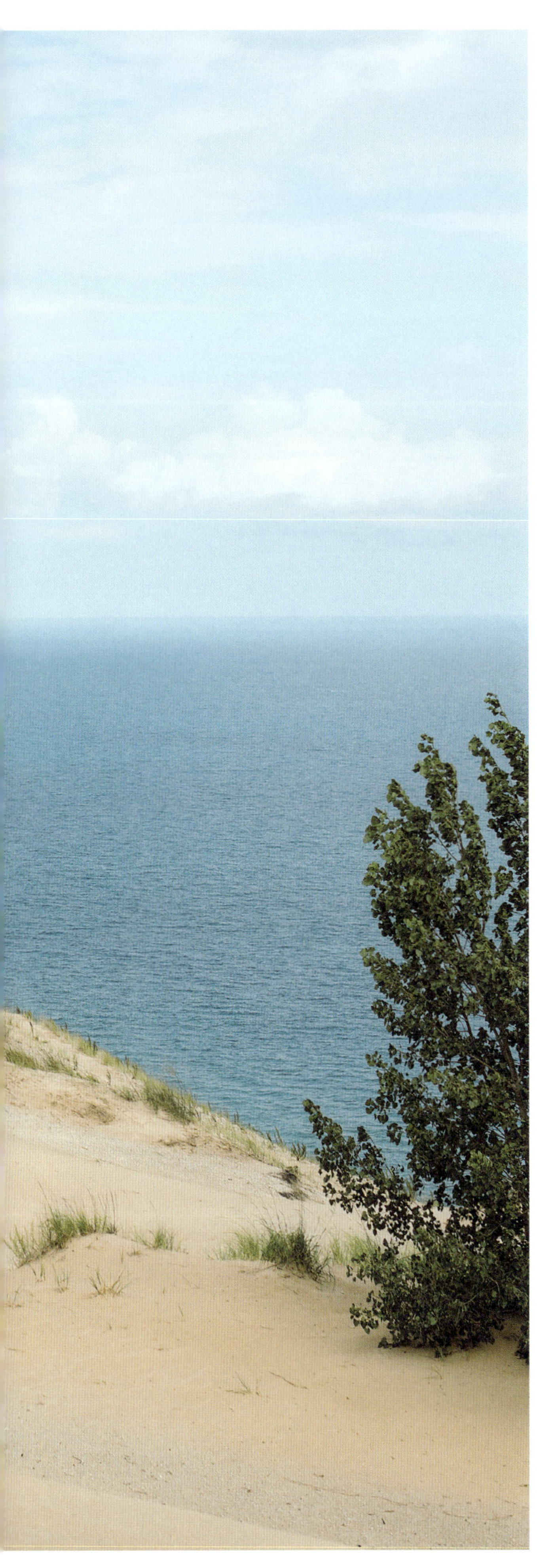

breathing, to hear the birds chirping, to notice the shapes of the clouds, to feel the earth around you—wind on skin, bare feet in grass, sand between fingers.

It's incredibly simple yet incredibly profound, and the benefits of grounding are endless. It's known to lower stress, stabilize the nervous system, lower blood pressure, reduce inflammation, balance circadian rhythms, support better sleep, and so much more.

Grounding is essential in our modern digital age, and arguably it's more important in the busy summertime than any other season. Luckily, it's also more fun in the summer when there's so much to feel and see and smell outdoors!

If you find yourself overstimulated this summer, let nature do its thing. Lie down in green pastures, walk beside still waters, and restore your soul.

summer grounding guide:

- Try to eat breakfast, lunch, and dinner outdoors for one day. Enjoy all three meals with a side of fresh air, sunshine, and deep breaths.
- Grow something. It can be as simple as one cherry tomato plant, one terra-cotta pot with basil in it, or one window box of flowers. Tending to something with your hands—watering, weeding, watching it grow, and maybe even eating its full-grown fruits—is deeply fulfilling.
- Make a sand angel (a snow angel on the beach), covering sweaty skin in sand, then race to rinse it off in the lake.
- Shop at the farmers' market exclusively for a week and plan your meals around what is being harvested locally.
- Try using your bike instead of your car for one day, one week, or as long as you can make it. Bike to the farmers' market, to the coffee shop, to a restaurant for dinner. Feel the wind in your face, the bumps in the sidewalk, every moment of the miles.
- Get caught in the rain. Stand outside in a sprinkle, close your eyes, and splash in puddles. If you're extra brave, skip the rain boots and go barefoot.
- Find a lakeside sauna and book a session. Enjoy the contrast of steam and sweat followed by a cold plunge in the lake.
- Read a physical book outdoors. It's such a simple thing, yet so understimulating in this day and age. Sit under the shade of a tree, watch the shadow and light dance across the words, and let a soft breeze turn the page for you.
- Go for a walk or hike and leave your phone at home. Just one foot in front of the other, fresh air, and the sounds of the world around you.
- Watch the sunset like a movie. Plan an entire evening around the sun; bring snacks and drinks, and watch the sky unfold from golden hour to a colorful canvas to a pastel dusk.

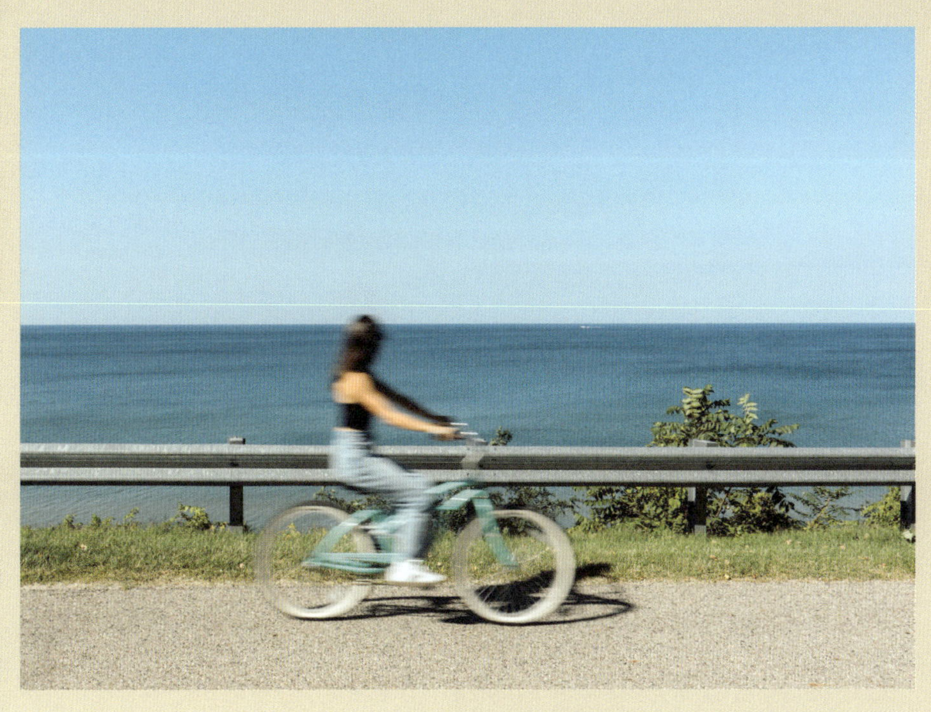

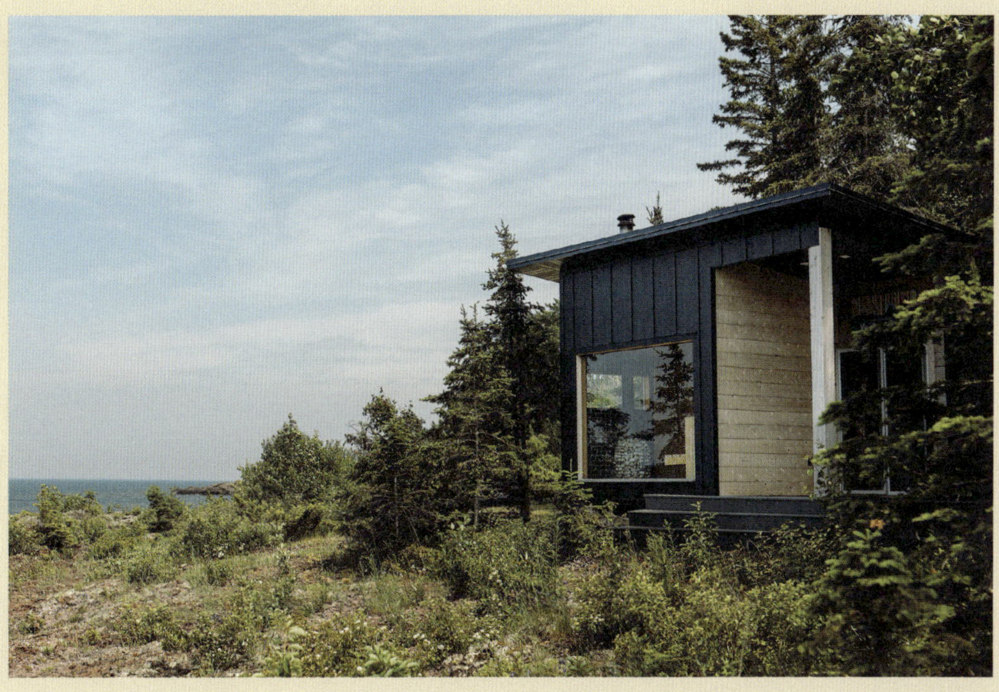

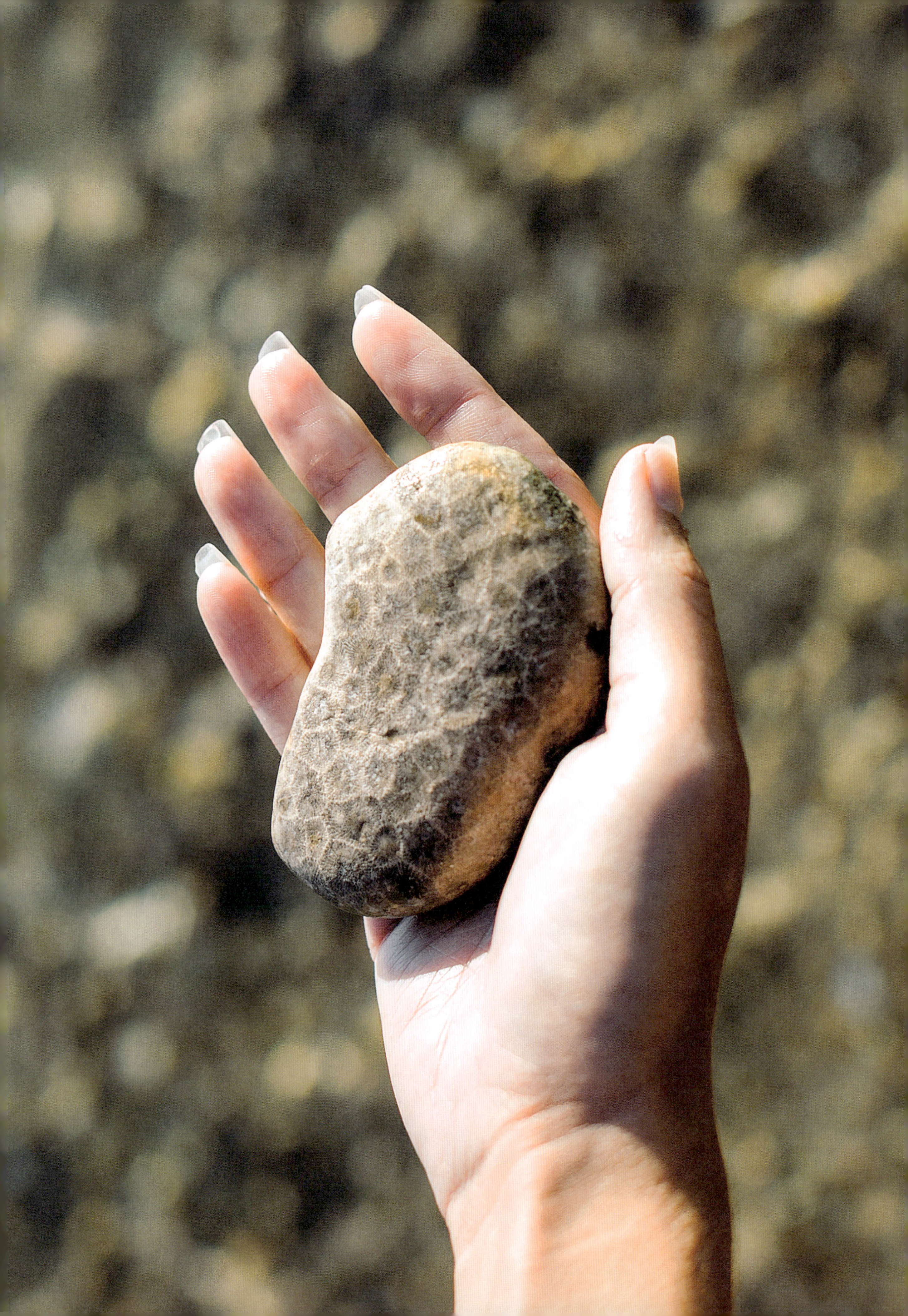

Petoskey Stones

TREASURES ON THE LAKESHORE

Hidden along the shores of Lake Michigan are unique gray stones. When drying in the sun, they might not look like anything special, but when dampened by the waters of the lake, their masterful designs are revealed: an invisible-ink, tie-dyed pattern, a secret underwater honeycomb, a grid of white sunbursts with no beginning or end.

Having grown up in Michigan, I've been familiar with Petoskey stones my whole life. I've known since my elementary years that they are the state stone. But recently, I became more curious.

On a hot summer day at the lake I discovered a palm-sized Petoskey stone with strongly defined patterns in the shallow water. It was remarkable, the first time I've ever found one of these rare treasures on my own. As I stared at the stone in my hand, outside the context of a classroom or a gift shop, I realized I had more questions than answers.... How are Petoskey stones made? Why are they only found in Lake Michigan? Are they still being formed, or is there a dwindling number of Petoskey stones left to discover?

This led me to do some research, and I learned that Petoskey stones are actually fossils. Legend has it, a shallow saltwater sea covered Michigan many years ago. Over time, the land shifted north, the sea gave way to the freshwater Great Lakes, and corals were fossilized in the process, turning them into Petoskey stones. Since there is no longer a tropical sea near Michigan and the type of coral that created them is now extinct, there are a limited number of Petoskey stones sitting in the belly of the Lake, washing up to the shore one wave at a time.

Rock hunting is a big thing in the Great Lakes region. At any given pebbly shoreline, you'll see people walking along the water's edge, heads bent down, searching for treasures. The avid rock hunters, often referred to as rockhounds, are spotted with

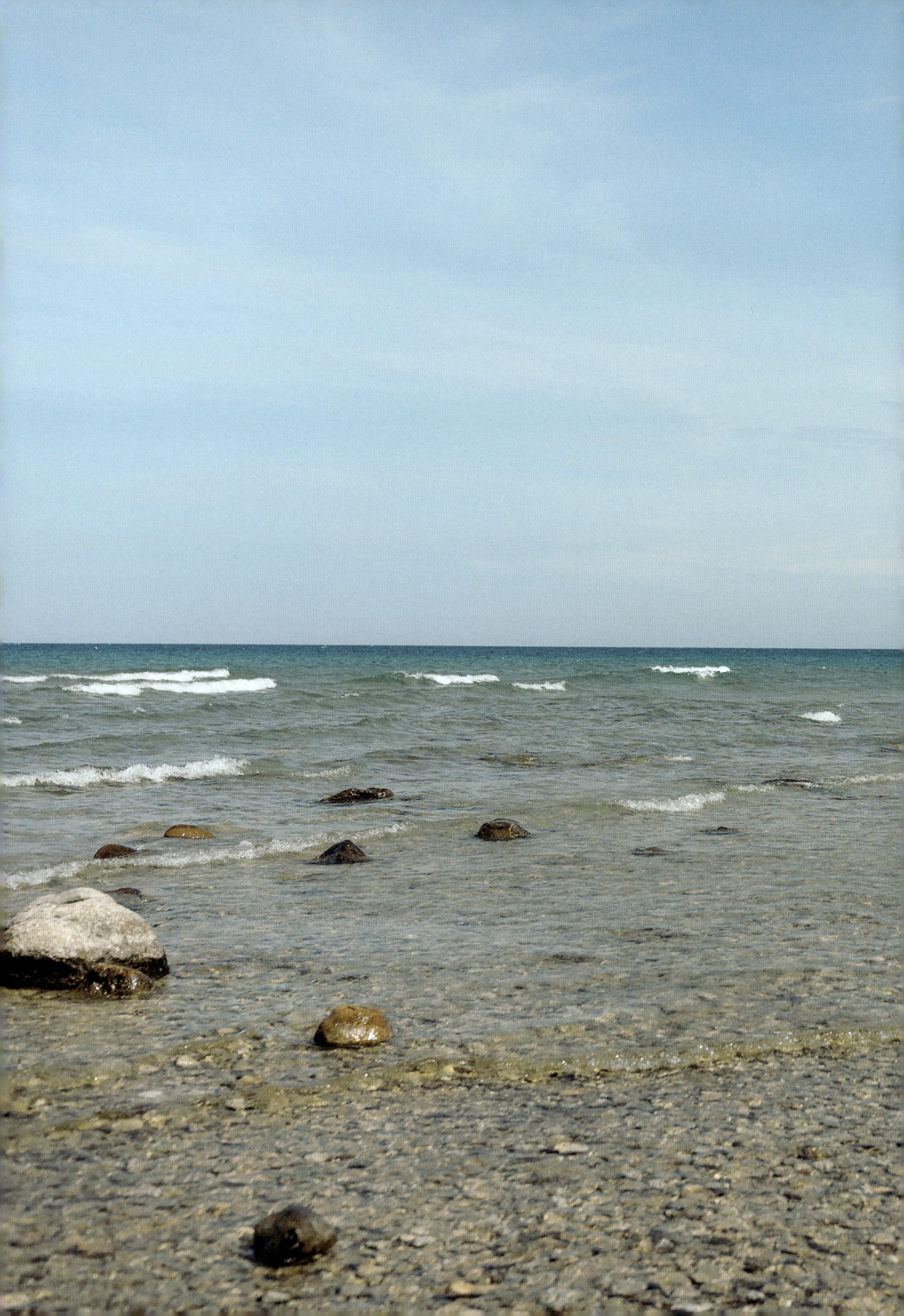

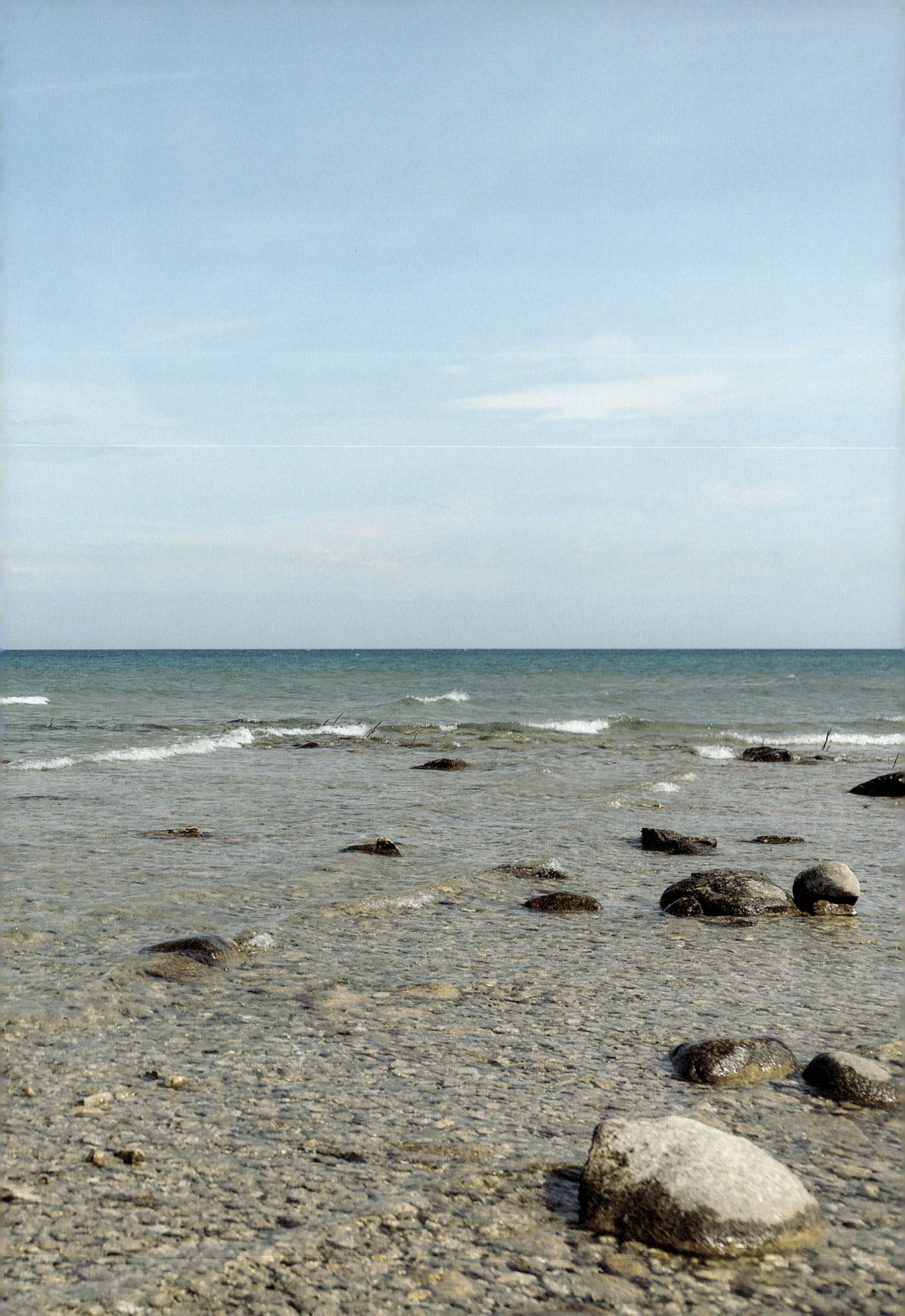

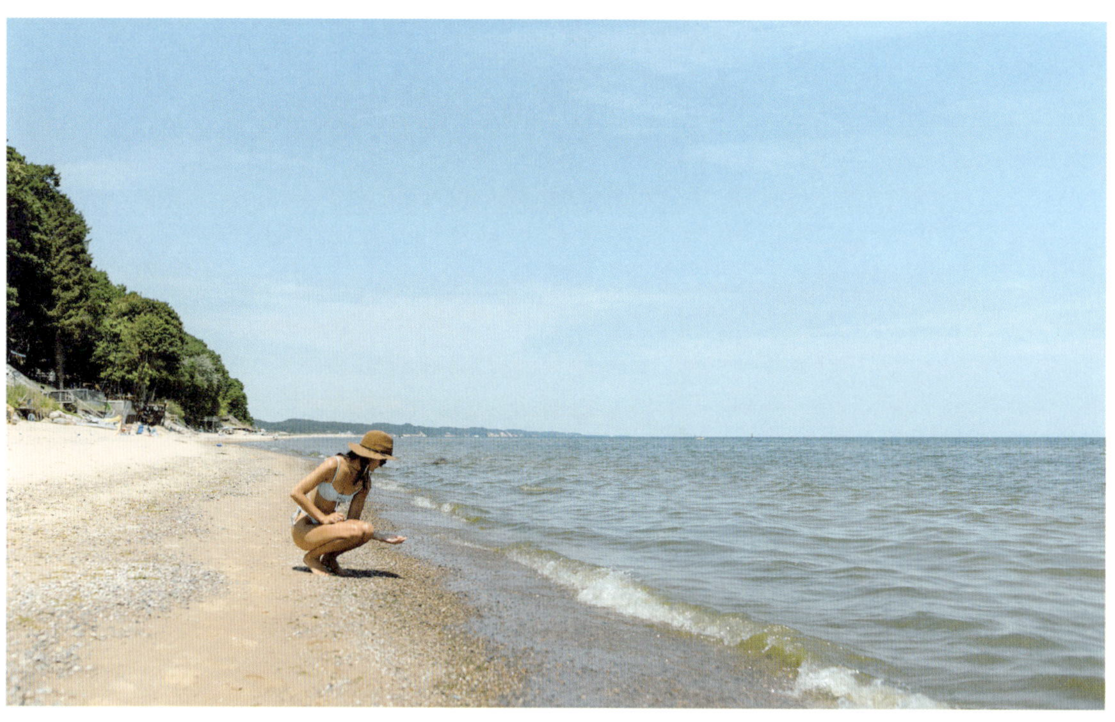

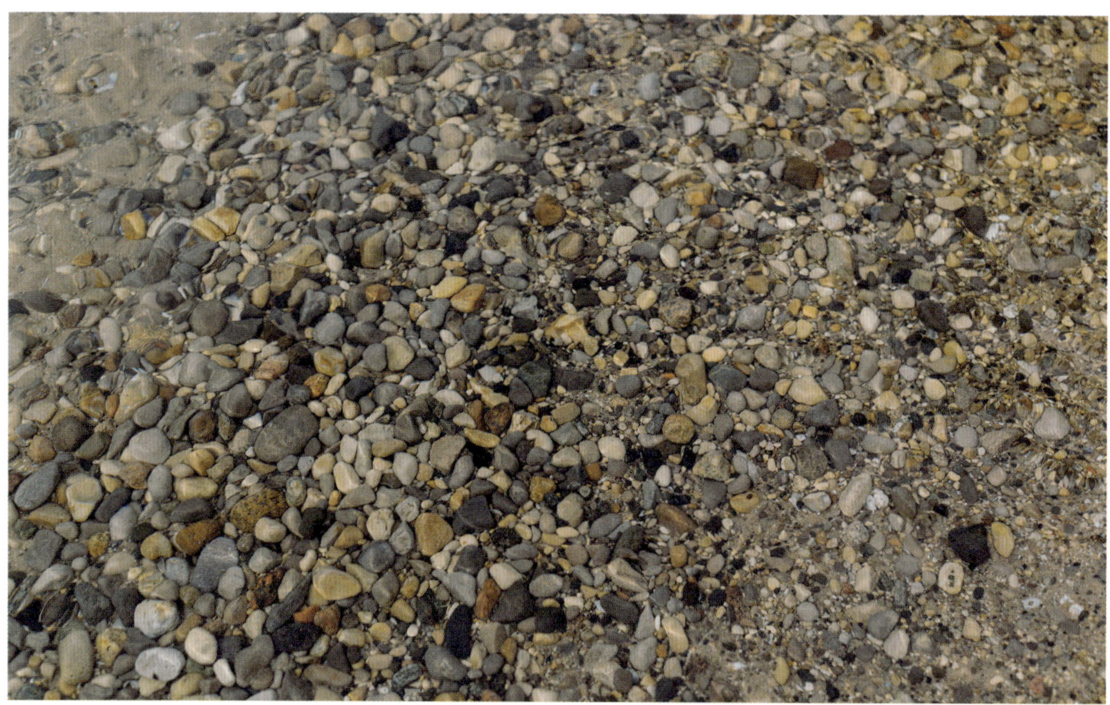

long rock-sifting contraptions, a pole with a strainer scoop at the end, and a collecting bag slung over their shoulders for the rocks worth keeping.

After finding this Petoskey stone, I'm starting to understand the rock hunting hype. It feels special to discover something rare, to unearth a treasure in the wild. And it feels even more thrilling now that I know the story behind this stone, the immeasurable miles and years it traversed, carried on the backs of ancient glaciers, letting erosion chip away at it over time, softening and rounding its edges just so that it could fit perfectly in the palm of my hand, here, now, today.

There are several other rocks in the Great Lakes with equally distinct appearances and interesting narratives. The Lake Superior agate is a beautiful red-orange rock formed from ancient lava flows. Leland Blues come in an array of swirling hues, and they are extremely rare since they were only formed over a fifteen-year period of local iron smelting in the 1800s. Septarian nodules, locally known as lightning stones, appear to have been struck by lightning with white bolts cracking through the brown prehistoric pebbles. Even something as simple as beach glass is highly sought after on the lakeshore. Whenever I find a smooth piece of colored glass, it leaves me curious how many decades it has been tumbling in the waves, pondering whether it was merely a piece of littered trash or carrying a heartfelt message in a bottle.

I read a memoir recently, *Bird Milk & Mosquito Bones* by Priyanka Mattoo. The title captured my attention, and I learned throughout the book that it's a phrase used to articulate something that is so rare and precious it seems unreal. It describes objects that are so scarce it's hard to believe they exist at all.

That's how it feels to find a treasure on the lakeshore.

Discovering something so small, antique, and unique in a world so large feels equally serendipitous and impossible. It causes me to consider all the years that have passed before me; this day, this moment, is like a single grain of sand in an eternal hourglass. It makes me marvel at how enormous the earth is, and yet our planet is a mere speck in the universe, like one tiny pebble in an infinite lake. It's a big feeling, remembering how small I am.

Your lakeshore likely contains something unique, too. A stone or shell or prehistoric fossil. Something unusual and uncommon with a fascinating origin story. Do some digging and search for the sweet thrill that comes from unearthing something precious. Bird milk and mosquito bones and Petoskey stones.

freshwater treasures:

Create a rock hunting wish list and try to collect them all. Include stones that are specific to your regional lakeshore and research their origins so that, if and when you find one, you'll get an extra thrill of wonder.

SOME OF THE MOST POPULAR FRESHWATER ROCKS IN THE GREAT LAKES

- Petoskey stones
- Charlevoix stones
- Leland Blues
- Lake Superior agates
- Frankfort Greens
- Keweenaw Greenstones
- Septarian Lightning Stones
- Yooperlites
- Pudding stones

MORE FUN TREASURES TO LOOK FOR IN ANY LAKE

- Beach glass
- Pottery pieces
- Geodes
- Fossils
- Freshwater shells
- Heart-shaped rocks

It's also important to be aware that rock collecting is restricted and prohibited in some areas. National parks and national lakeshores have regulations against removing any natural resources, and so do certain state lands and historical sites. Taking rocks from private property is also prohibited without permission from the landowner. Michigan even has an annual rock-collecting limit of twenty-five pounds per person per year. So be sure to research regulations in your area before rock hunting and respect the rules.

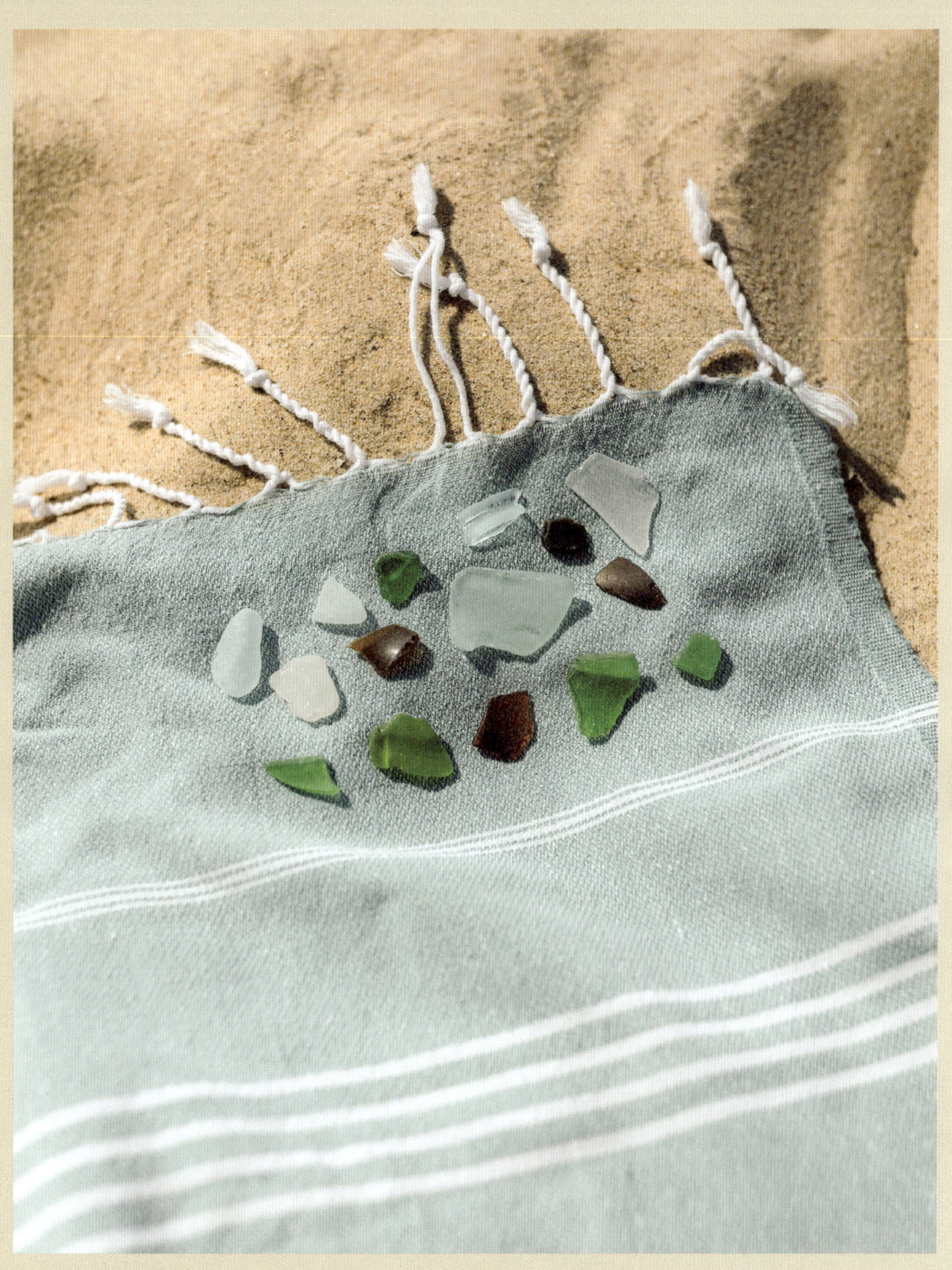

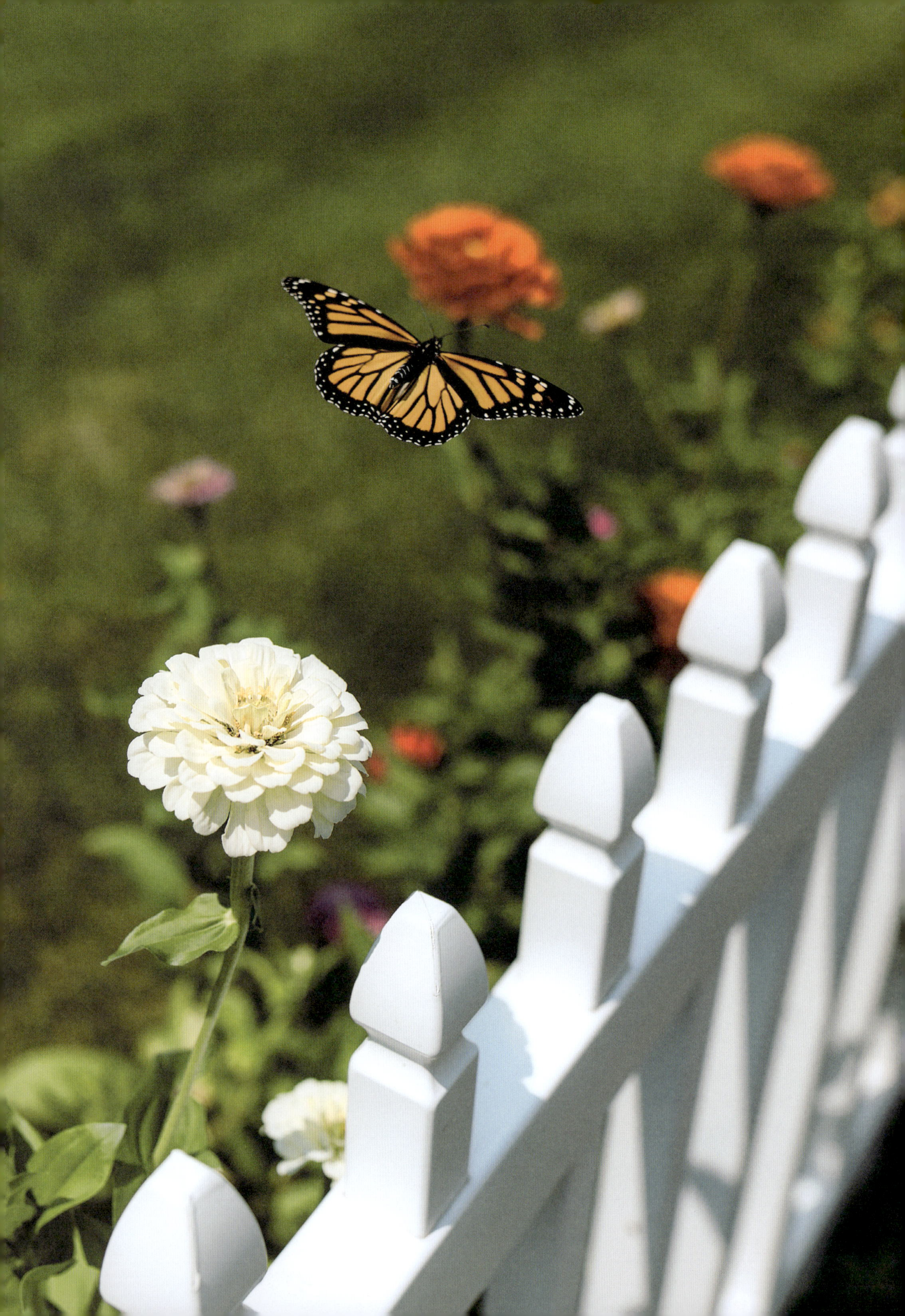

Butterflies

ON BEING A KID AGAIN

My childhood consisted of bug nets and running barefoot in pursuit of my new best friend. Some kids have imaginary friends; I had butterflies.

Orange monarchs, yellow tiger swallowtails, black swallowtails with blue-dotted wings. I spent my summer days chasing butterflies, and I'd often sneak them into the house and let them fly around my bedroom.

I have memories of sitting on my bed, reading a book, while a butterfly or two or three was fluttering around me. I'd set out vases of fresh wildflowers for them to sit on and sliced oranges for them to drink the juice from. I'd delicately hold them and let their strange, grippy insect legs crawl all over my fingers. Eventually I'd set them free, because half the fun was searching for a new one anyway.

Whenever I see a butterfly today, flapping its wings in the summer months, I'm instantly taken back—back to my humble childhood home with the barn that was bigger than the house, the gravel driveway off the dirt road, the open field where I'd chase butterflies. To memories of playing with my brothers in the backyard, of summer days and sprinklers under the trampoline, of my tiny upstairs bedroom with the low slanted ceilings, monarchs and swallowtails flying around me. Back to when we had three acres, two parents, one family.

Perhaps that's why we all love summer so much. The places we find ourselves, the sights and smells, the bugs, the butterflies, the dirt roads...they spark memories, they trigger nostalgia, and they invite us to be a kid again. Here's how to accept the invitation.

summer activities for rediscovering childlike joy:

- Visit an ice cream shop and order the treat you used to get as a kid. The cone with rainbow sprinkles, the sour green slushie, the root beer float, the banana split.
- Try playing in nature with bare hands and bare feet. Splash in a puddle, build a sandcastle, chase butterflies. You might be surprised by how great it feels.
- Think about a game you loved playing with your siblings or childhood friends in the summertime. Try getting everyone together again for one more round, or teach it to your own kids, nieces, nephews, or neighbors.
- Climb a tree again! Be safe, of course, but see how high you can go and relax on a branch for a while.
- Pick a fluffy dandelion and make a wish.
- Eat a PB&J for lunch today.

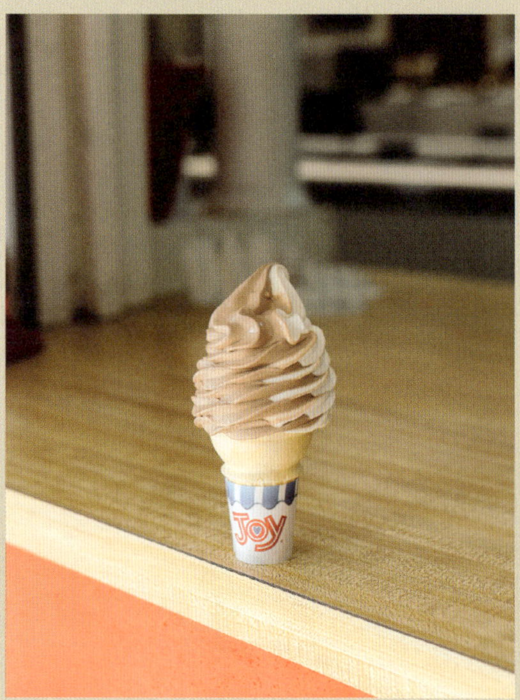

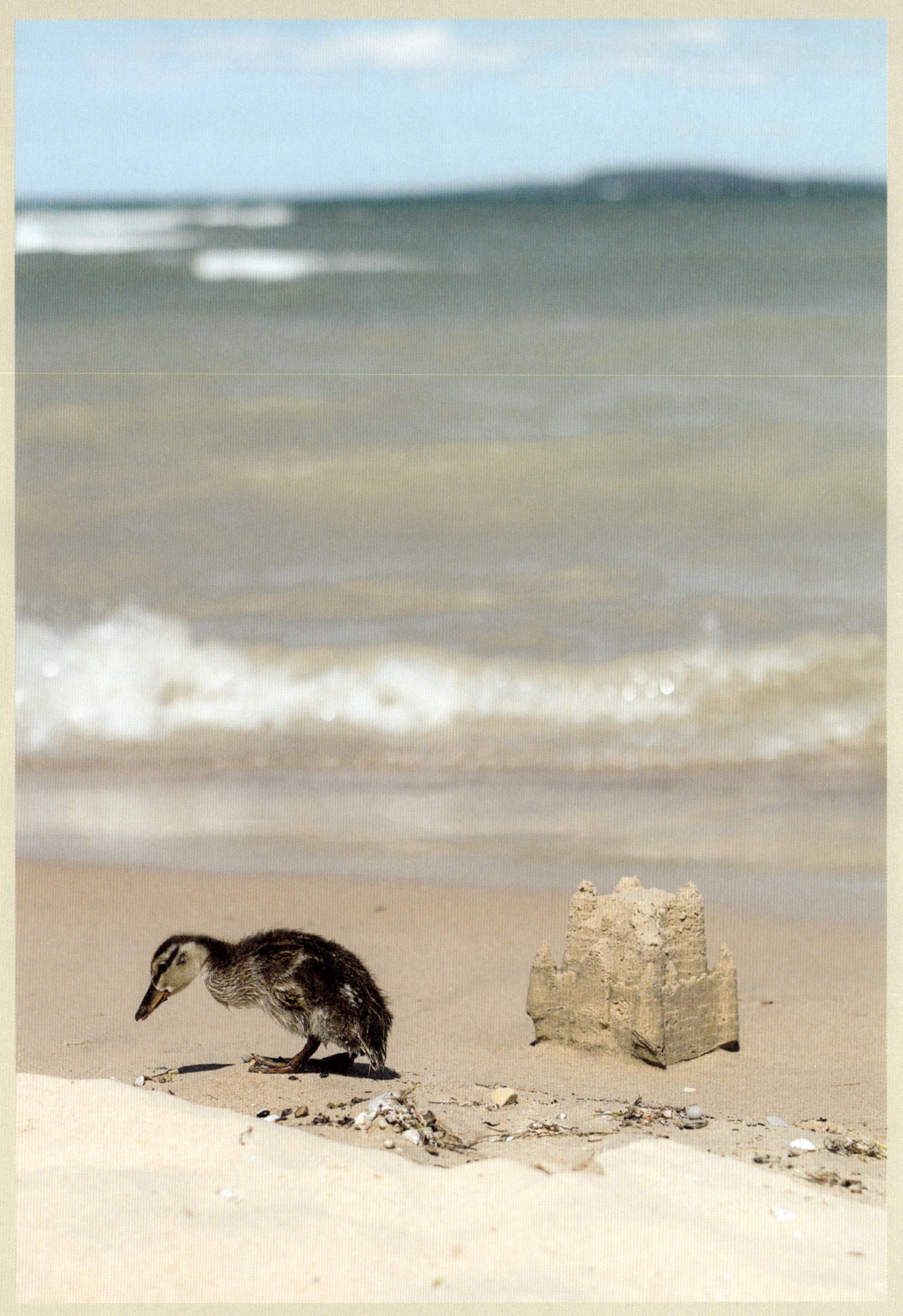

Lighthouses and Lake Towns

SUMMER EXPLORATION

One of my favorite things to do in the summer is visit lighthouses. There's something about the unique swirly architecture and circle porthole windows, the mysterious histories and quaint keeper's quarters, the picture-perfect lakeside landscapes.... It all sparks so much curiosity and imagination.

Plus, it's amazing how many lighthouses there are in the Midwest. With 129 in Michigan, and a total of 388 in the Great Lakes, I'll likely never see them all, but that's the beauty of it—there's always more to discover.

On a warm clear day last summer, I checked a new one off my list: Big Sable Point Lighthouse. I was particularly excited about exploring this one because, while many lighthouses nowadays have a parking lot steps away, Big Sable Point can only be accessed by hike. It remains separated from civilization, and therefore feels like a step back in time. Volunteer lightkeepers still live in it to keep the gift shop and lamp running. They often say they are paid in sunsets.

With my water bottle filled, sunscreen applied, and swimsuit underneath my clothes (just in case), I followed the brown state park signs toward the trail. After two miles on a sandy path, I eventually spotted the black-and-white-striped lighthouse peeking out above the dunes.

I climbed the claustrophobic spiral staircase up Big Sable's tower, crawled under low hatches, glanced through the portholes, and finally stepped out onto the observation platform where the wind and the view took my breath away.

A landscape of creamy rolling sand dunes was blanketed in beach grass, and cascading white-crested waves coasted in toward the shore. The sand at the bottom of the lake rippled in its own wavy design, a mesmerizing pattern that I never could have detected from the ground. I also noticed the varied colors of the water. What appeared to

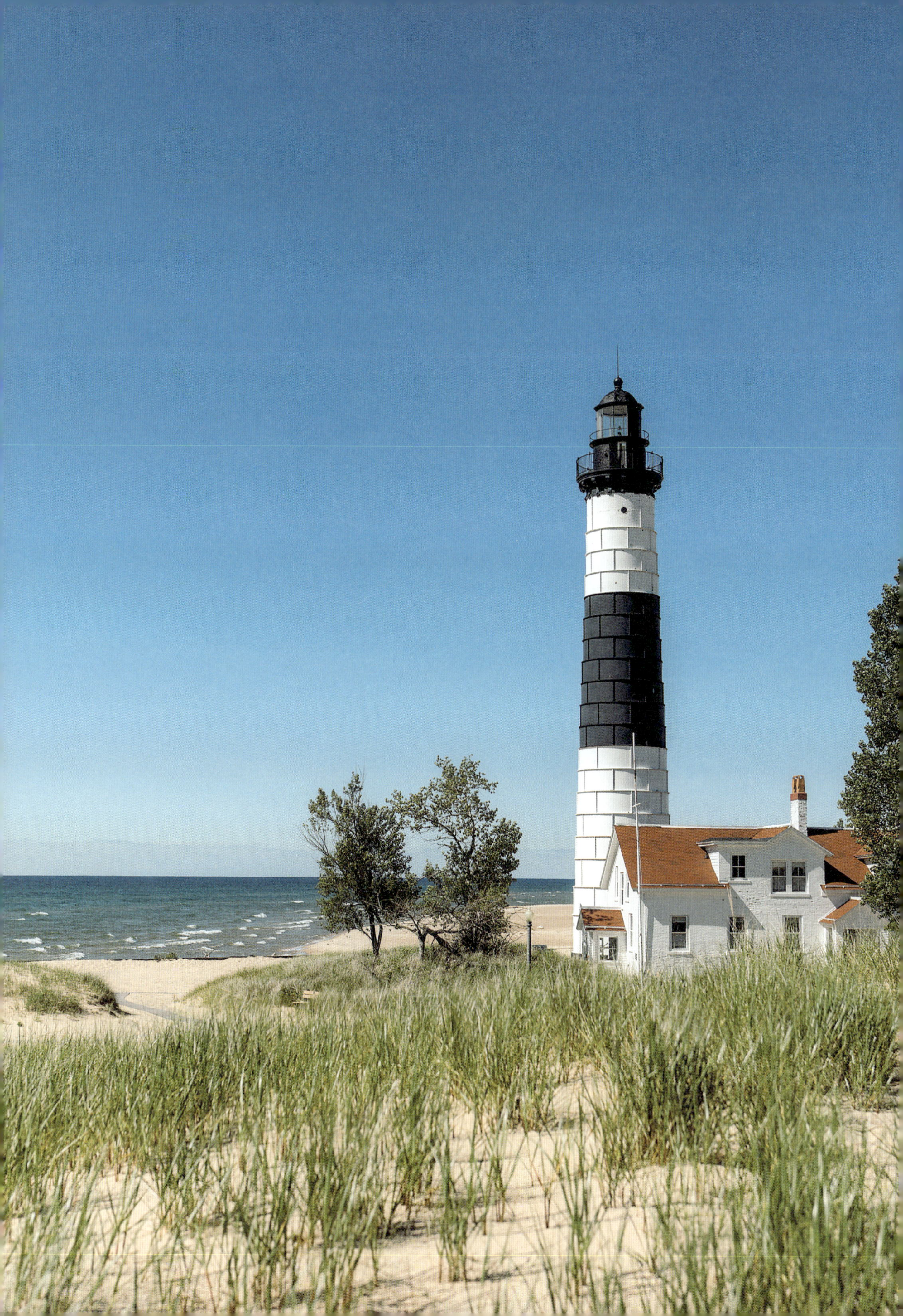

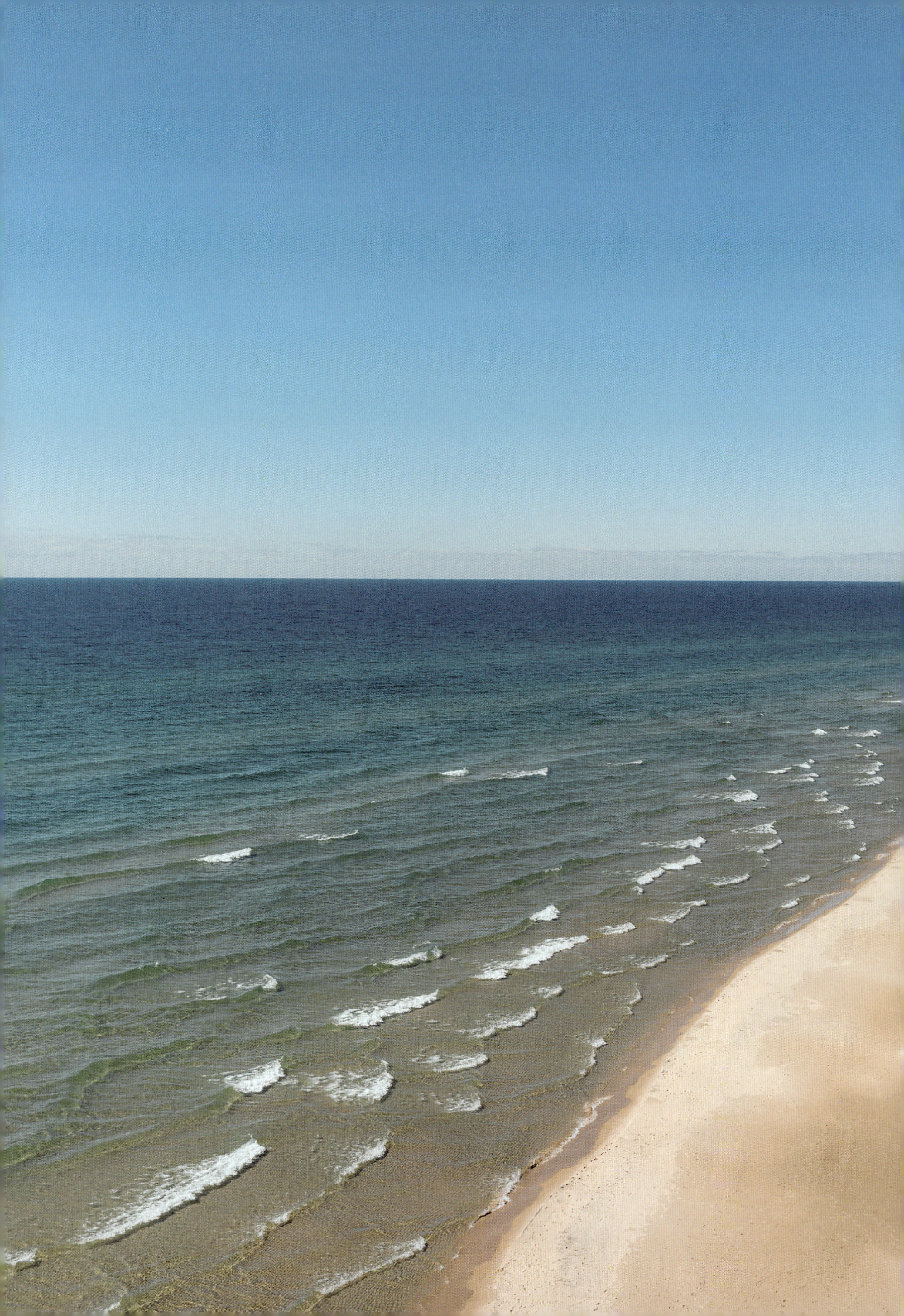

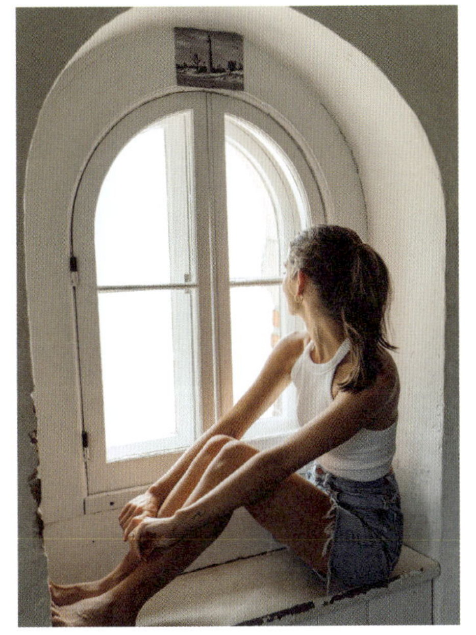
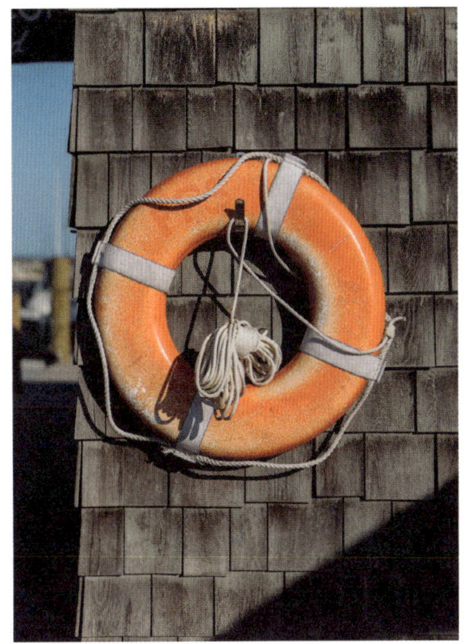
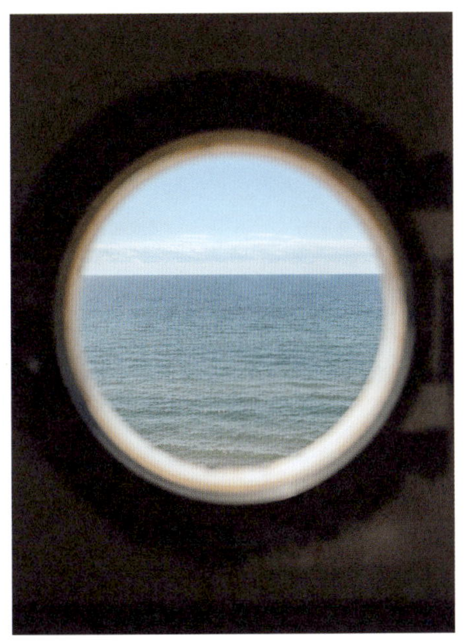
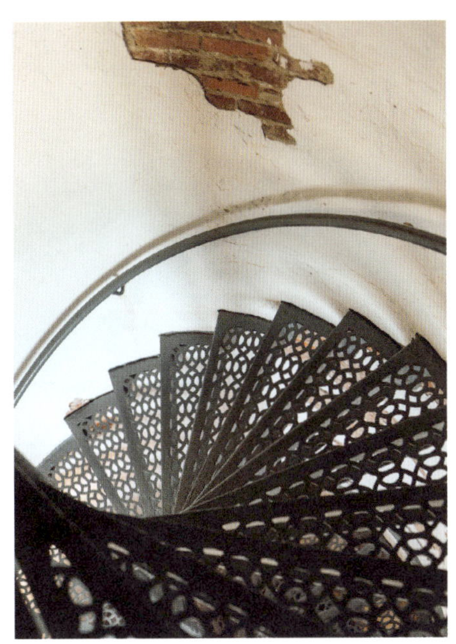

be simply blue from below had now multiplied into a kaleidoscope of shades—deep nautical navy and Caribbean aqua, robin's egg pastel and tropical turquoise. It's like the lake donned different outfits according to the dress code of each sandbar.

Climbing to the top of lighthouses is not for the faint of heart or those afraid of heights, but it's always worth it for the view. At shore level, with our feet in the sand, it's hard to capture the full picture. But from above, we can see how everything fits together, and it's often more beautiful and colorful than we ever could have imagined from below.

On another day and another lighthouse adventure, I drove to the Grand Traverse Lighthouse and my route took me right through Northport, a quaint town I had never heard of before. Cute boutiques lined the streets with their doors propped wide open. Cafés and restaurants had inviting outdoor bistro sets and wooden picnic tables. A charming little library sat next to a historical post office. It was so lovely that I immediately decided to park the car and check it out.

There's a certain kind of wonder and bliss that comes from stumbling upon a new place with no agenda and zero expectations. As I leisurely walked up and down the streets, in and out of shops, taking it all in, I marveled at the reality that even in my home state, there's always more to

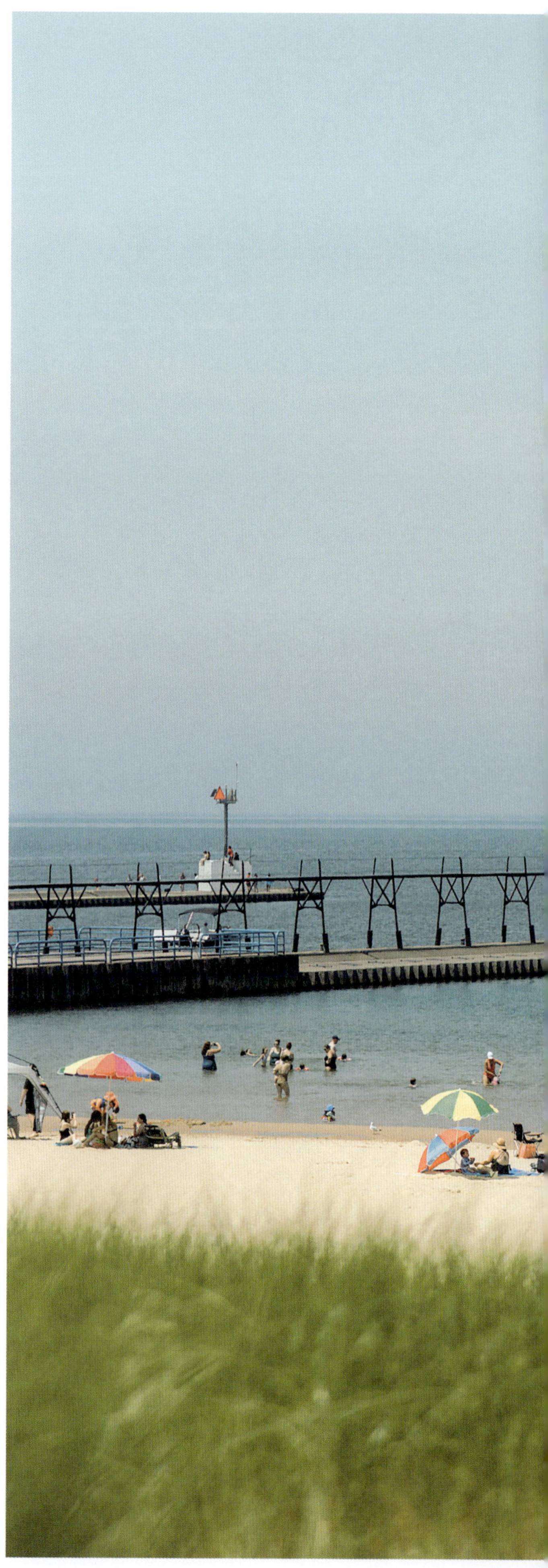

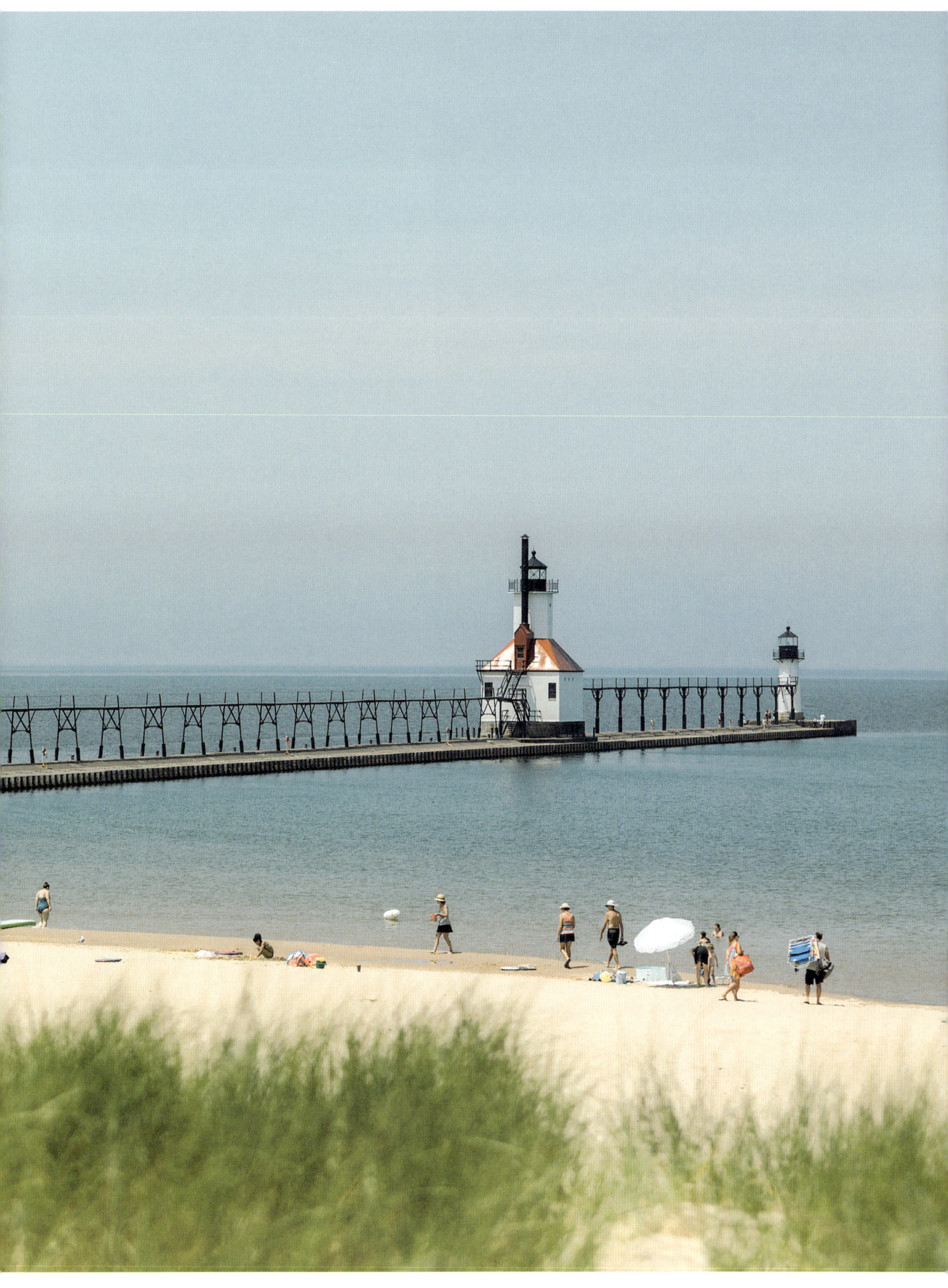

There's a certain kind of wonder and bliss that comes from stumbling upon a new place with no agenda and zero expectations.

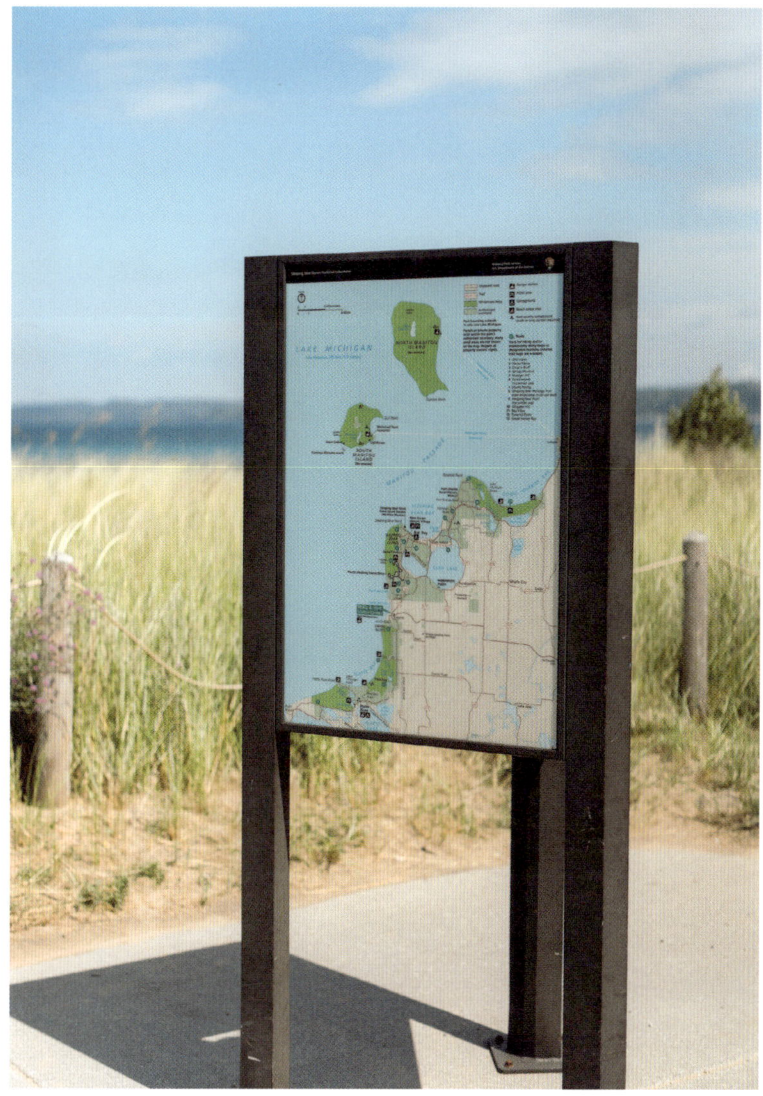

see. There's so much I have yet to explore in Michigan, in the Great Lakes region, in the Midwest. So many photos yet to take, beaches yet to swim, foods yet to try, adventures yet to find, and that's what summer is for—unexpected discoveries, pursuing curiosities, and endless exploration.

You never know what you might find if you pick a lake town you've never been to before and spend an agenda-free afternoon exploring. Or visit a lighthouse, climb to the top, and take in the view. Book a boat tour or dune ride, and be a tourist for a day. Pull over for a roadside farm stand or quaint country market. Go on a road trip without every detail planned, and let curiosity be your GPS. Try a new hiking trail, a different biking path, or simply walk on the other side of the street. There's always more to explore right where you are.

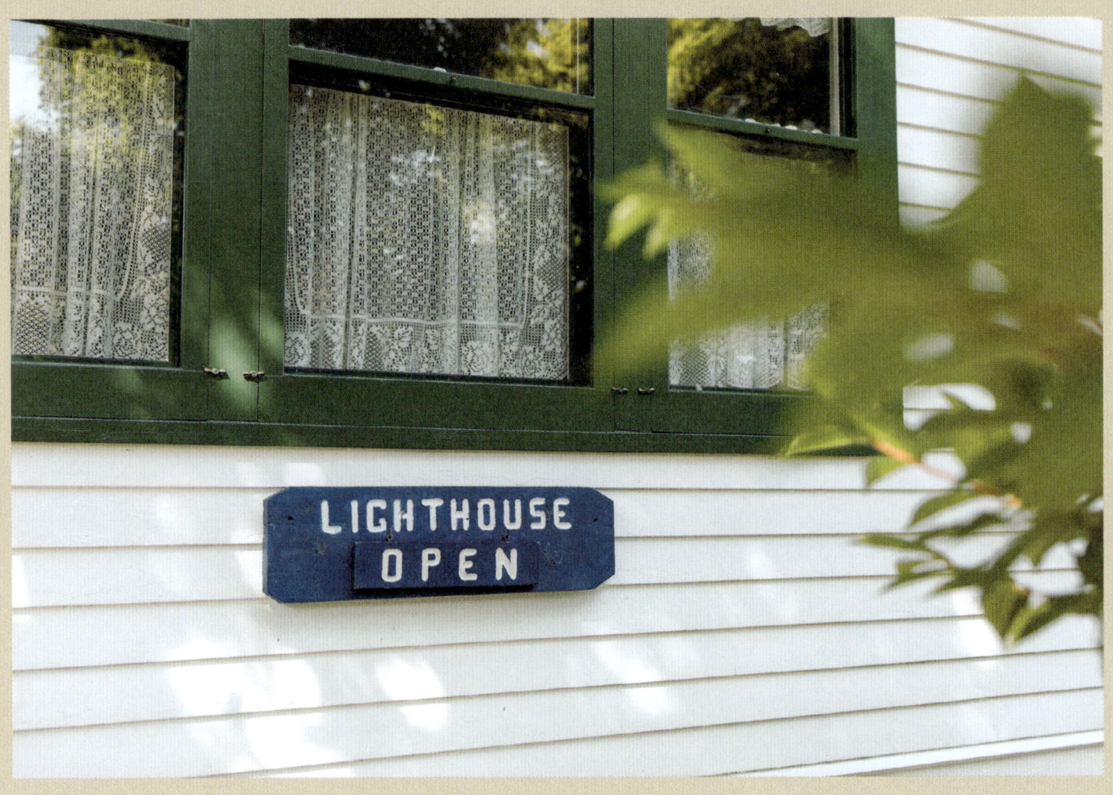

my guide to exploring the lakeshore:

Here are some of the places in Michigan that I love to explore on a summer's day. This isn't a comprehensive list; there are many more wonderful lighthouses and lake towns to discover throughout the Great Lakes region, so pull out a map and find your own favorites, too!

LIGHTHOUSES

- Mission Point Lighthouse
- Grand Traverse Lighthouse
- Little Sable Point Lighthouse
- Big Sable Point Lighthouse

LAKE TOWNS

- Suttons Bay
- Leland
- Glen Arbor
- Saugatuck
- Pentwater

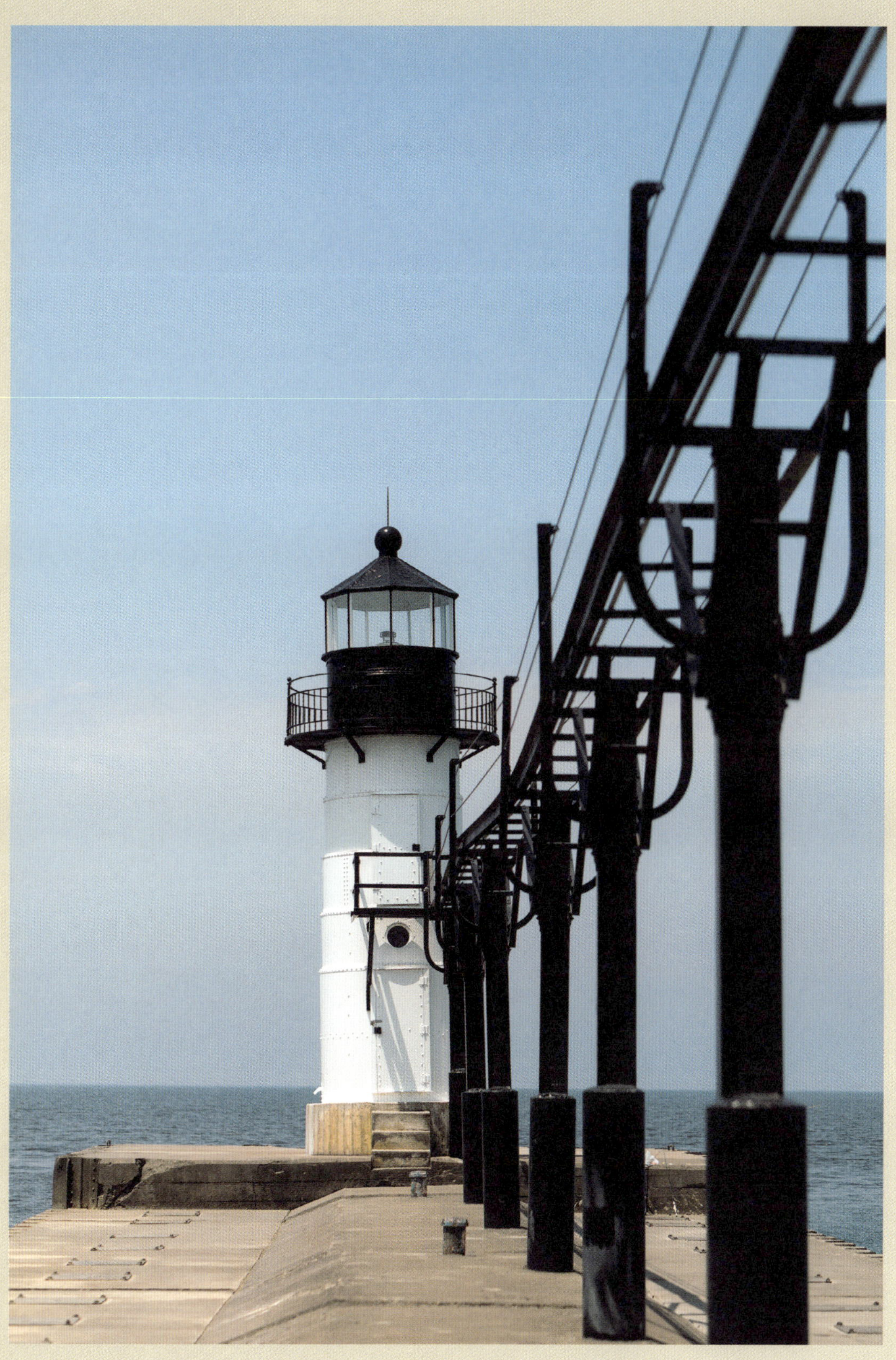

barbecue on the bluff

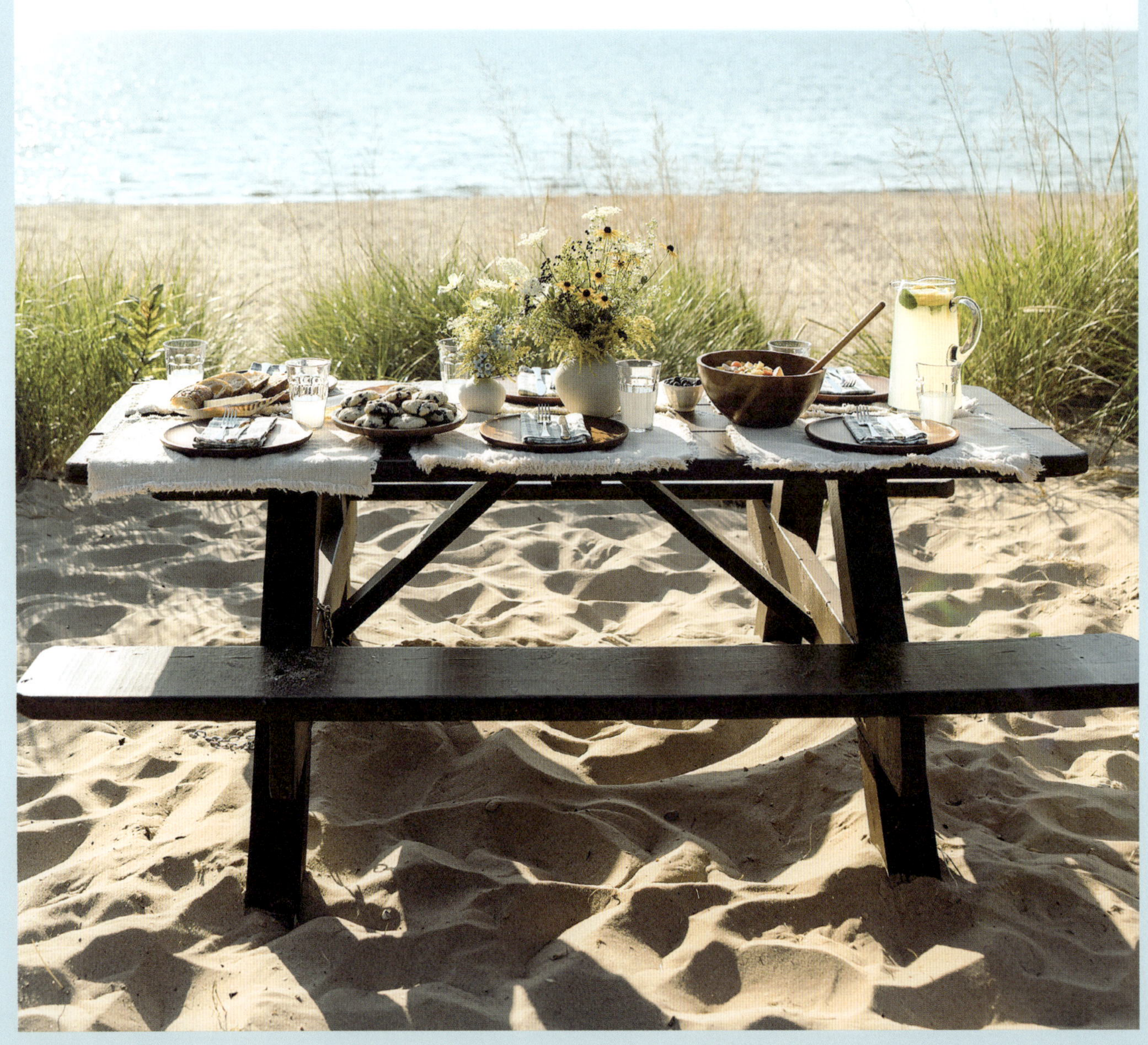

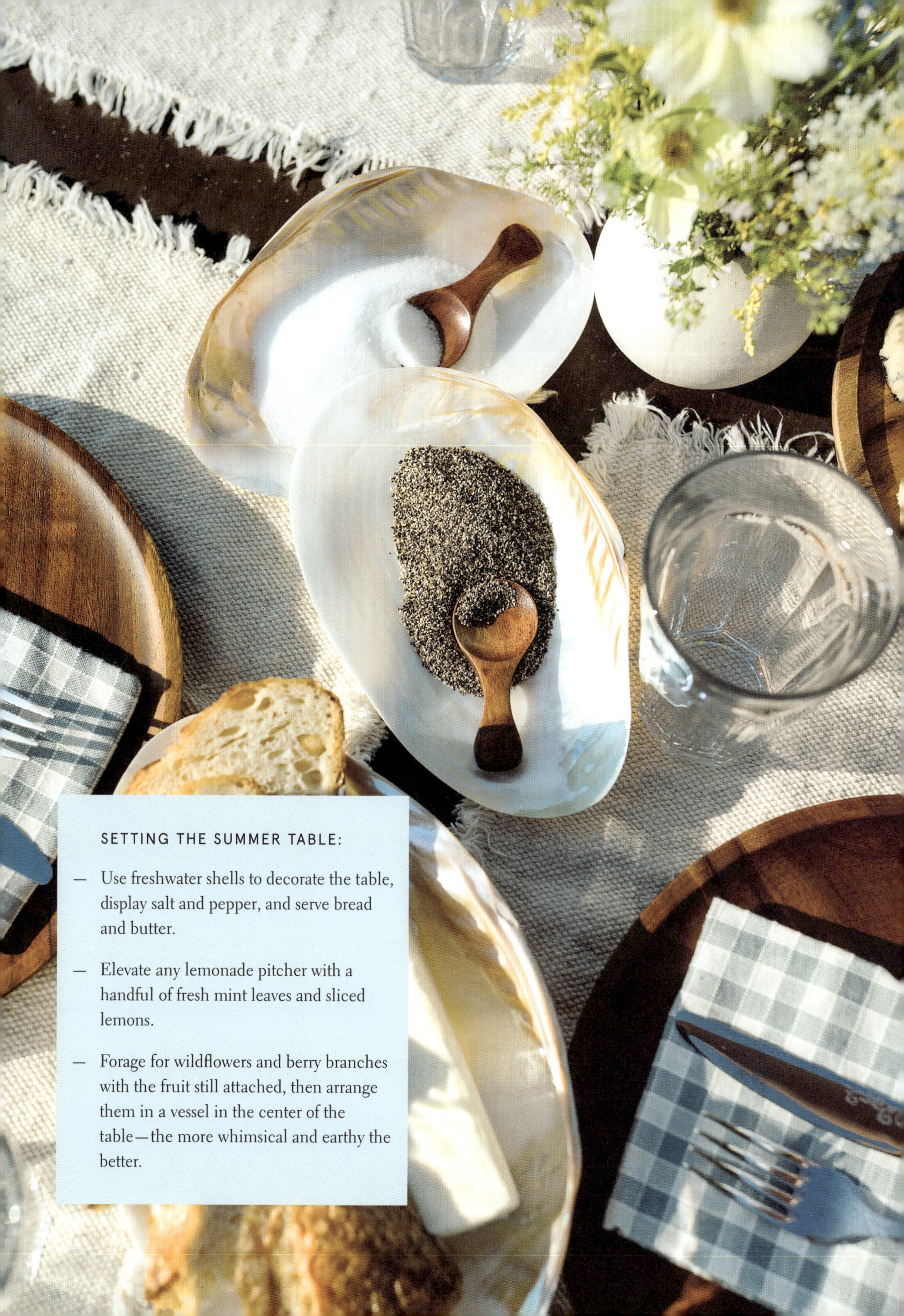

SETTING THE SUMMER TABLE:

- Use freshwater shells to decorate the table, display salt and pepper, and serve bread and butter.
- Elevate any lemonade pitcher with a handful of fresh mint leaves and sliced lemons.
- Forage for wildflowers and berry branches with the fruit still attached, then arrange them in a vessel in the center of the table—the more whimsical and earthy the better.

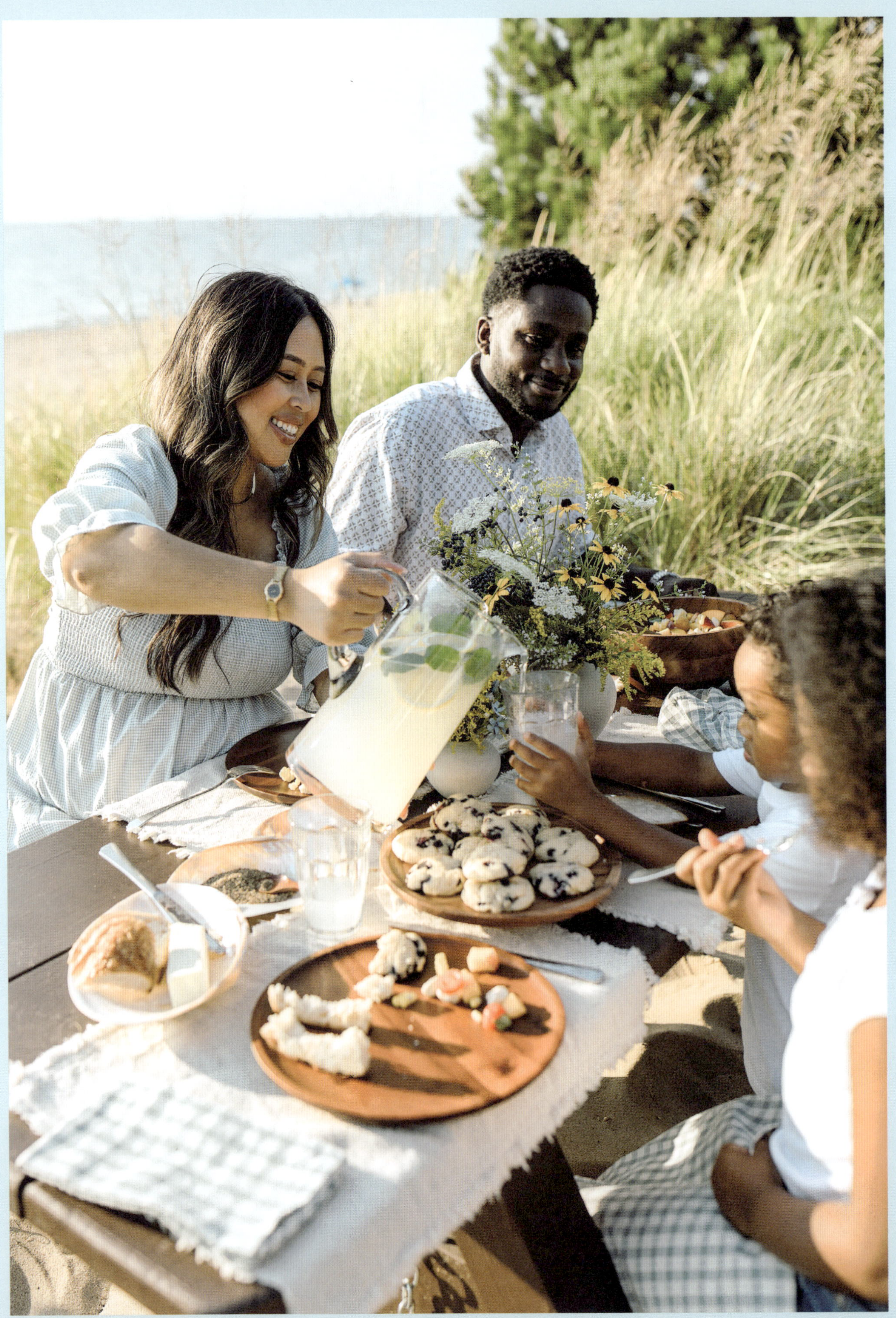

Peach Sweet Corn Salad

SERVES 4 TO 6

This is a fresh and colorful side to complement any summertime meal. It's also a great fit for August when peaches, tomatoes, and sweet corn are at their peak and ready for harvest!

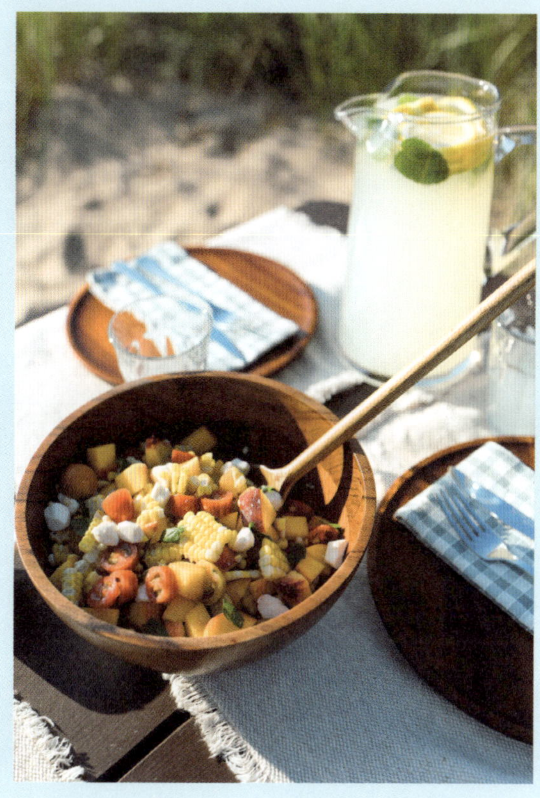

FOR THE SALAD

2 ears sweet corn, husked
1 cup (145 g) cherry tomatoes, halved
2 ripe peaches, pitted and chopped
1 (8-ounce/225 g) package mozzarella pearls
2 tablespoons chopped fresh basil leaves

FOR THE DRESSING

2 tablespoons olive oil
1 tablespoon white balsamic vinegar

Salt and pepper

Make the salad: Cook the corn however you please (boiled, grilled, or microwaved). (I promise fresh corn tastes so much better than canned—don't cheat!) Let cool slightly, then cut the kernels off the cobs and place them in a salad bowl. Gently stir in the tomatoes, peaches, mozzarella pearls, and basil.

Make the dressing: In a small bowl, whisk together the olive oil and vinegar.

Drizzle the dressing over the salad and toss to combine, then finish with salt and pepper.

Blueberry Cardamom Cookies

MAKES 16 COOKIES

I love incorporating floral flavors into foods in the summertime, and cardamom is one of my forever favorites. These cookies have the moist, fluffy texture of a muffin, and they taste so bright and flowery. Such a unique summer treat!

- 2½ cups (315 g) all-purpose flour (you can substitute gluten-free oat flour)
- 2 teaspoons ground cardamom
- 1½ teaspoons baking powder
- ¼ teaspoon salt
- ¾ cup (1½ sticks/170 g) unsalted butter, at room temperature
- ½ cup (100 g) granulated sugar
- ½ cup (110 g) light brown sugar
- 1 teaspoon pure vanilla extract
- 1 large egg
- ½ cup (120 ml) whole milk
- 1 cup (145 g) fresh blueberries

In a medium bowl, combine the flour, cardamom, baking powder, and salt. In a separate large bowl, using a handheld mixer, beat the butter, granulated sugar, and brown sugar until creamy. Add the vanilla and egg, and mix for just a few seconds, then slowly mix in the dry ingredients. Add the milk and mix until just combined. Be sure not to overmix; the dough should be very thick and sticky. Gently fold in the blueberries, then refrigerate the dough for 30 minutes.

Preheat the oven to 350°F (180°C) and line a baking sheet with parchment paper.

Using a melon baller or tablespoon, scoop the chilled dough onto the prepared baking sheet. Bake for 15 to 20 minutes, until the edges are golden and a toothpick inserted into the center of a cookie comes out clean. Let cool completely before enjoying. Store in an airtight container in the fridge for up to 1 week or freeze for up to 1 month.

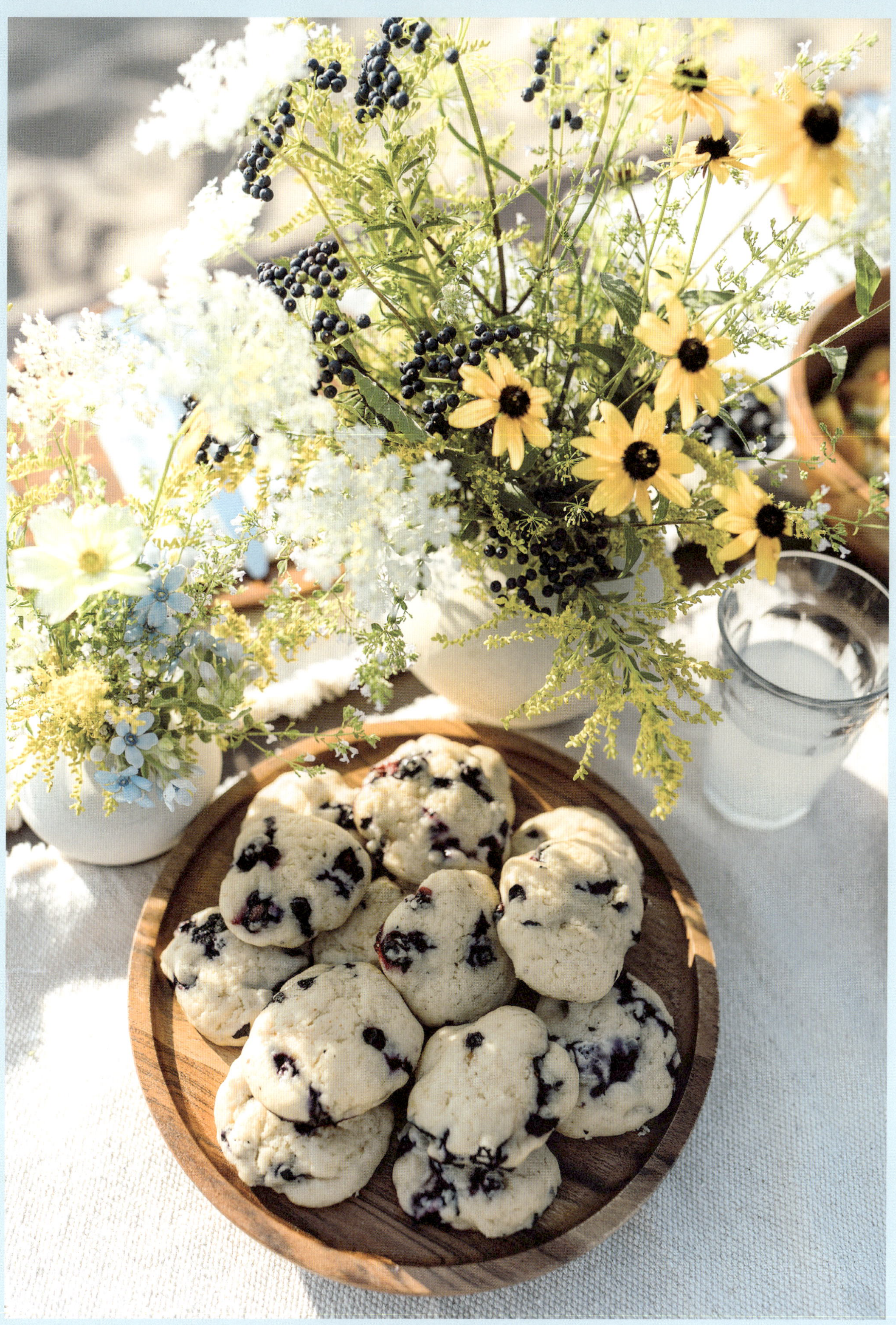

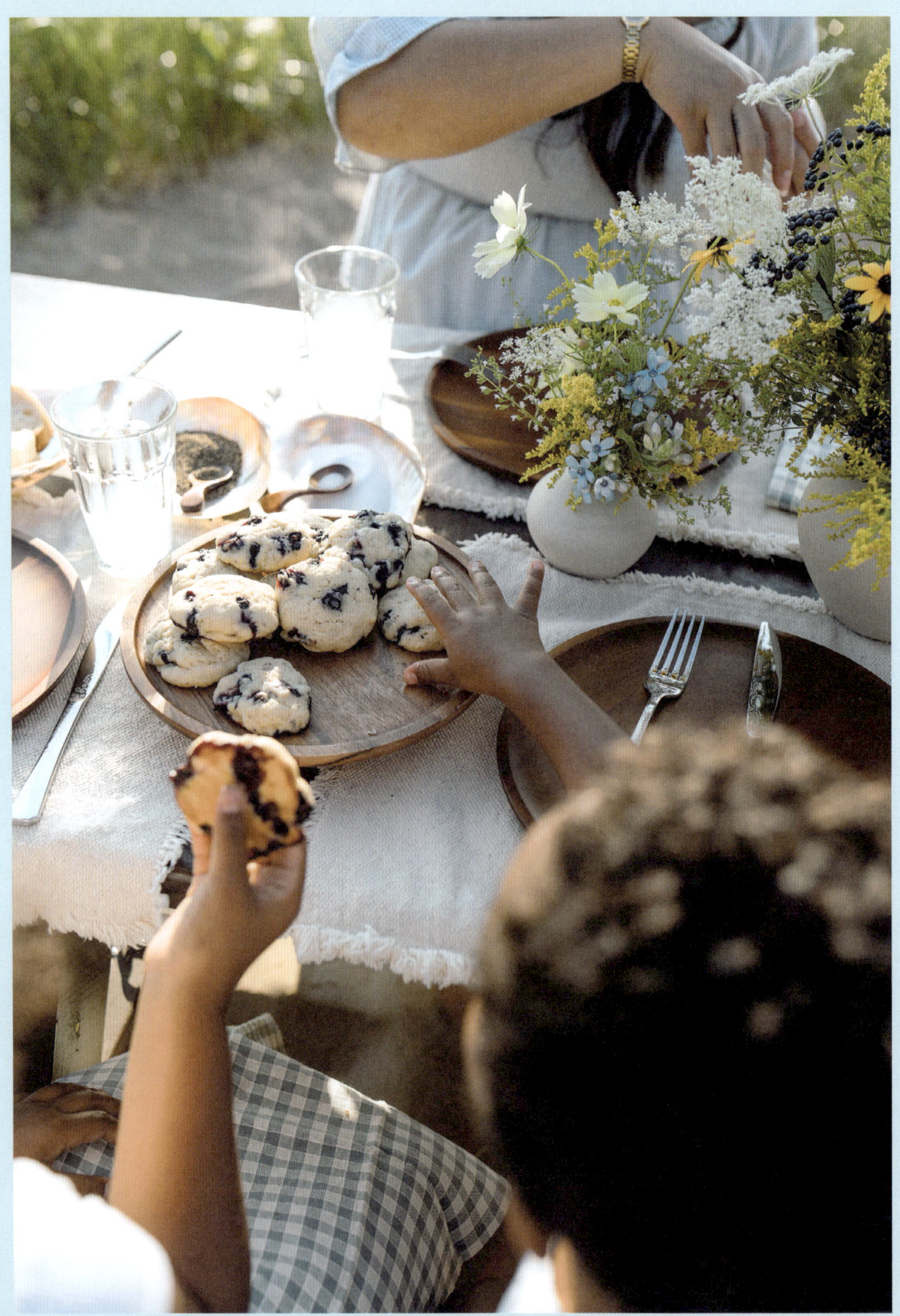

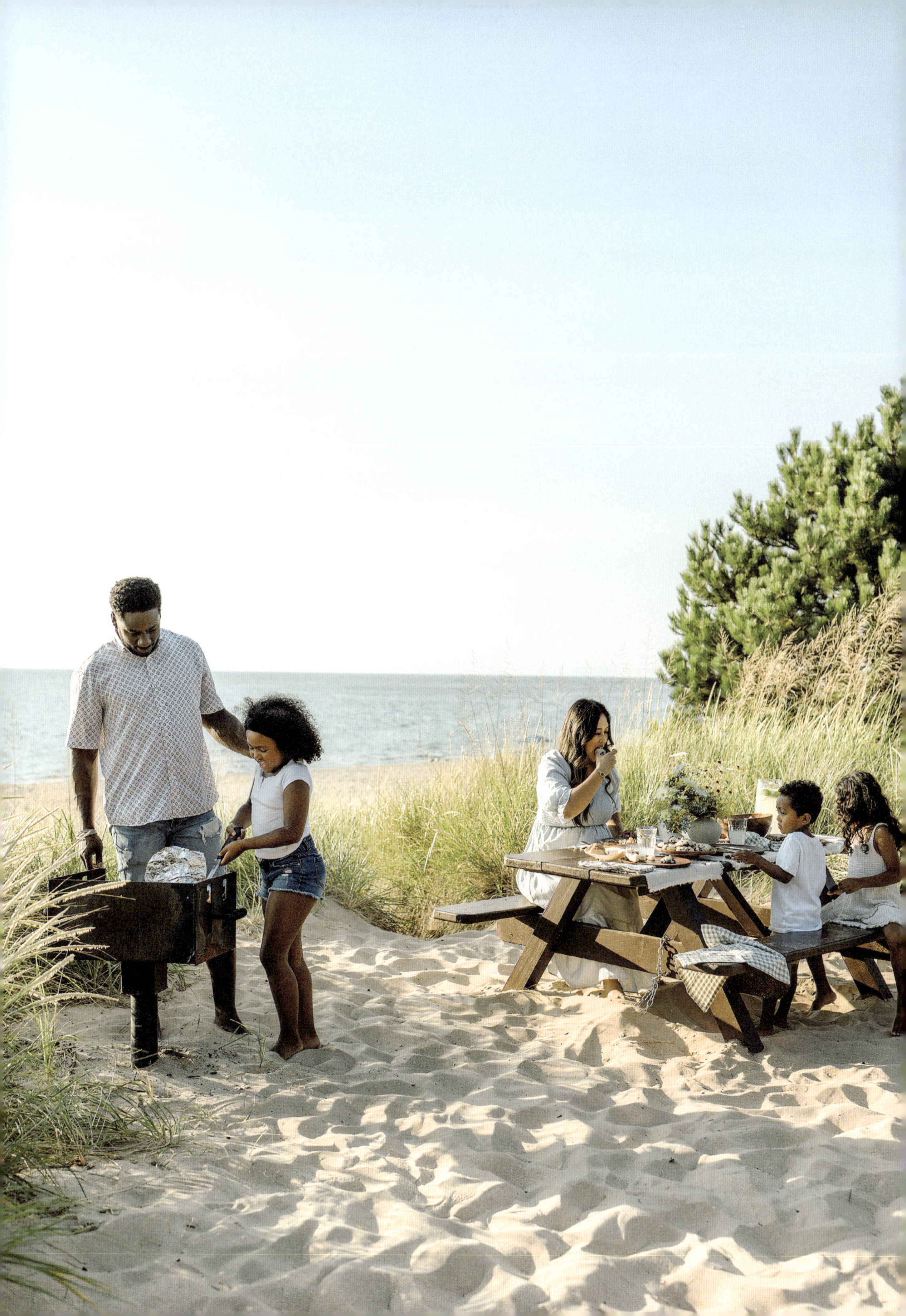

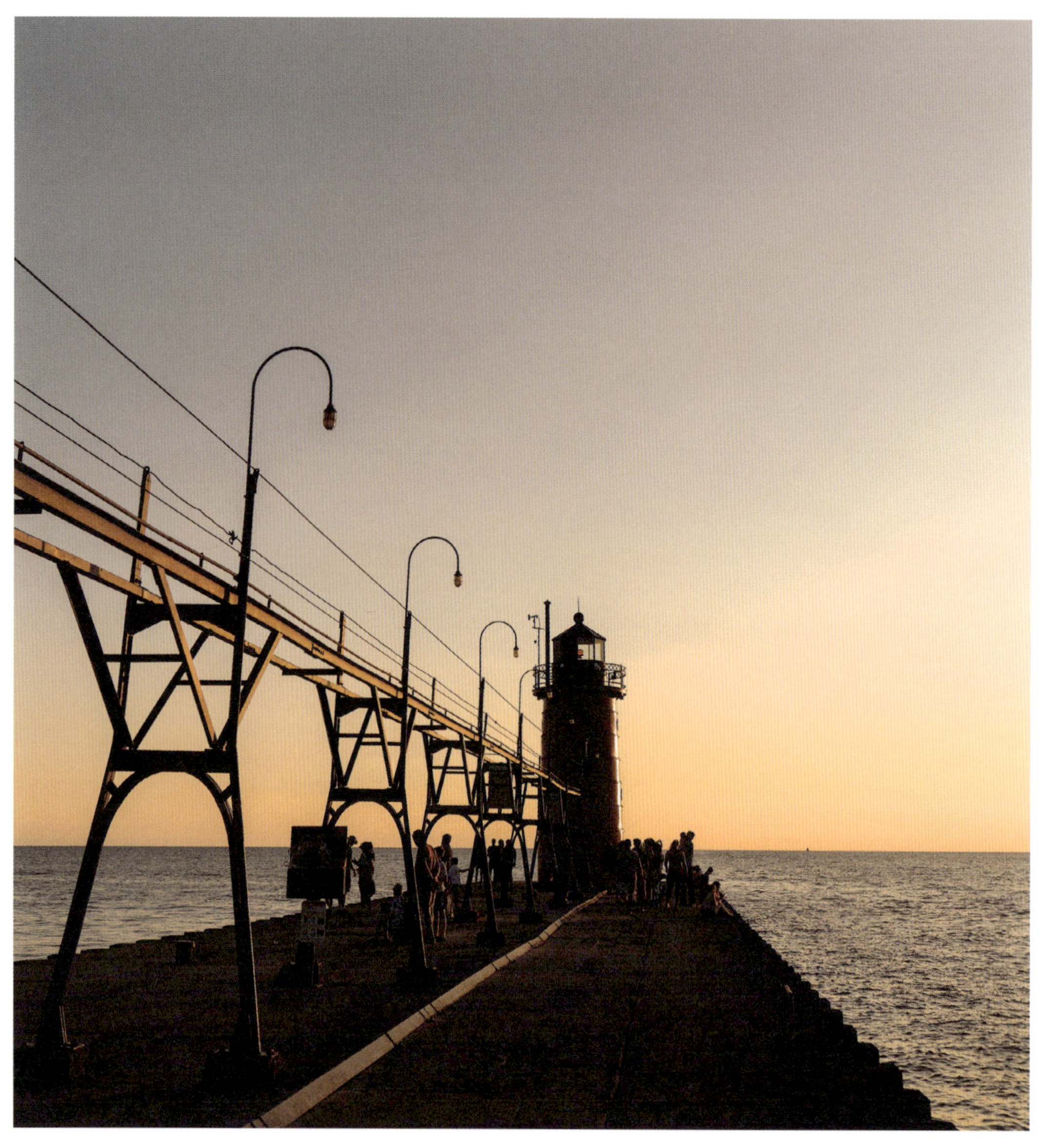

September

September at the lake is the final hurrah. On summer nights we gathered around to watch the sunset, standing on lighthouse-laden piers and westerly shores to see the sun sparkling on the lake as it made its way to meet the surface. With each passing minute colors appeared in the sky; some nights vibrant red-orange graffiti, other nights delicate pastel watercolors. As the last sliver of sun sank into the waves, we often joined in on a spontaneous round of applause, clapping instinctively, a collective hallelujah. After all those sunset standing ovations in June, July, and August, summer performs a much-longed-for encore: September. September brings bonus beach days and bathtub-warm lake water. It grants us one more boat ride, a final float on the paddleboard, and a few more bonfires with blankets on our laps and our chairs inching closer to the warmth. September is for wearing a sweatshirt over your swimsuit after one last swim and driving home with sandy bare feet on the pedal. A countdown is taped to the local ice cream shop window in September: "23 more days until we are closed for the season," a cruel but motivating reminder to order an extra scoop and savor every last lick. September is for migrating; birds fly south, and we walk west, watching the sun set on another summer.

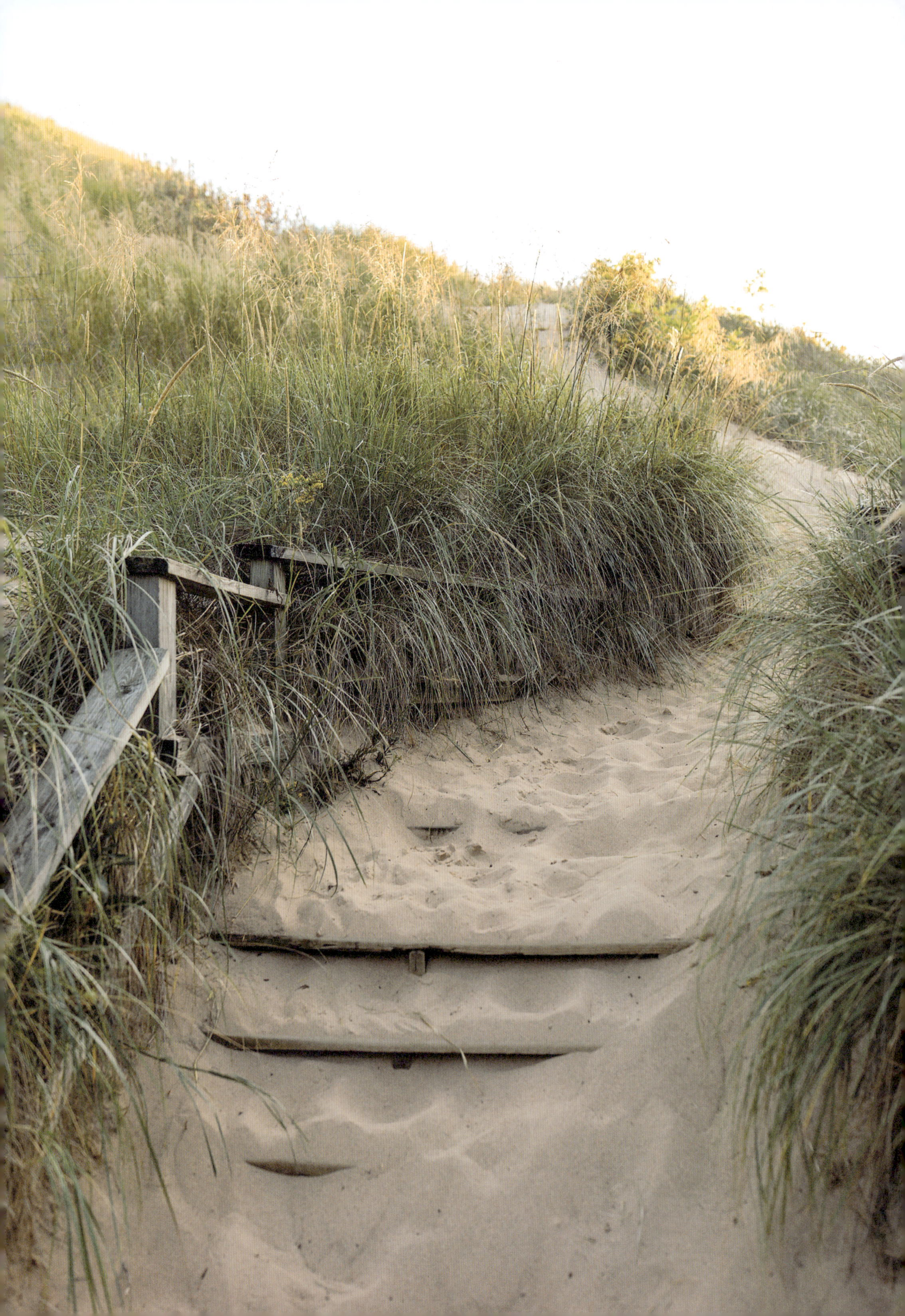

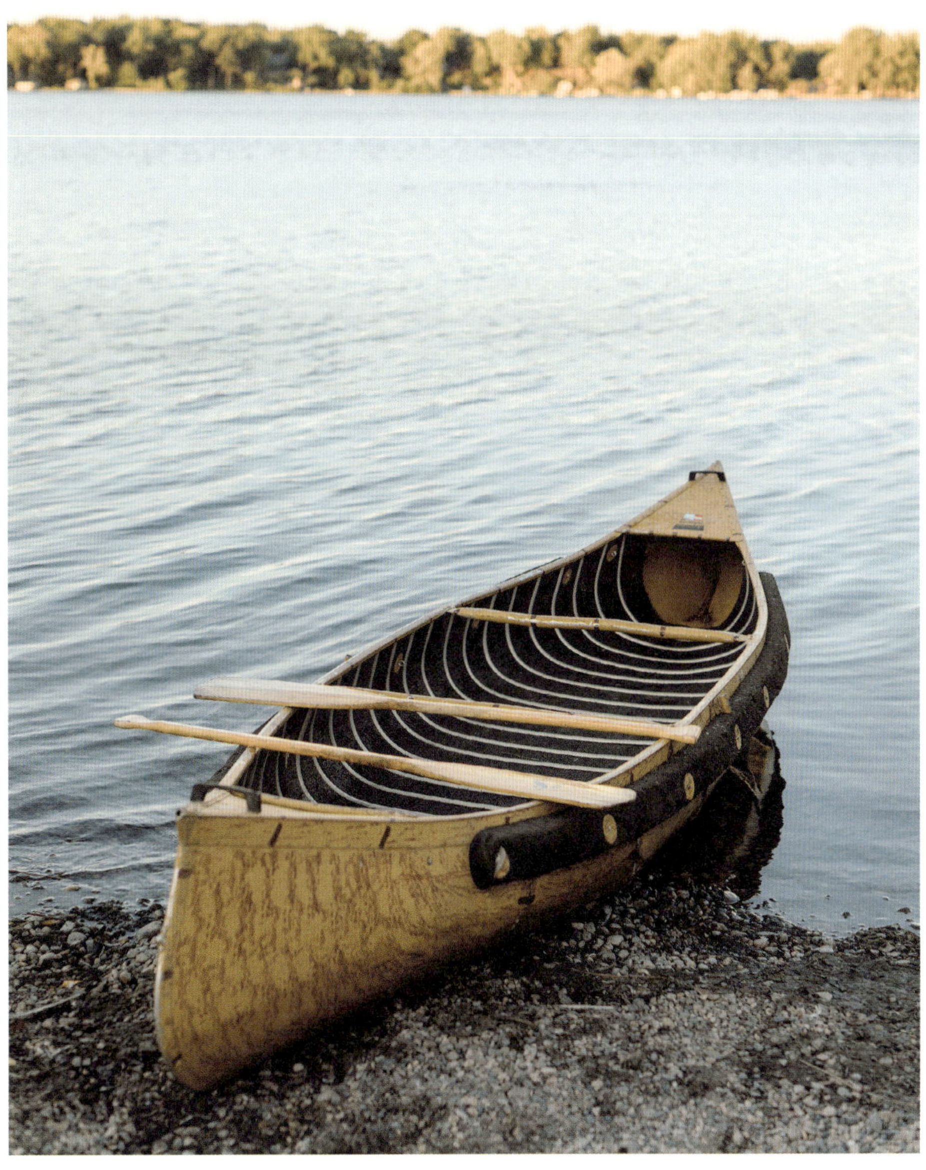

Mementos

REMEMBERING SUMMER

Because it's a crisp day, I have a familiar sinking feeling in my stomach.

Because a palette of pale dying colors taunts me from outside my window, I feel slightly uneasy.

Because the sun now sets before 7:00 p.m., I'm anxious about all the darkness to come.

I used to absolutely dread winter. I would entirely miss out on the beauty of autumn because I was fearfully anticipating the coming cold.

For many years I fantasized about moving to warmer climates and ditching my Midwestern roots. I wanted to be free from Michigan and the cold dark doom that constitutes a quarter of each year.

But somewhere along the way, my mindset shifted. I still get a little angsty at the end of summer, but I'm growing to tolerate winter and, at times, even enjoy it.

I now hold a certain reverence for it—for the coziness that can only come from a dark, snowy day spent by the warmth of my fireplace, for mugs of steaming-hot tea and flickering candlelight, for extra-heavy blankets and hardcover books.

I've started to consider winter a rite of passage, a small price to pay for the perfect summer lake days and living within close proximity of my entire family. I could never leave this community. I could never leave this town. I could never leave this lake. Therefore I must learn to welcome winter, to embrace lakeside living the rest of the year.

Creating summer mementos has helped me make this switch. I like to be reminded daily, especially in the winter season, of the glorious golden months at the lakeshore. The canned fruit jams in the pantry, the collection of lake treasures on the shelf, the piles of colorful Polaroids, the

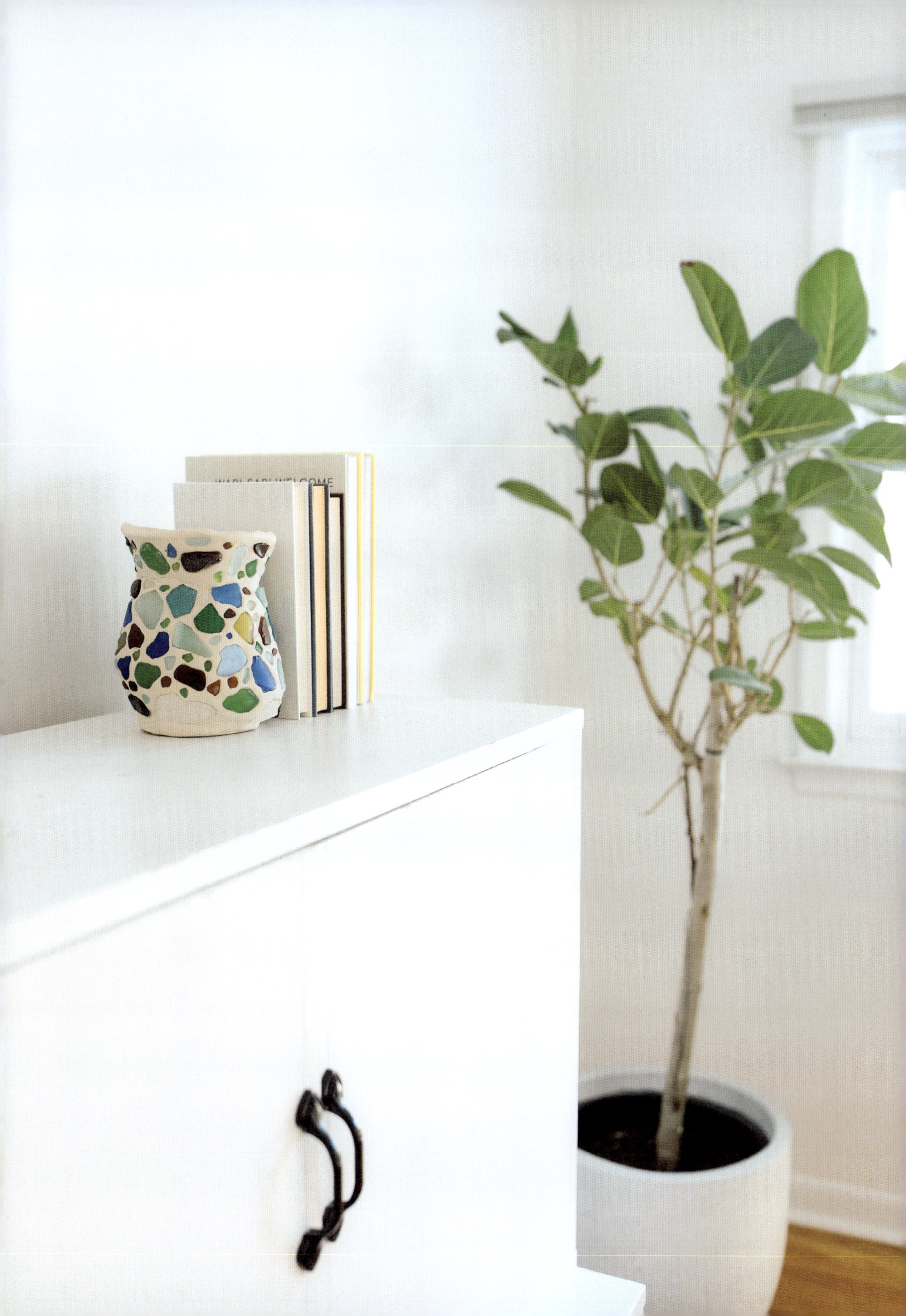

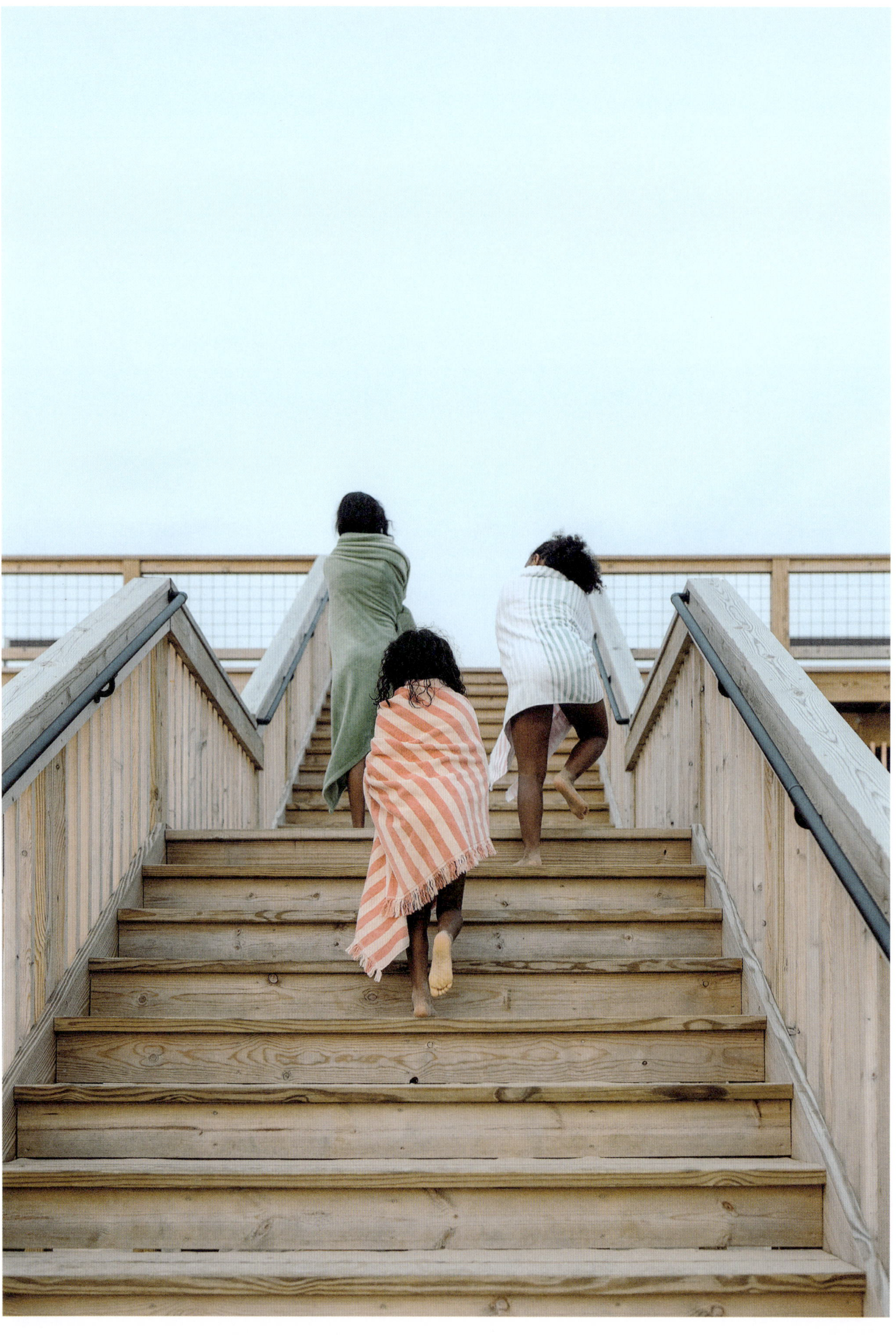

dried summer flowers—all serve as reminders throughout the remainder of the year. Memories of what has been and what will be again.

If you also live somewhere with brief summers, and if you share a complicated love-hate relationship with winter, just know that you can always bottle up some sunshine to sustain you year-round. Summer may be a brief and beloved season, but its memories hold a significance strong enough to keep us here and carry us through until next year.

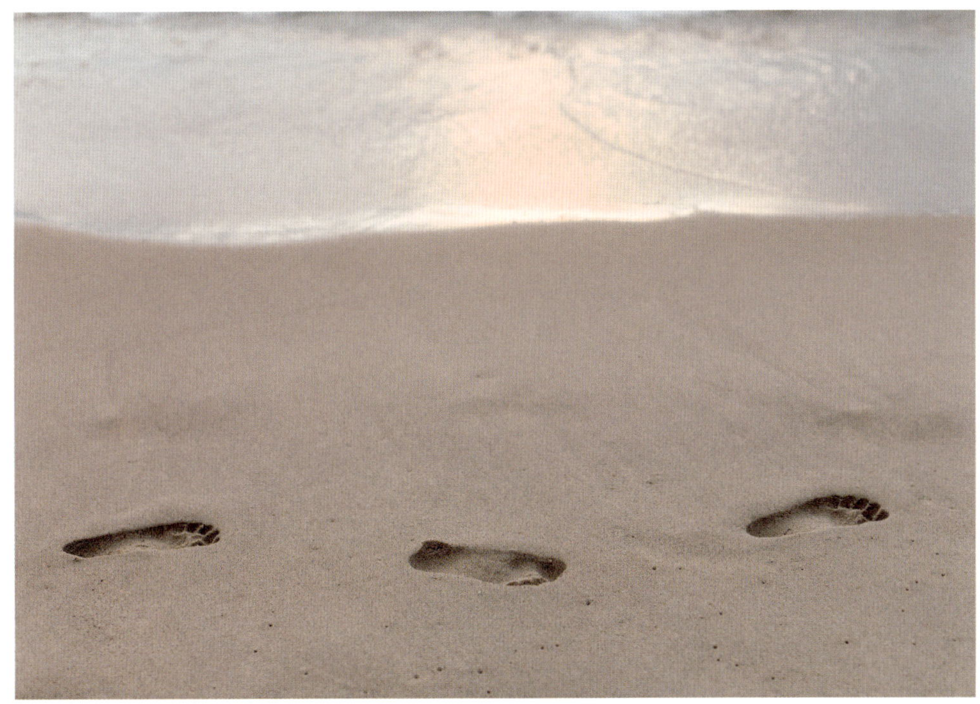

making summer mementos:

- Rather than keeping your beach glass collection in a closet or drawer, put it on display. Organize it in a glass jar or vase, or use air-dry clay to create a pot or dish and press some pieces into it.
- Preserve summer's sweetness for a dreary winter day. Make jams and jellies with summer fruits, or pickled veggies and salsas from the garden.
- Put a few late-summer hydrangea stems in a vase with no water. Let them dry out and keep them on display through the fall and winter.
- Freeze some fresh-picked berries for winter baking and smoothies.
- Display all of the warm, colorful Polaroid photos you captured this summer in a shell or ceramic to peruse on the coldest, grayest days.
- Arrange and frame your rock treasure collection in a satisfying shadowbox gradient.
- Let this book be your bottled sunshine! Keep it on your coffee or console table, flipped open to your favorite page, keeping your heart warm until summer's return.

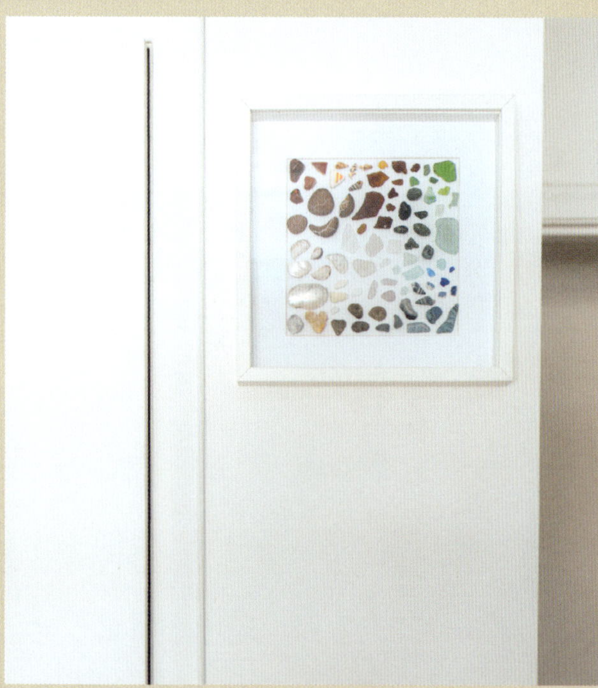

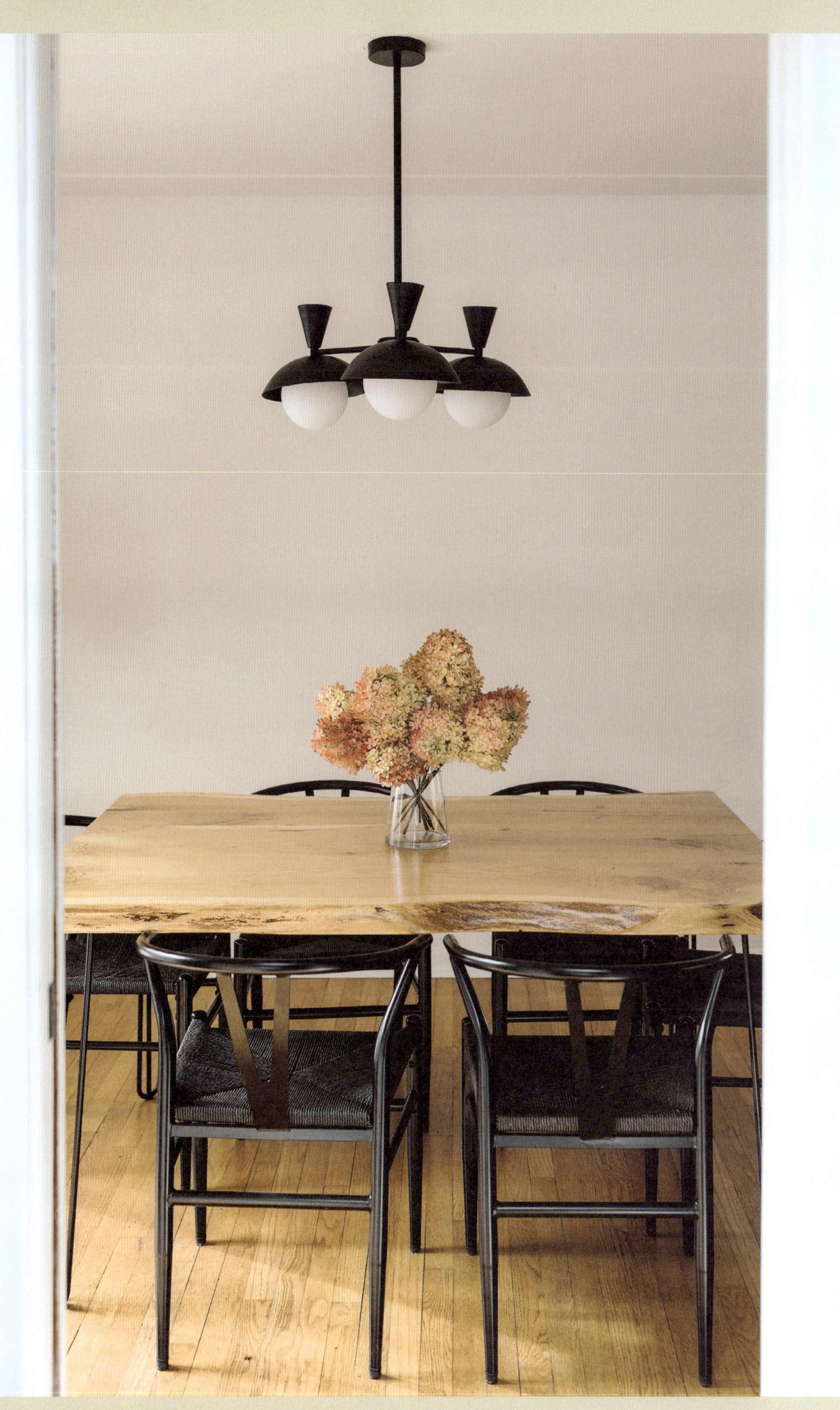

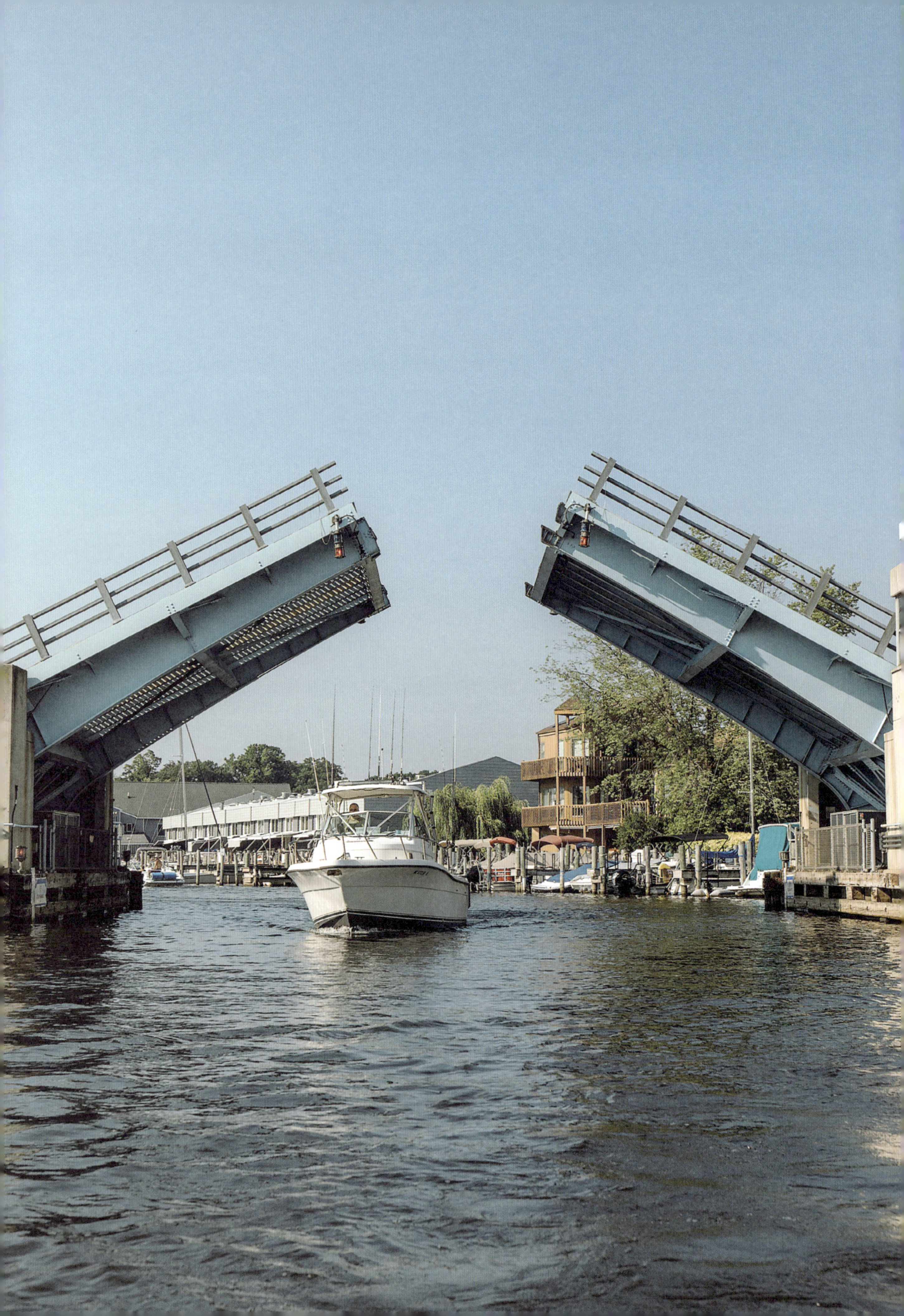

Drawbridge

LIVING ON LAKE TIME

South Haven, Michigan, is a popular lake town and boating destination with a drawbridge. It's one of those rarities where a heavily trafficked main road is stopped every half hour so that the bridge beneath can open up, splitting the pavement in two and pointing the road upward toward the sky, allowing boats to pass through the channel below.

All day, every day, this drawbridge alternates between pausing boats so that pedestrians and cars can pass on the road above, and pausing pedestrians and cars so that boats can pass through the waters beneath.

It is quite the phenomenon, a testament to how slow-paced the lifestyle is here. No one in South Haven is in that big of a hurry, and if they are, they surely aren't taking Dyckman Avenue.

On a lovely late-summer weekend, I sat at a high-top table by the channel, snacked on a burger and fries, and watched the drawbridge lifting and lowering on repeat. Walkers, bikers, and cars crossed above while boats bobbed in the waves below, awaiting their turn. Then boats floated through while the road split in two, and flashing red lights stopped all traffic above.

Everyone seemed to be on lake time. Both the boaters and the pedestrians appeared to be in no rush; they were relaxed and easygoing, willing to take the scenic route. They would laugh and chat while they waited, leaning over the bridge railing and watching the world go by, rolling down their car windows and turning up the music, or opening another drink and kicking up their feet on the boats. No one seemed too bothered by the waiting; if anything, they appeared to welcome the hiatus and delight in the delay.

This is how I want to live my life year-round: unhurried and carefree.

Autumn seems to be a time when our pace quickens, our to-do list lengthens, and our responsibilities get heavier by the day.

This time of year, we start easing ourselves back into real life similar to how we waded in the water all summer long, gradually getting deeper and deeper back into work, school, routines, obligations, commitments.

Before you realize you're up to your neck in the waves, stop and think of the drawbridge.

Consider what you will allow on your autumn agenda and what you can leave out, bobbing or braking on the sidelines. Choose what you dedicate yourself to this season, and what to let go of in return. Decide how you want to live, who you want to be, day by day, and season by season. As one of my favorite authors, Shauna Niequist, writes in *Present Over Perfect*: "My goal upon returning to real life after lake life is to keep my summer heart—my flexible, silly, ready-to-play, ever-so-slightly irresponsible heart."

As you transition into the rhythms of a new season, let the habits you've cultivated in summer stay with you throughout the remainder of the year. The summertime lakeside lifestyle can be maintained year-round if you keep a slow pace, a spontaneous spirit, and remember that the scenic route is always worth the view.

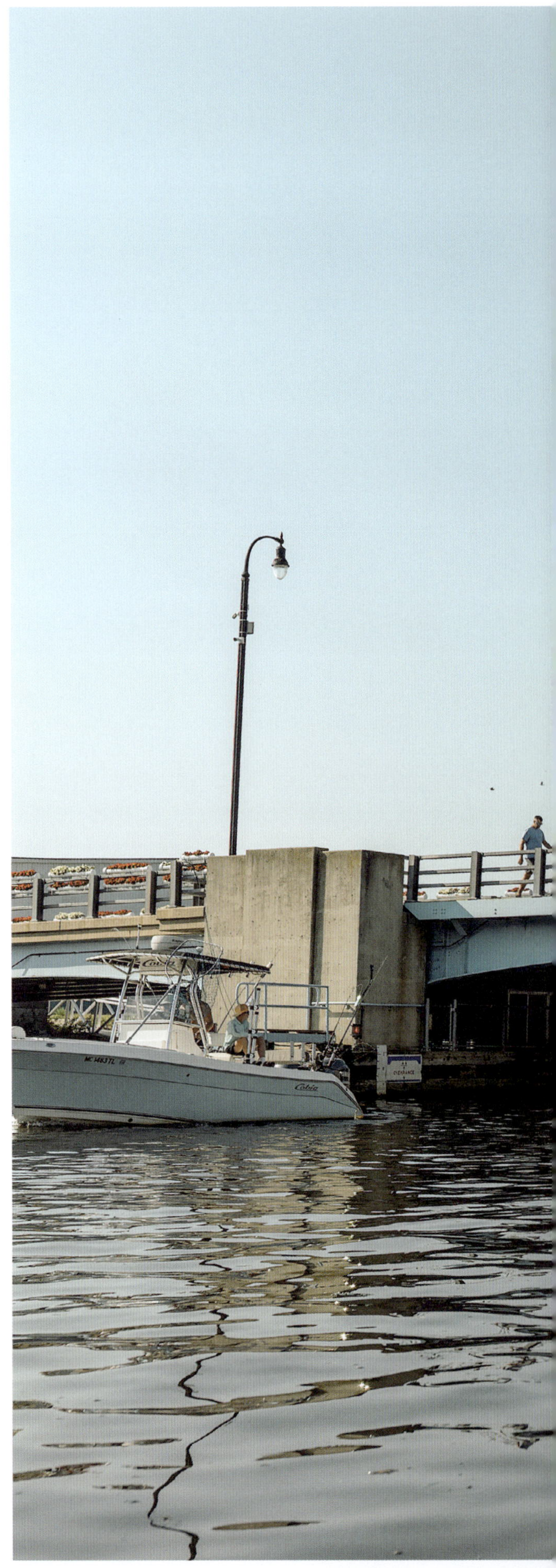

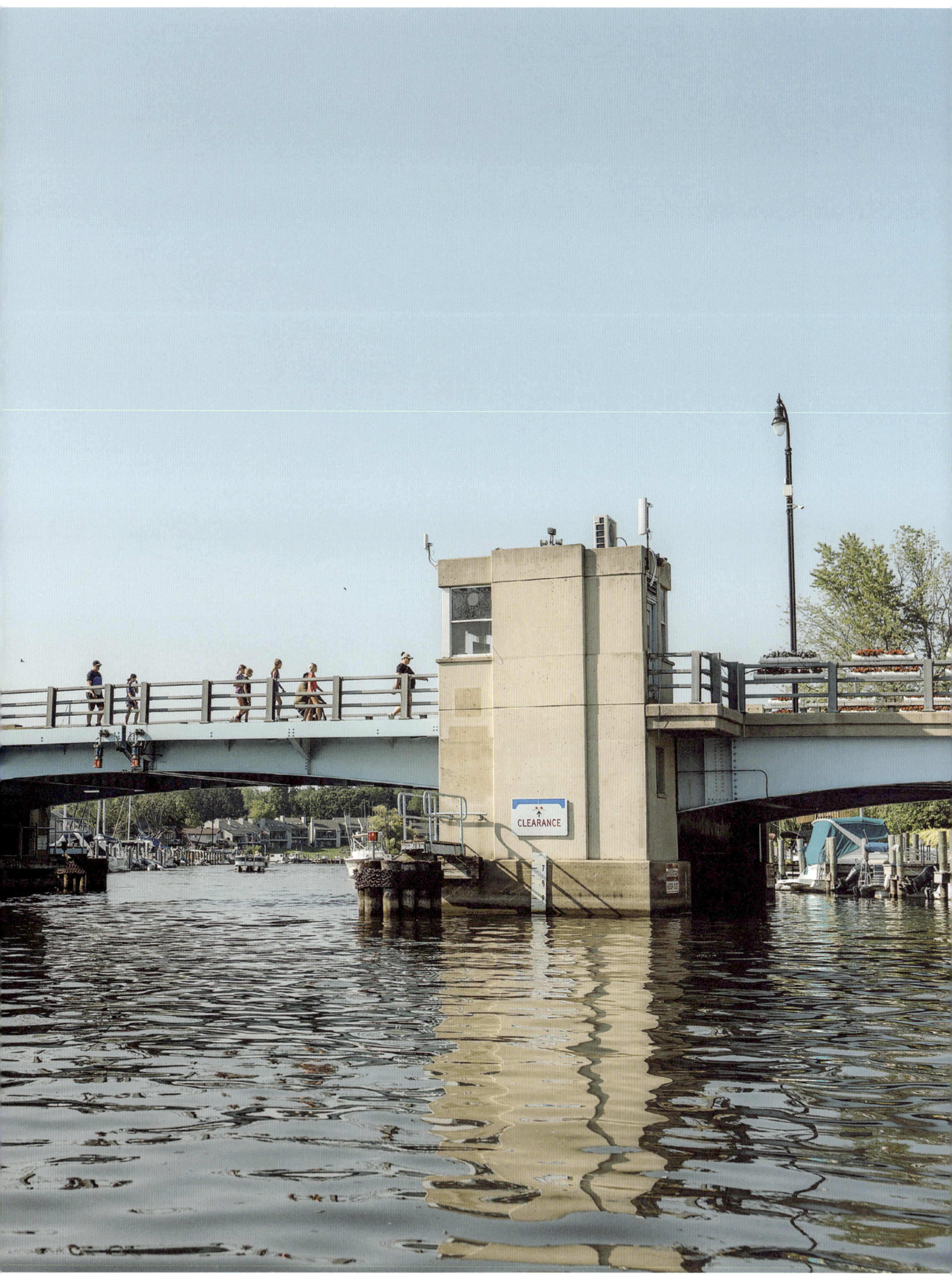
CLEARANCE

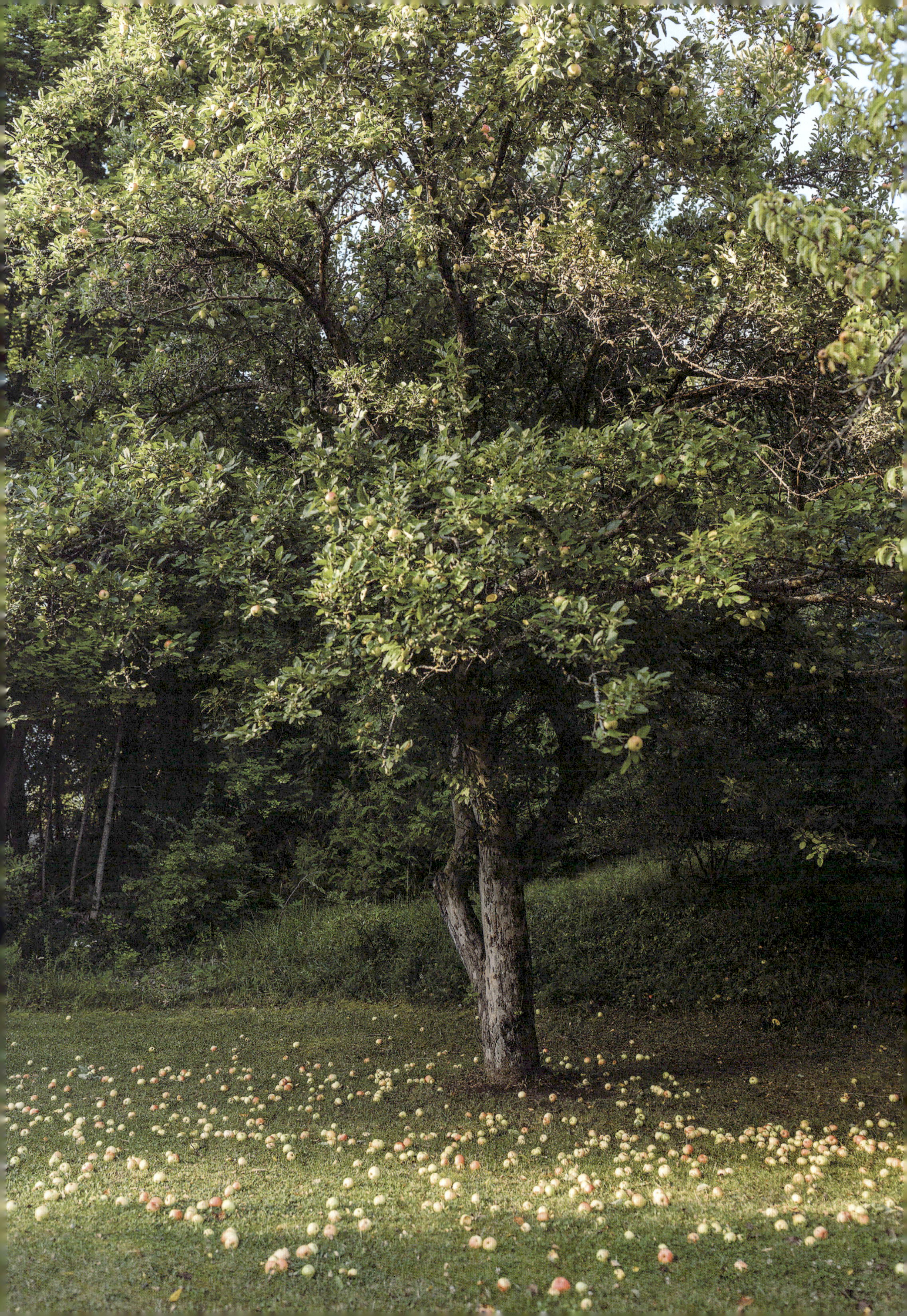

Seasons

SAVORING THEM ALL

As a lifelong Midwesterner, my entire existence has been a ceaseless cycle of seasons.

Every year, like clockwork, I've felt the rain and sun and wind and snow. I've planted and weeded and raked and shoveled. I've witnessed the budding and blooming and falling and stillness. I've embraced the growth and abundance and descent and darkness.

I've seen the lake with frozen gray waves and sheets of ice covering the lighthouses, and I've beheld it bluer than the sky, splashing and spraying in summer abandon.

I've witnessed baby bird eggs hatch, heard them chirp, watched them fly south, and listened to the world go silent. Year after year, again and again.

Living in Michigan, I experience all four seasons in full force. As the world keeps spinning, so does this carousel of seasons. But whether or not you live somewhere with four seasons, your life is surely composed of seasons, too.

Spring is the fresh starts, the new beginnings, the blossoming hope.

Summer is the celebrations, birthday candles and wedding cake, the golden days.

Autumn is the slow decline, disheartening downturn, blustering winds of change.

Winter is the long dark nights, the chilling barrenness, the trials and tribulations.

Life is nothing more than a compilation of seasons—joyous ones followed by heavy ones, bitter ones interwoven with sweet ones, spring and summer, autumn and winter. And here's what I've learned from 120 seasons of living: You can't appreciate the first warm wind without having felt the frostbite, and you'll never be utterly grateful for the sun unless you haven't seen it for all of January.

Starting around April or May, Michiganders say things like, "I'm about to remember why I live here." Although it's a subtly somber thing to say, it has some truth to it. We put up with brutal winters and lake-effect snow, months of temperamental weather and gray skies, all for the luxury of perfect summers—not too hot, not too humid, with lavish green landscapes and a boundless freshwater playground. But dark seasons foster a deeper gratitude for the bright ones.

I'm continuing to learn that every season of life serves a purpose and holds potential. A season without hope is like a year without summer—it doesn't exist. There will always be something warm and golden on the horizon.

They say how you spend your days is how you spend your life. I say how you savor your seasons is how you savor your life. So savor this one, and the one after it, and the one after that, because none of them lasts forever.

This season is just a chapter in your book, just like the last one was, just like the next one will be, and your story is beautiful, because of and even though.

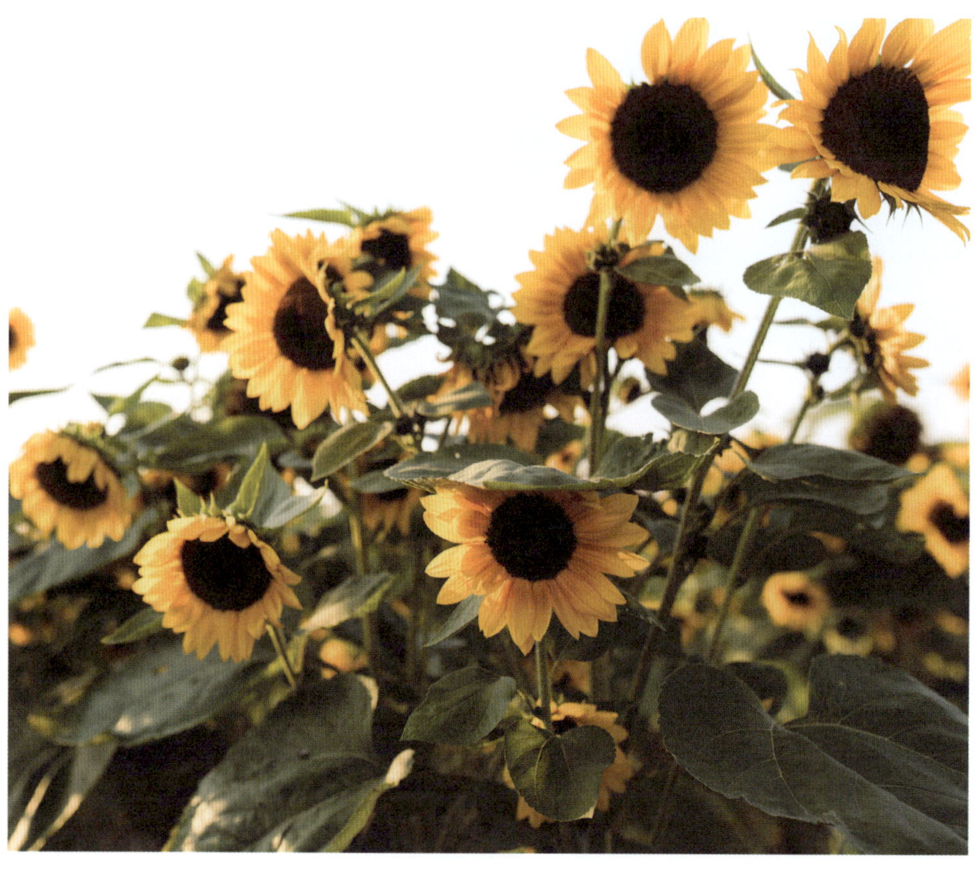

A season without hope is like a year without summer— it doesn't exist. There will always be something warm and golden on the horizon.

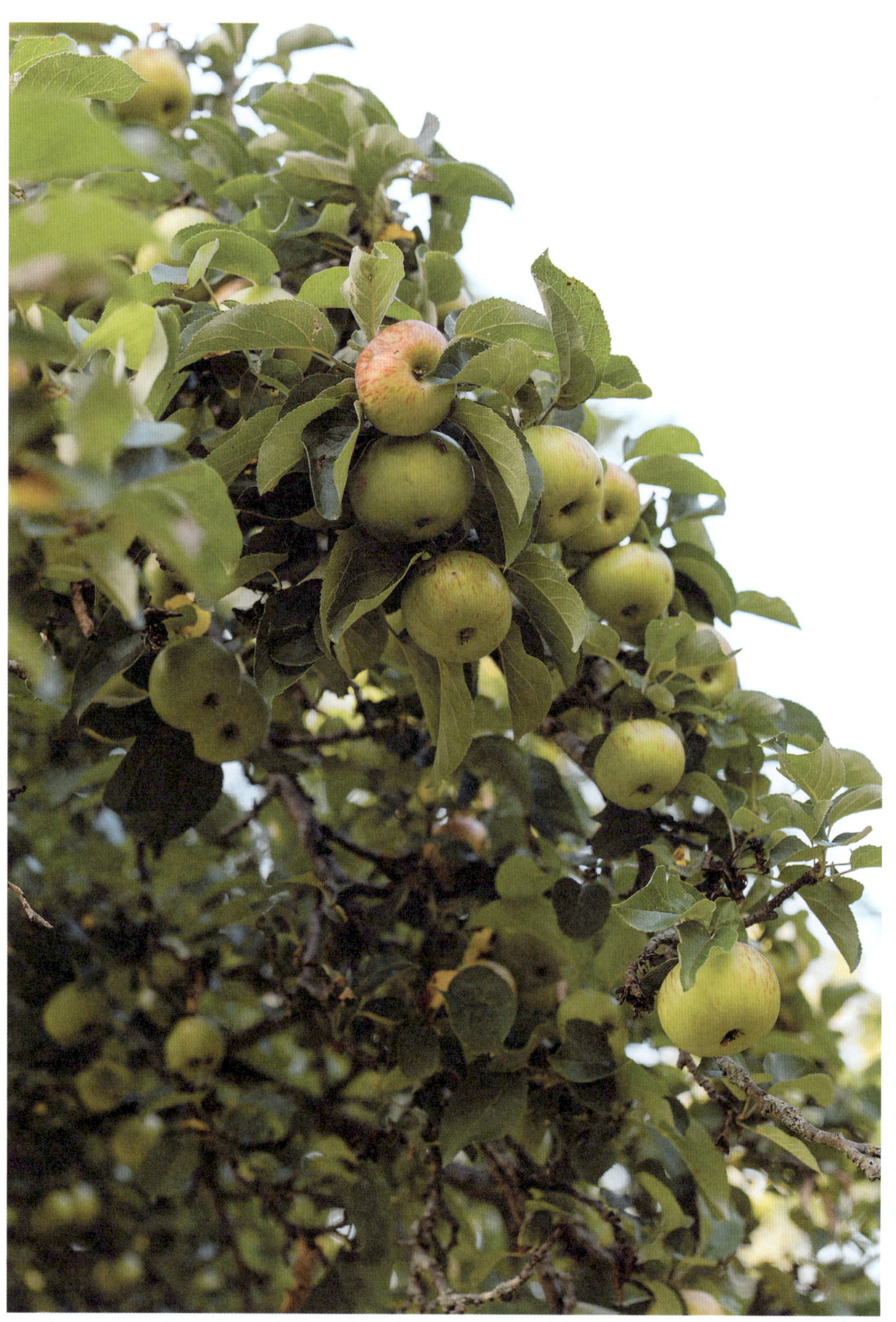

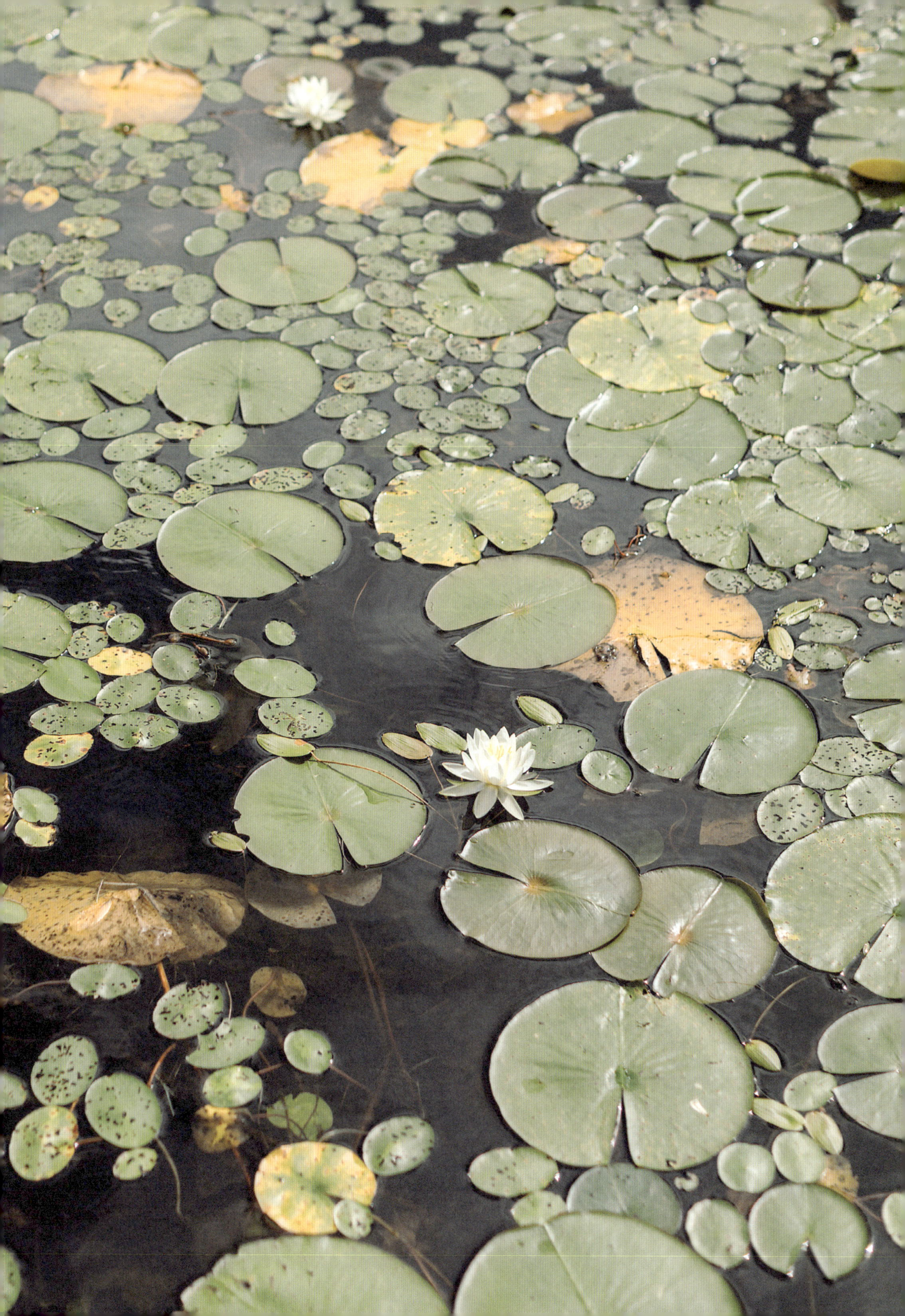

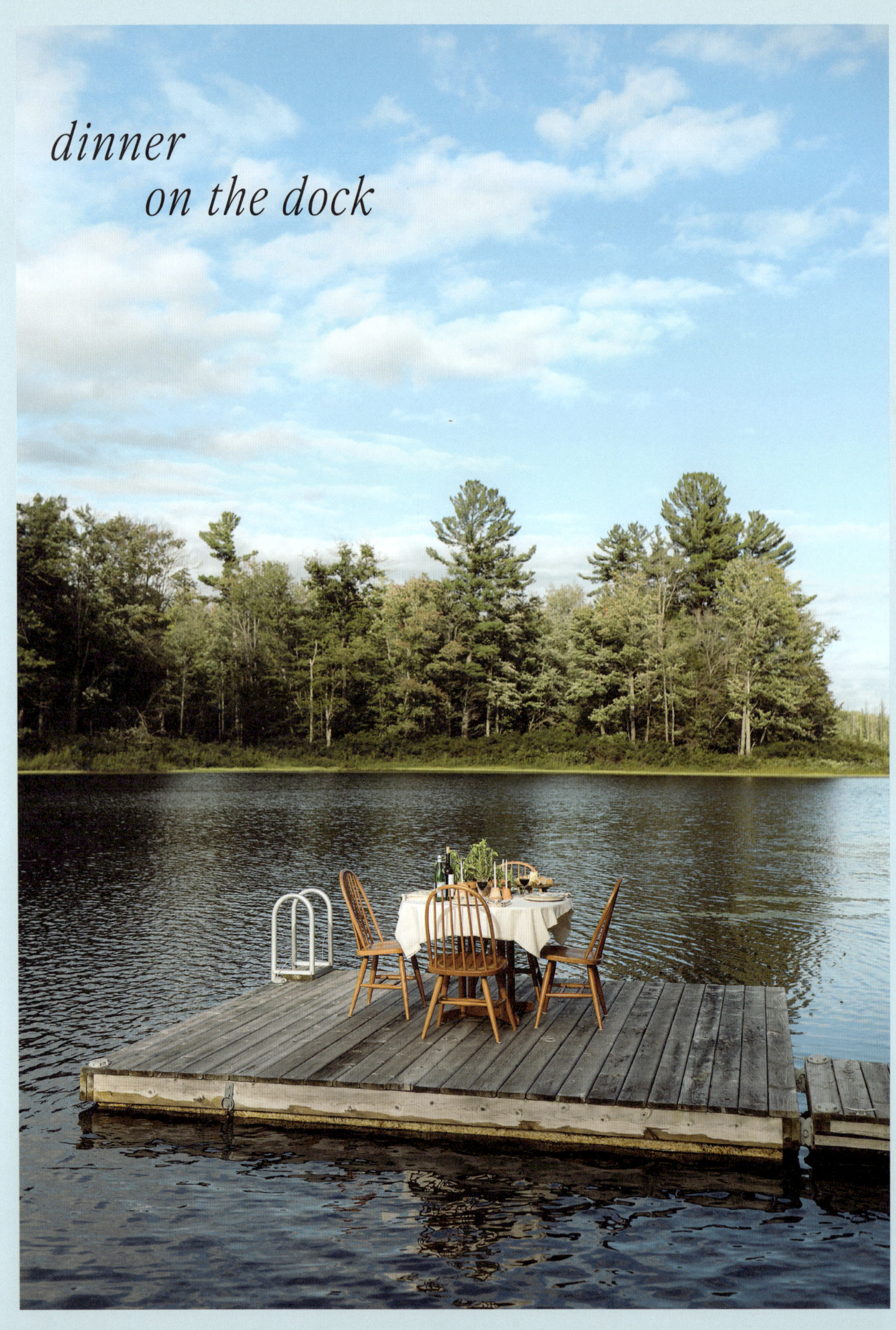

dinner
on the dock

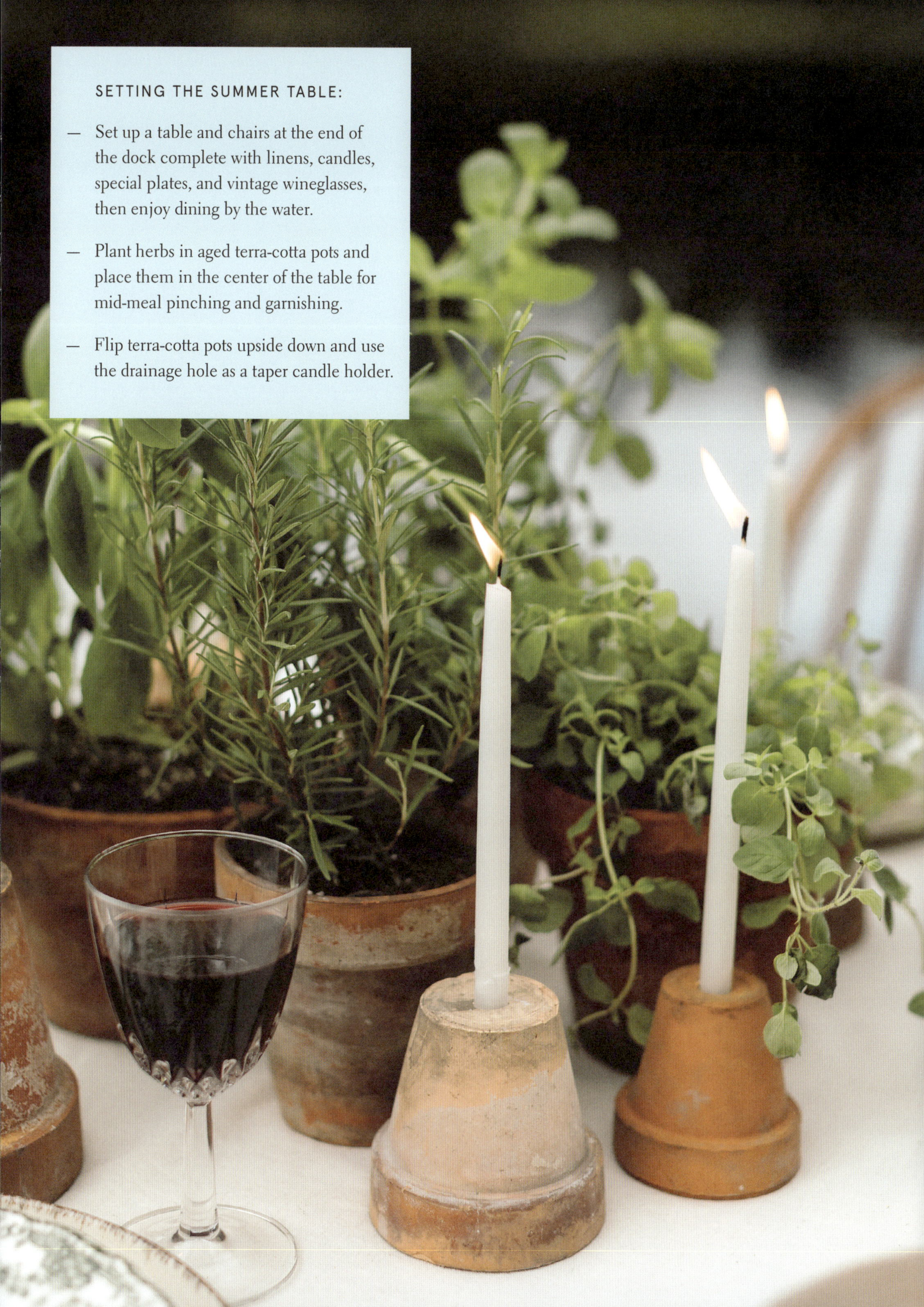

SETTING THE SUMMER TABLE:

- Set up a table and chairs at the end of the dock complete with linens, candles, special plates, and vintage wineglasses, then enjoy dining by the water.
- Plant herbs in aged terra-cotta pots and place them in the center of the table for mid-meal pinching and garnishing.
- Flip terra-cotta pots upside down and use the drainage hole as a taper candle holder.

Garden Tomato Pasta

SERVES 4

This has become a frequent dinner in my home over the past few years. You can make it year-round, but it's especially yummy in the summertime when made with ripe juicy tomatoes and fresh herbs from your backyard! It's hard to get sick of it when there are so many ways to customize it. Plus, it's great for the end of summer when the garden and farmers' markets are overflowing with tomatoes of all shapes and sizes.

1 (8-ounce/225 g) block feta cheese
2 cups (290 g) fresh tomatoes (I prefer heirloom cherry tomatoes for this recipe, but Roma, vine, or other small varieties are also great)
2 tablespoons olive oil
Salt and pepper
1 (16-ounce/455 g) package pasta of your choice (I usually use penne, rigatoni, or rotini)
Optional add-ins: grilled chicken, chicken sausage, broccoli, mushrooms, spinach
Fresh basil leaves
Balsamic glaze

Preheat the oven to 375°F (190°C).

Place the feta in the center of a square or rectangular medium baking dish. If using cherry tomatoes, place them in the baking dish around the feta; for any other tomatoes, chop them into large chunks, then add them to the baking dish. Drizzle the olive oil over the feta and tomatoes, then sprinkle with salt and pepper. Bake for about 30 minutes, until the tomatoes have softened and their juices are bubbling.

Meanwhile, cook the pasta according to the directions on the package and prepare any other add-ins (cook the chicken or chicken sausage, steam the broccoli, sauté the mushrooms, and so on).

Remove the baking dish from the oven and use the back of a spoon to pop and squish the tomatoes, then stir until creamy and incorporated with the feta.

In a large serving bowl, combine the feta-tomato sauce, the pasta, and any add-ins. Top with basil, drizzle with balsamic glaze, and finish with salt and pepper.

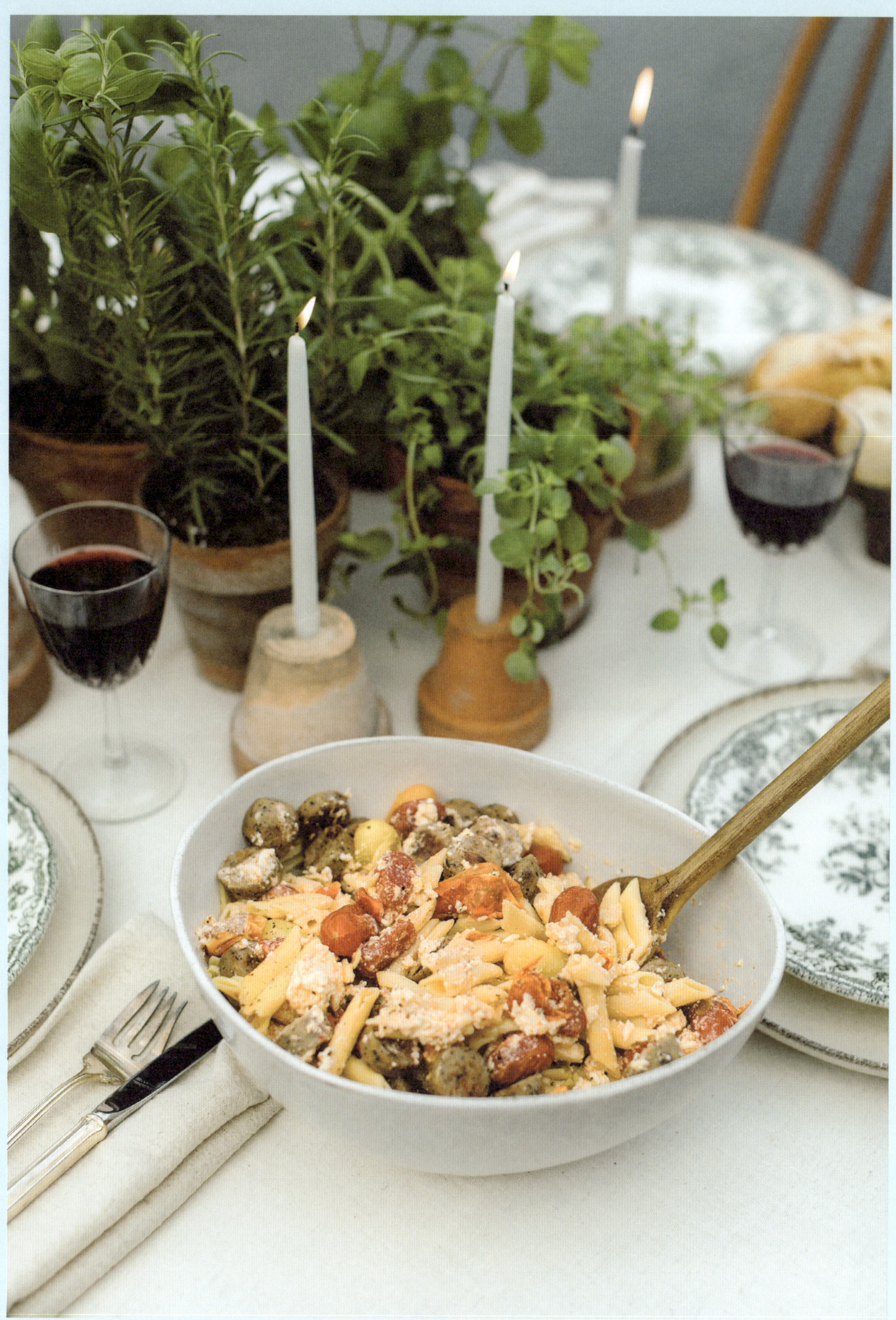

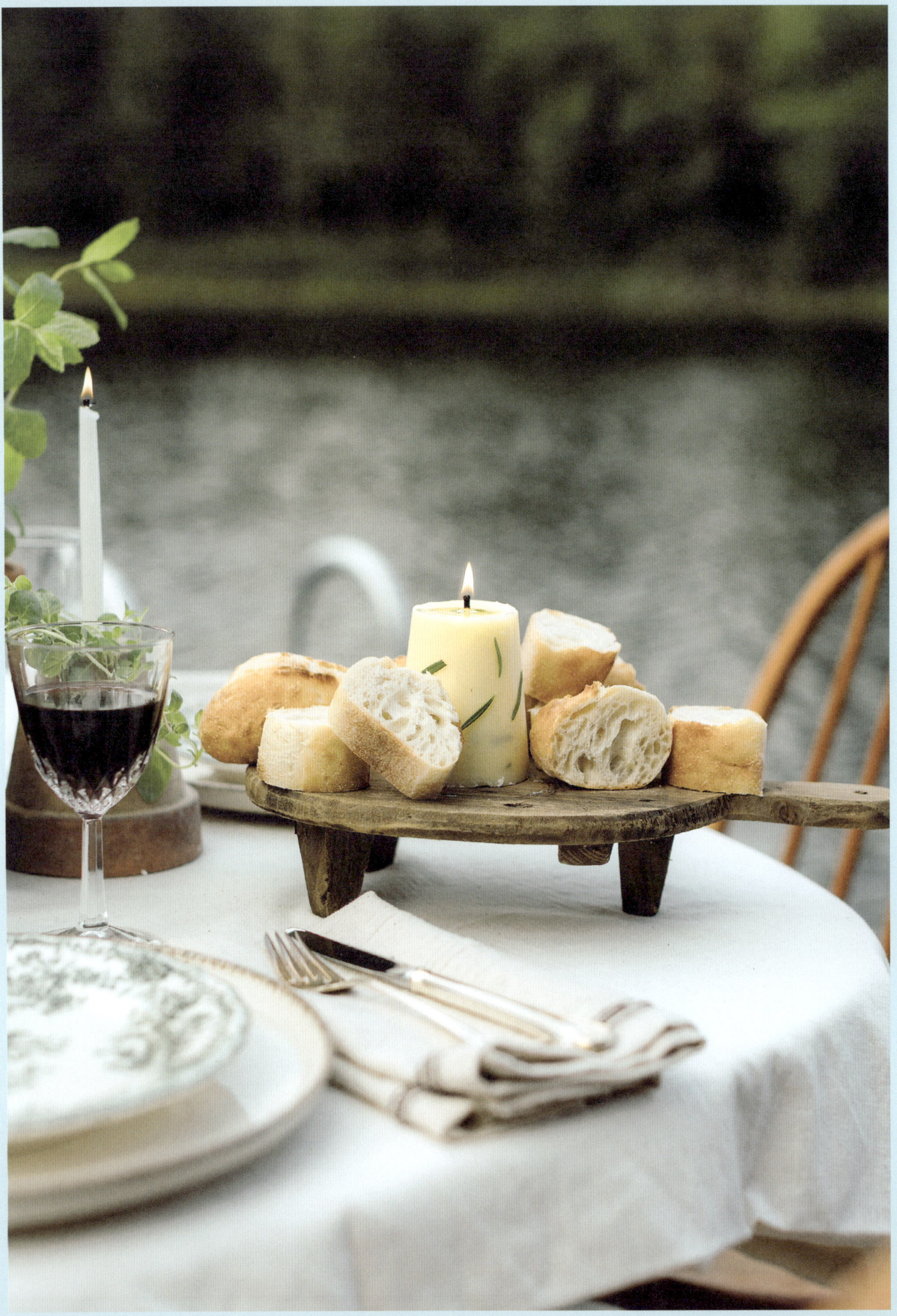

Herb Butter Candle

MAKES 1 CANDLE

No dinner table is complete without some flickering candlelight, bread, and butter. . . . So why not make all three in one? Such a simple concept, yet it will truly wow your guests. This is my party trick!

- 1 (12- or 16-ounce/355 or 475 ml) paper cup
- 1 food-safe candlewick (such as hemp candlewick)
- 1 cup (2 sticks/225 g) unsalted butter
- ¼ cup (45 g) fresh herbs, chopped (rosemary, oregano, or thyme work well)
- Fresh sourdough bread or baguette, for serving

Poke a tiny hole in the bottom of the paper cup, just big enough to pull the wick through. (If it's too wide, butter will seep out.) The wick tip should extend from the bottom of the cup by a couple of inches (about 5 cm; the cup will be flipped upside down). Tie the wick around a Popsicle stick or plastic knife and center the wick in the cup.

In a small pot, warm the butter over low heat until just melted. *Don't heat too fast, and don't overmelt!* The butter should be thick and creamy, just barely stirrable. If you overmelt and it's too liquidy, just pop it in the fridge for a few minutes at a time until it's at the correct consistency.

Stir in the herbs and mix for a minute until they are covered in butter. This keeps them suspended throughout the candle as opposed to floating to the top. Pour the butter mixture into the paper cup around the wick, then immediately pop it into the freezer for 10 minutes. Transfer it to the fridge and let it chill for another 2 hours before serving.

Just before serving, cut or tear away the paper cup, remove the Popsicle stick, and trim the wick as needed, leaving about ½ inch (1.25 cm) at the top to light. Stand the butter candle upright on a serving plate or wooden board. Light the wick so the butter starts melting. Serve with fresh sourdough or baguette slices for dipping into the melted butter as the candle burns down.

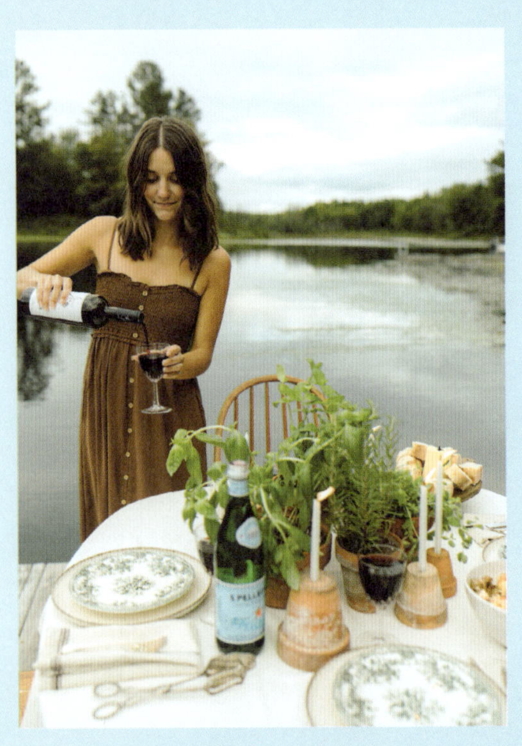

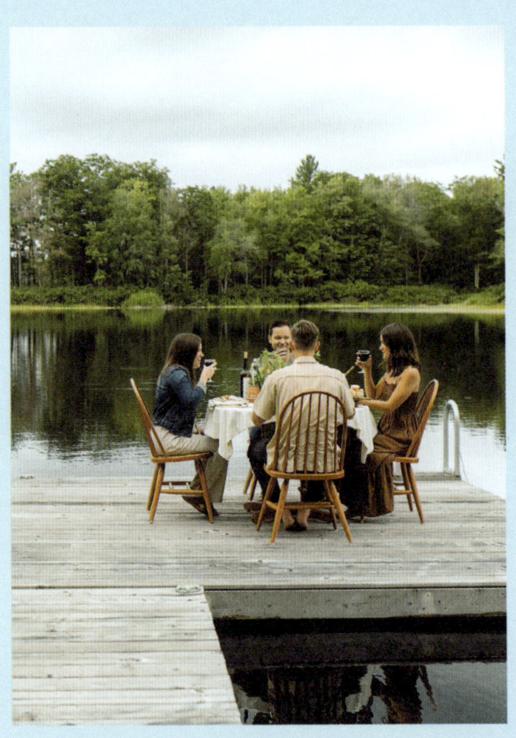

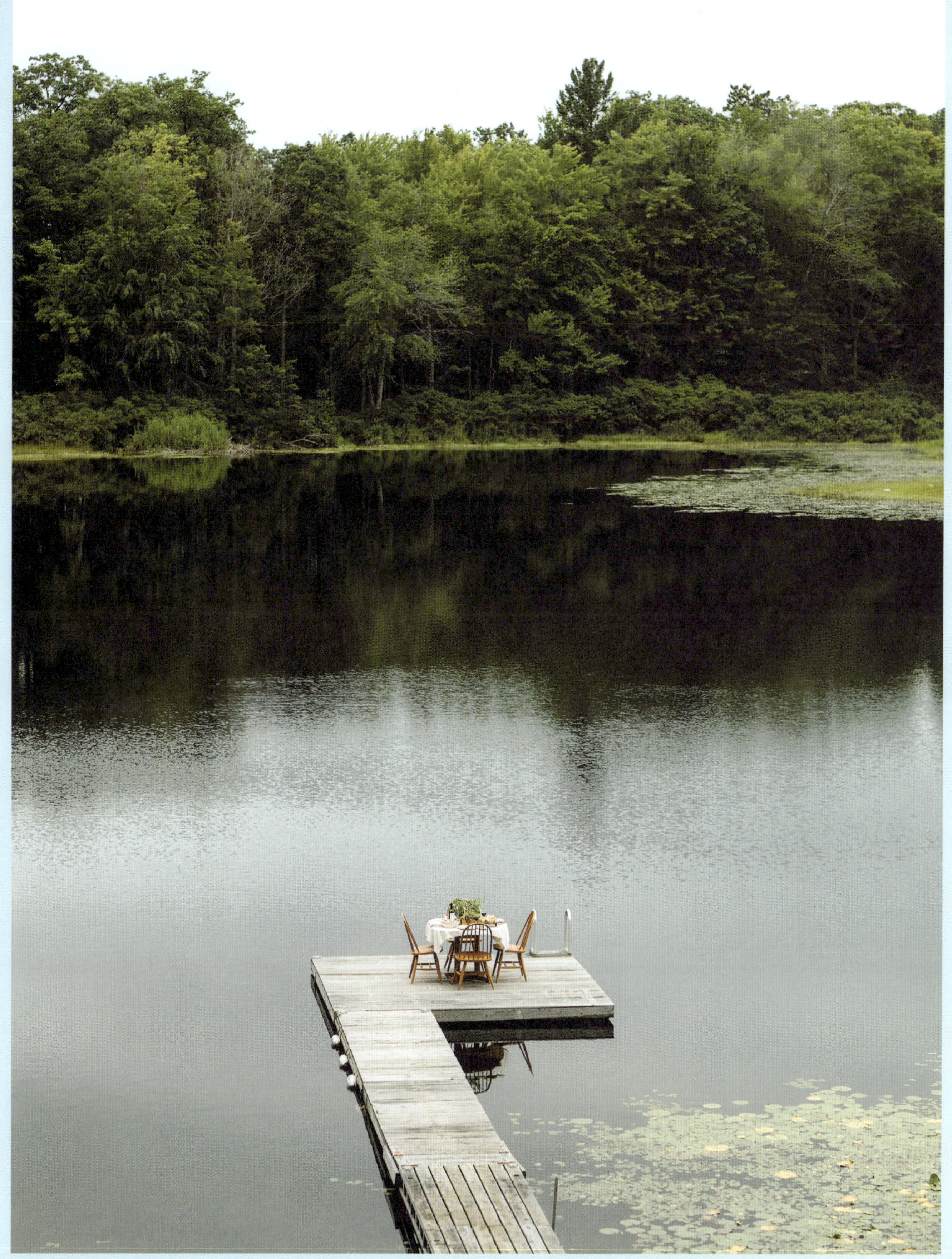

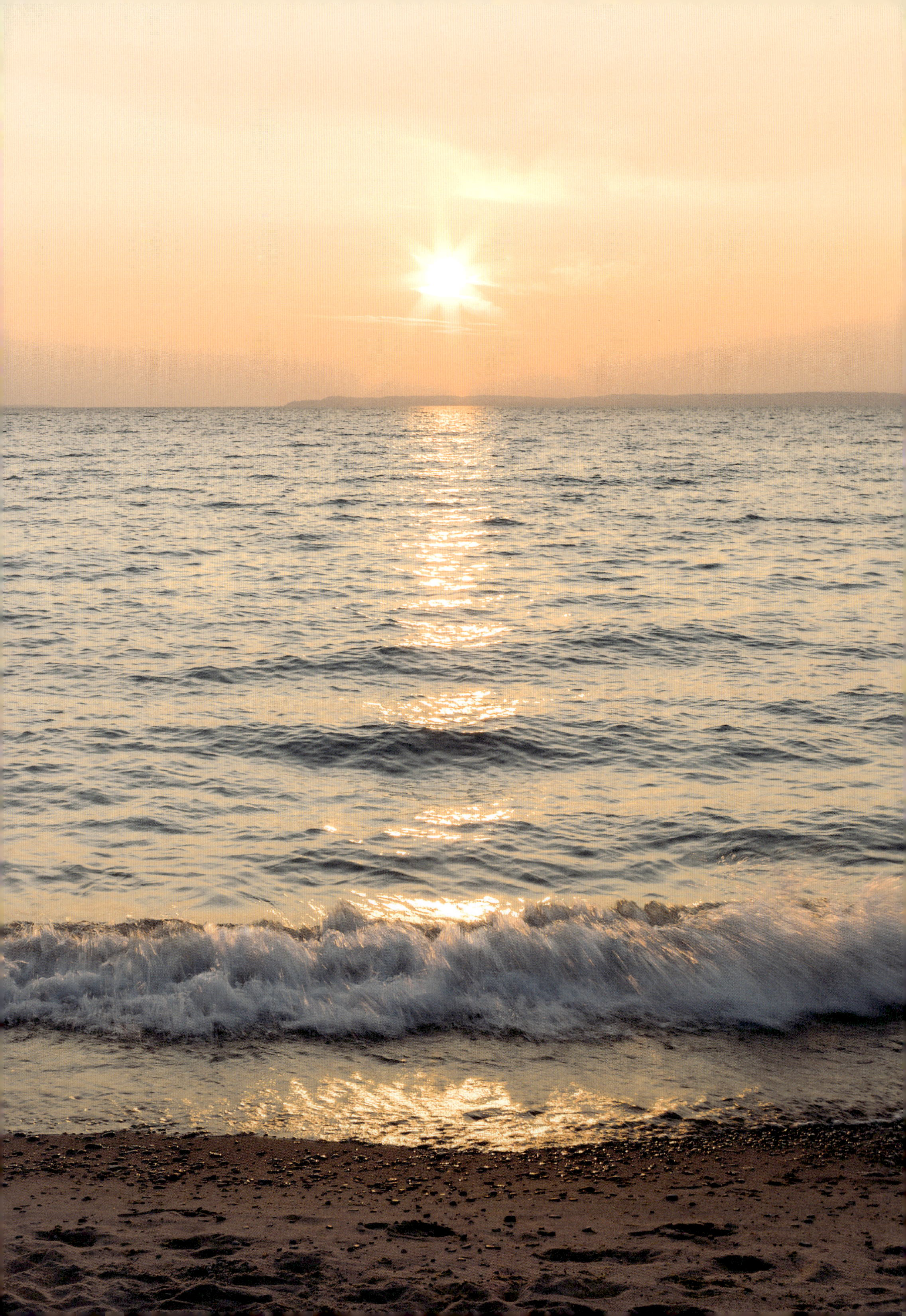

The End of Summer

Eventually, the colorful summer sunsets trickle into the trees, with shades of red and orange and golden leaves that rival the best July sky.

Open windows are traded for open fireplace flues. Barefoot beach walks are replaced with socks and boots. Front-porch iced coffees become fireside mugs. Outdoor dining is swapped for soup and Sunday football.

Less warmth, less green, less daylight; more clouds, more routines, more layers.

The end of summer feels like the end of a vacation; we never wanted it to end, but we always knew it wouldn't last forever. However, you don't love something less just because it doesn't last forever. If anything, you love it all the more fiercely for the short time you do have—holding on with both hands, hugging with both arms, making every moment count.

This summer, I hope you ate most meals alfresco and ordered the extra scoop. I hope your fingers were berry-stained and your tan lines well defined. I hope you jumped in even when—especially when—the water was cold. I hope you stayed up late with your favorite people, and I really hope you were the last to leave. I hope you did something brave, something childlike, something nostalgic. I hope you re-created fond memories and formed new ones, too. I hope you said yes to spontaneity and discovered somewhere new. I hope you made it to your Up North, the more times the better. I hope you smelled the flowers, felt the grass, and listened to the waves. I hope you watched many sunsets, face turned west, warmed by its rays.

I hope you checked off your summer bucket list, but even if you didn't, that's okay, because there's always next summer.

As sure as the waves on the lakeshore, summer will keep coming back to us, over and over and over again.

As sure as the waves
on the lakeshore, summer will
keep coming back to us,
over and over and over again.

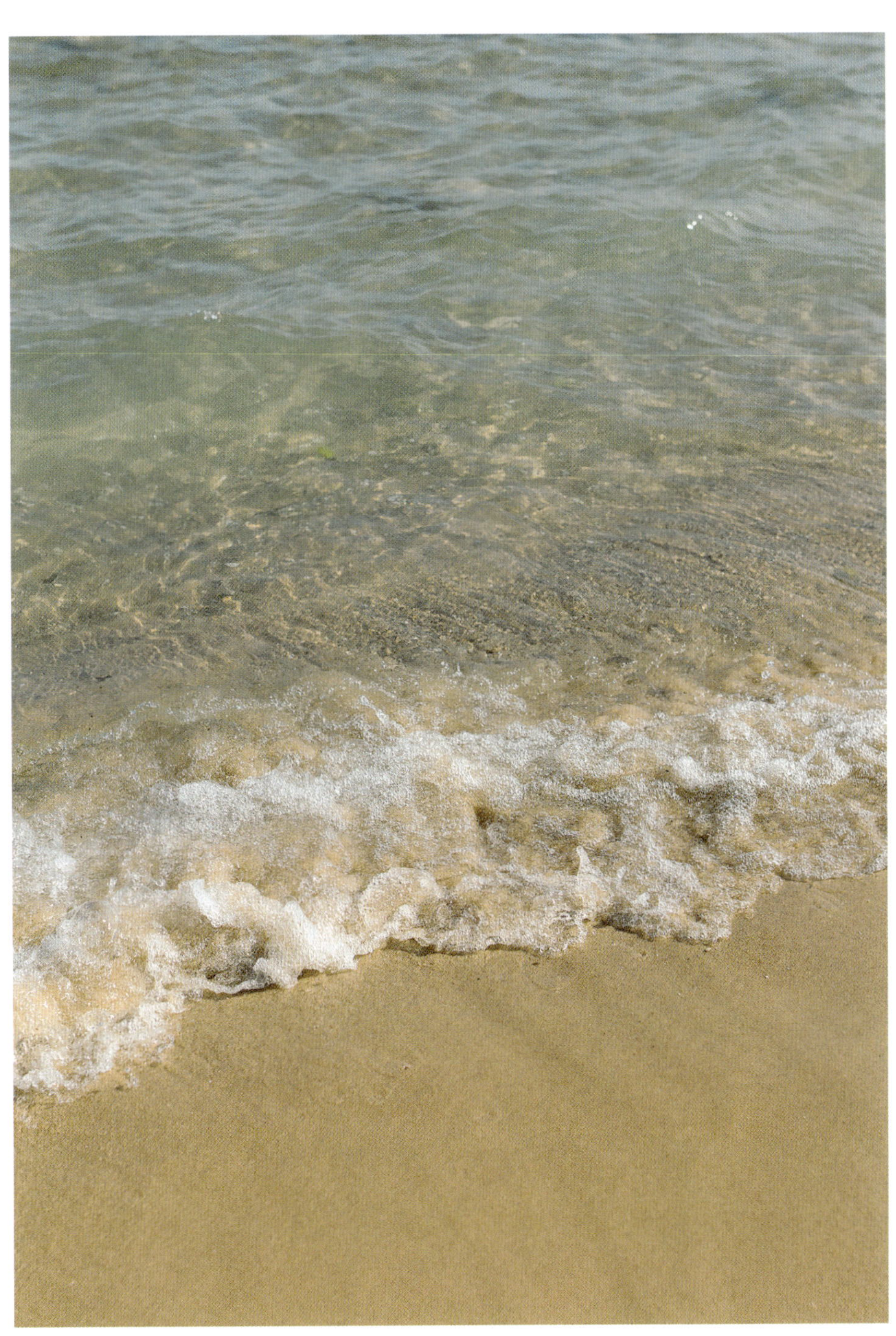

Acknowledgments

There are so many people to thank for helping make this book what it is today. They say it takes a village; I say it takes a cozy lake town. Here's mine:

First and foremost, thank you Joy Eggerichs Reed for being the most incredible agent, for believing in me and sharing my affinity for Michigan summers. I never knew it would be possible to find an agent as wonderful as you. Thanks for being a mentor and inspiration for me, not only in the writing world, but in all realms of life. I'm eternally grateful for you, and none of this would exist without you!

Thanks also to Amelia Graves for your editing expertise. I appreciate your reading the earliest (ugliest) versions of these essays. Thanks for every suggestion and correction, as well as the times you chose to look the other direction at the improper grammar that I like to call my *artistic style*.

Special thanks to Shoshana Gutmajer, the most wonderful editor. Endless gratitude to you for seeing the potential in this book and having an even better vision for it than I did at the time. You're a true visionary and a pleasure to work with. Thank you for making my dreams come true!

To the entire Artisan team, thank you for bringing this book into the world. Thanks to Lia Ronnen for believing in this book and giving it a chance, to Jane Treuhaft for designing each page and piecing together the puzzle, to Abby Knudsen for your helpful edits, to Philip Verdirame for your support, to Suet Chong for your artistic direction, to Hillary Leary for making sure every detail was just right, to Donna Brown for making sure every page shines, to Moira Kerrigan, Allison McGeehon, Mackenzie Collier, Maya Donchez, and Cindy Lee for getting this book into the hands of lake-loving readers, and to every other Artisan team member who played a part in this project! I am so blessed to work with such an experienced and talented group of people.

Thanks to my friend and fellow author Jade Havenaar for your invaluable feedback

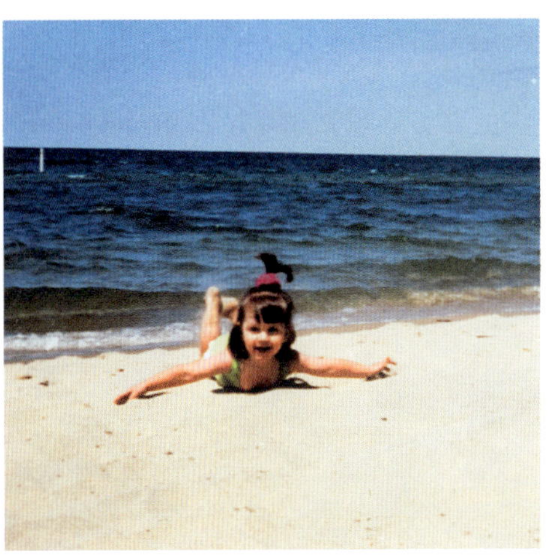

on my early manuscript and your companionship at every (often awkward) writerly event.

Thanks so much to Macy Jean Temrowski for all of your design advice along the way. I'm so lucky to have such a talented and trendy sister-in-law!

To all the creatives (credited on the following page) who helped make this book so wonderful, thanks for sharing your talents and for making this book more beautiful.

My deepest gratitude to every single person who "modeled" for me. Whether it was around a table, on a boat, or in the waves, your lakeside lifestyles are the heartbeat of this book. Thank you for showing us the way! Thanks also to those who opened the doors to their cottages and inns, offering me a place and space to be inspired.

To my family and friends (you know who you are), thank you for your unwavering support and belief in me from the beginning of time. For always putting up with my camera in your face, and occasionally pressing the shutter when I'd say "Push this button while I go jump off that dock!" To the original 10:00 a.m. prayer ladies, and my recipe testers, and my book club girls, thanks for all the ways that you each have encouraged me through this journey.

The greatest thanks goes to my husband. This book is dedicated to him because it certainly wouldn't exist without him. Gavin, thanks for always affirming me and my dreams, and selflessly helping me pursue them. For reminding me every day, for celebrating every milestone, and for holding my hand when I couldn't do it alone. From running down a pier with a camera in one hand and a dripping ice cream cone in the other, determined to help me get the perfect photo before the sun sets; or kayaking, biking, cliff jumping, and other various activities you got roped into; or driving me thousands of miles across the Midwest and parking the car on the side of the road whenever I wanted just one more photo . . . thank you, you're my best.

Finally, thanks be to God for painting every sunset, you deserve the glory.

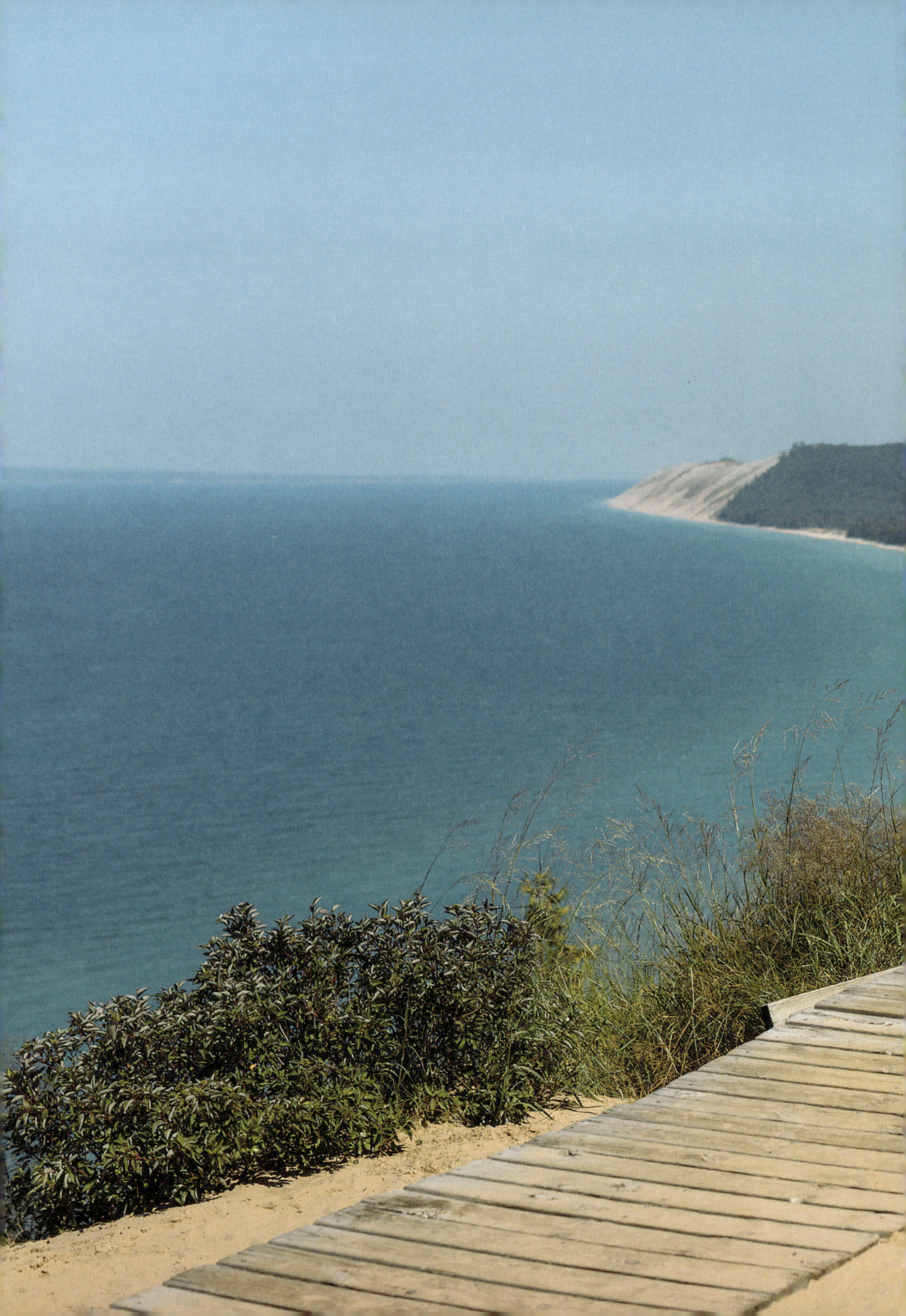

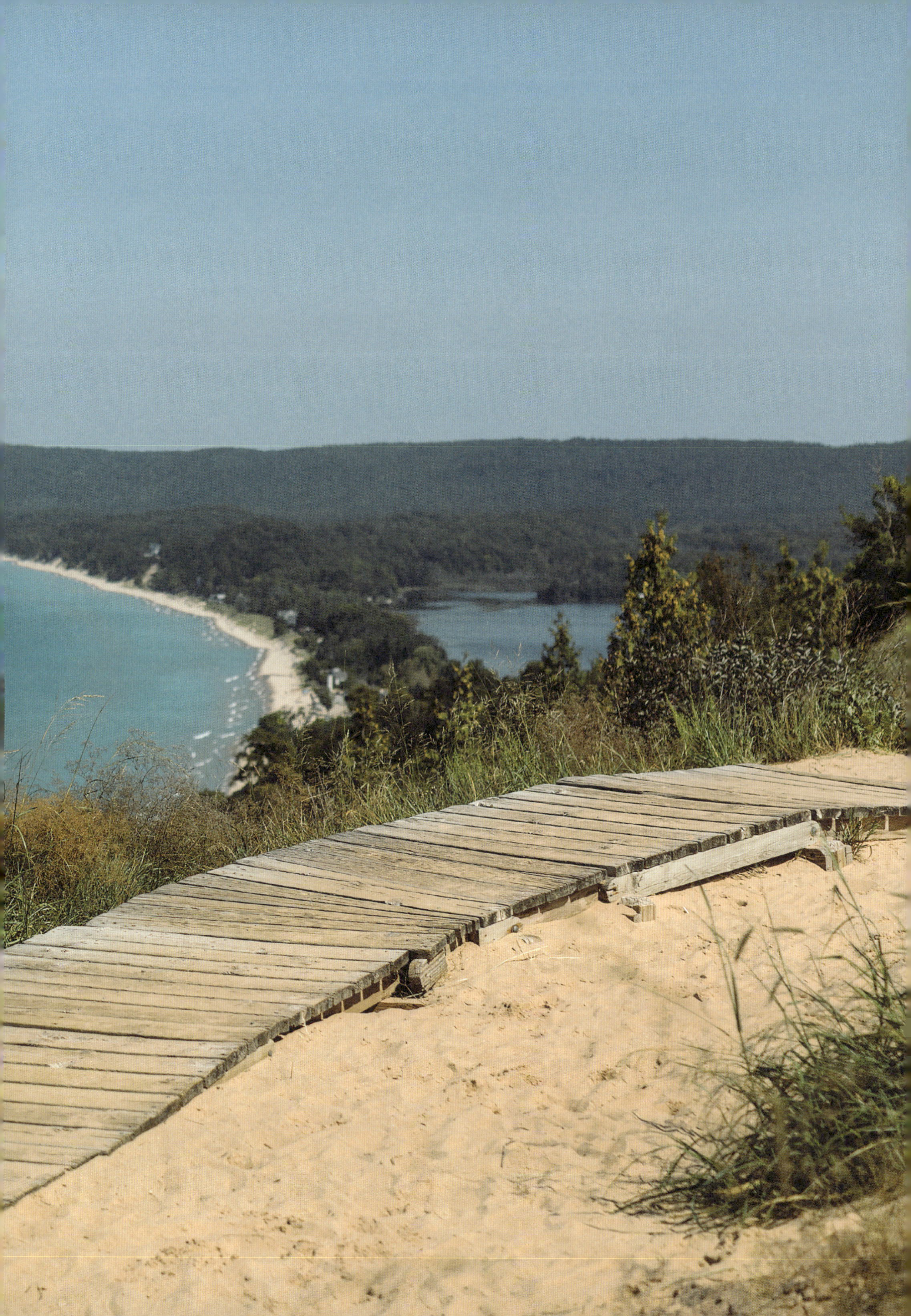

credits

I want to give credit to all the designers, artisans, and creatives who helped make *Life on the Lake* so beautiful. Their talents are a true blessing to this book and the world.

- **Anchor Inn:** The cozy scenes on pages 79 and 81 were taken at Anchor Inn in Traverse City, Michigan, which has been renovated, designed, and styled by husband-and-wife team George and Alyssa Brittain. Many of the lakeside moments and musings in this book were inspired by my summer days at Anchor Inn.

- **Emily Rae Design:** Emily styled and curated each of the monthly recipe photo scenes. The table settings and decor are as aesthetic and exceptional as she is. Thanks for everything, Emily!

- **Joy & Bloom Design Co.:** Alicia is an incredibly talented florist, and she put together all of the floral arrangements for the monthly recipe photo scenes. Thanks for bringing my vision to life!

- **Lake Shore Resort:** The beautiful space mentioned and showcased on pages 48 and 49 was reimagined and renovated by motelier Andrew Milauckas. The family business started as a lakeside getaway built by his grandparents in 1952, then passed along to his parents, and now to him. Thanks for breathing new life into freshwater shores. You've created one of my favorite places.

- **Takka Saunas:** The stunning lakeside sauna pictured on page 123 was designed by Jason and Lynn Makela. They brought such a unique experience to the shores of Lake Superior.

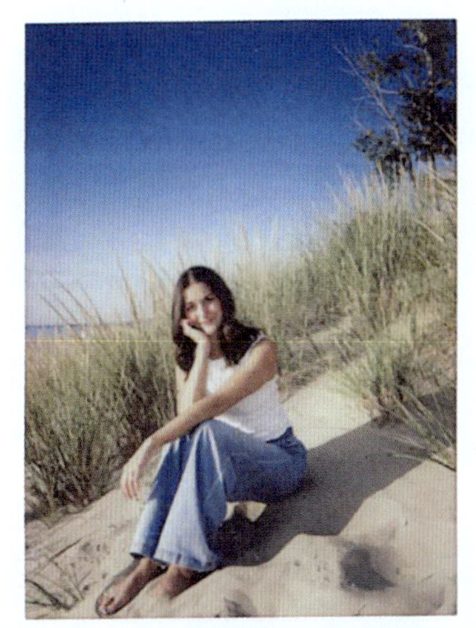

Tylee Shay is a writer and photographer with a passion for pairing prose and photos to create a compelling story. She is equal parts world traveler and homebody, with a love for trips to Europe as well as sunny days spent at Lake Michigan. Tylee's words and photos have been published in *Midwest Living*, *Grand Rapids Magazine*, and more. She writes on her Substack, *Prose & Photos*, and lives in Grand Rapids, Michigan, with her husband, Gavin. Learn more at tyleeshay.com.

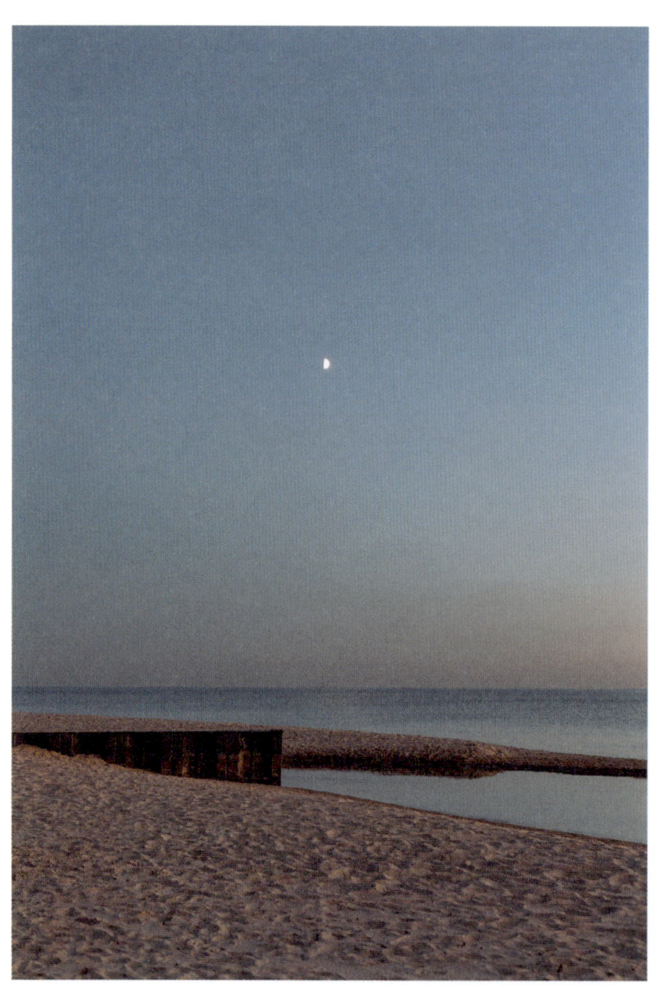